6/9/79

To Bert and Fe

Next year
we'll create a few
tales of our own—
full of Schnitzel,
Schlag, und toate.

Love,

Bob

BOOKS BY

Sarah Gainham

The Habsburg Twilight

The Habsburg Twilight

TALES FROM VIENNA

Sarah Gainham

Atheneum   New York

1979

Library of Congress Cataloging in Publication Data

Gainham, Sarah.
  The Habsburg twilight.

  Includes index.
  1. Vienna—Civilization.   I. Title.
DB851.G3   1979   943,6'13   78-7308
ISBN 0-689-10957-1

Contents

Illustrations

The Habsburg Twilight

Foreword

THERE are two tenacious legends about Vienna; one that there was a long, conscious and documented decline in the Habsburg Empire or Dual Monarchy of Austria-Hungary and the other that Vienna was an especially gay and frivolous place and that its frivolity showed some relation to its disappearance. The decline was not protracted, it was sudden. But there was a consciousness of great change coming in the future, that it would be 'the end of an era' when the old Emperor Franz Joseph died. This feeling was mainly caused by the sheer length of Franz Joseph's reign. From December 1848 when the new ruler was proclaimed to 1916 when he died on 21 November, is exactly sixty-eight years. Many millions of people had never known any other ruler; not only young people but those already elderly could not envisage their world without Franz Joseph. The fear that his death would be the end of the world rather than the end of an age, which it was bound to be, did not become deep or widespread until after the beginning of the First World War, or as it was more graphically called until 1939, the Great War. That war was rightly called the Great War because it destroyed Europe and no matter how terrible the Second World War was, and it was indeed terrible, it was really the aftermath of 1914–18. The Austro-Hungarian Empire collapsed under the hammer blows of a four-year war on three fronts and for no other reason. The evidence of a long twilight was mainly constructed afterwards by politicians for their own reasons. It was a matter of interpretation and of leaving out all evidence about the other countries of Europe. Except for the serious loss of confidence that followed the death of the Crown Prince in 1889, almost all evidence of decadence current before 1914 proves, on examination, to be the product of Russian and Serbian panslavist propaganda beginning with Danilevsky in 1869. It was not countered from Vienna for reasons of a perhaps rather disdainful unconcern.

The second half of the nineteenth century was a period of continuous reform of administration and government in all the highly developed countries of Europe under the pressures of industrial and economic change. This was so of Great Britain, France, Germany and Italy as well as Austria-Hungary. Dates naturally varied, and the forms of new arrangements differed according to the customs of the country concerned; the process itself was contemporaneous and almost the same everywhere. Where it did not take place it was either because there was no major economic change, as in Spain, or where the system of government was so rigid that it could not change itself, as in Imperial Russia. In fact, universal male suffrage, then generally agreed to be the attainment of real parliamentary democracy, came earlier in Austria-Hungary than in Britain. The Emperor himself forced general and secret suffrage through in 1906 in what turned out to be a last attempt to break the outdated grip of Hungarian oligarchy by using the weight of the mass-vote. In the Hungarian half of the Dual Monarchy large numbers of non-Magyar subjects were until then unenfranchised. The large body of the new voters must inevitably have produced new forms of a Danube federation, but the outbreak of the 1914 war ended the development. In the Austrian half of the Empire the situation was somewhat different because the Bohemians or Czechs were economically and socially more developed than either the transylvanian Rumanians or the South Slavs and the old restricted franchise based on taxation or the ownership of property was therefore more widespread. The Bohemians were also heavily represented in administration and this gave them much quiet influence so that the German-Austrians were not in the perman-

ent overweight of power as the Magyars were in their side of
the realm. The form of government was what we are nowadays familiar with as presidential cabinets in which the ruler –
in this case an hereditary monarch – appoints his cabinets at
his own judgment and not necessarily from the elected assembly
or parliament. This seems, to judge by modern France
and the United States, to result in parliaments becoming permanent oppositions to governments, and this was the case in
Austria-Hungary. The oppositional stance of both national
parliaments in Vienna and Budapest was much increased by the
unceasing squabbling over language questions which fragmented
the assemblies into helplessness because they were divided not
only by political views as in all elected assemblies but by language or 'national' status as well. This quarrelsome fragmentation
was the real cause of the frequent suspensions of parliament:
whenever urgent and essential business had to be transacted,
such as financial estimates and budgets, parliament had to be
bypassed in order to get anything done.

Instead of a widening liberalization through elections, the
outcome of the 1914–18 war produced a collection of small,
internally inchoate and mutually hostile states which were supposed to be language units. This was in practice impossible because there are no ethnic barriers in the central European
populations and language, clan and family relationships were
inextricably mixed. None of the new 'nations' was strong or
coherent enough to dominate the Danube. These Succession
States were established in 1919 and twenty years later all
collapsed. This happened because the ancient co-ordination of
the Danube basin was broken and a vacuum of power existed.
Power is as much a fact of nature as air or water and nature
abhors a vacuum in this as in any other element. Of all the
regions and clans that formed the Successor States to the old
Danube Empire the only part that has regained any real control over its own destiny is Austria itself. This is sometimes
believed to be some kind of luck, an extension of 'tu felix
Austria' but luck does not exist historically; it is in fact the

result of careful and tenacious good judgment, the inherited ability to manage circumstances. Not for nothing did this German clan dominate the Danube for a thousand years.

As to the second legend, that the Austrians in general and the Viennese in particular are more gay and frivolous than other people, that too turns out to be a tenable view only if Vienna is considered in isolation. It is true that the Viennese like to enjoy life. But a general survey of European societies in the nineteenth, and for that matter the twentieth, century, shows that Catholic Europe has a higher standard of enjoying life for the sake of living than countries dominated at some time by a form of puritanism. This seems to be independent of wealth and climate, for stern Geneva has a better climate than Vienna and is much richer. The highest level of individual wealth in Europe obtains in Sweden, but if the Swedes enjoy life more than the Italian or Austrian Alpine peoples, who have an equally abominable climate, then they succeed in hiding their enjoyment pretty well completely. Everywhere mankind is born to sorrow as the sparks fly upwards, but Catholic mankind seems to be able to enjoy living between the sorrows better than Calvinists or Lutherans.

The actual cause of the legend of 'gay Vienna' is undoubtedly the series of immortal melodies connected with the names of Johann Strauss father and son, and their successors. The dances and songs were mostly adapted from traditional country dances, the waltz, the mazurka, the polka and so on and were written mainly for what we now call musicals. The quality of the music belongs to the Danube tradition and as soon as restrictive, and essentially puritanical, musical snobbery is abandoned one may slide from Haydn, Mozart and Schubert to Strauss and Lehar and back again without frontiers. How often have I sat with a glass of wine in the sunshine and enjoyed peasant tunes that sounded like familiar friends! It was a long time before I recognized that I had listened to them glorified by Beethoven and Schubert in concert halls, years before I heard their ancestral voices. There are many phrases from Haydn symphonies that sound back and forth in the time-space continuum without any need for Einstein's mathematics. The grip at the heart in Schubert's music for Heine's 'Doppelgänger' is deeper but not different from the equally erotic fury of jealousy in Lehar's 'Ich gehe zu Maxim'. It is not necessary to choose between them; one can have both and to enjoy both is not frivolity but wisdom.

A less obvious cause of belief in Viennese light-heartedness is a tradition that has now almost entirely disappeared, of beautiful manners and superficial conversation. Small talk was an art in Vienna, an applied art and a useful one. It grew from the polyglot nature of official society at all levels. Careers were open to the talents for generations and anyone of ability could rise in the official scale, whether military or civil, if he possessed a grasp of the German language and pledged complete loyalty to the state. Since the state, which is to say the Imperial house, was the source of security, prestige, influence and sometimes power, the loyalty shown was real and rewarded. It would be impossible to mix with half a dozen different nationalities with differing mother tongues in office or garrison all day and every day without developing pleasant and neutral manners and a collection of subjects to talk about. The subjects must also be neutral, of universal if slight interest. The situation can be seen clearly by contrasting it with a different Imperial tradition. In the British Empire the ruled were almost completely divided by rigid barriers from the rulers and where the ruled were included in the processes of administration they performed subordinate functions only. Therefore a series of set phrases in English was sufficient and led to the terse, clipped speech needed for clearness with 'natives' who did not really understand the language; this became the manner so often called the stiff upper lip. The German language on the other hand was in Austria-Hungary a universal second language above peasant level; all educated people were at least bilingual and often multilingual, using French and Italian as well as the domestic vernacular as easily as German. Senior administrators and officers could well come from outlying parts of the realm and carry real authority requiring real respect. A junior might carry an older name and belong to a family of power but he was required to treat his superiors with deference, naturally not only out of the tradition of good manners but for the pressing reason that his superior could make life hell for him at that moment. This constant cross-intercourse made sharp tongues and rough manners professional disadvantages and differing local customs made outspokenness unwise on many subjects. If the Colonel's wife came from Transylvania one did not make jokes about backwoodsmen to the Colonel. These rules and their origins were operative throughout the entire official structure and therefore spread to society as a whole. It was often said by strangers that Austrian good manners were false and they often were, but good manners are usually to some extent insincere for few of us really want to be pleasant to those about us all the time. The arrogance of rank and the stratification of society were just as strong in Austria-Hungary as elsewhere at the time but were expressed with a conciliatory easiness that kept others at arm's length without offending them. Differences of class were very subtle and, as in England, people were able instantly to recognize them. This, like the constant use of several languages, kept wits sharp and increased the interest of everyday life. Nothing is more boring than a society in which everyone is the same, unless it is a society in which everyone says what he means.

The legend of decadence, of waltzing on the powder barrel until the shots at Sarajevo on 28 June 1914 blew it into the air and the dancers with it, was constructed after 1919. Somebody and something other than the new politicians must be blamed for the disaster. Some intellectual bastion must be built against that fear of the future which hag-rides those who know that their defences have disappeared. The co-ordination of the Danube basin was gone and loudest of all those who constructed the responsibility of the old Empire for its going were paradoxically those who believed that they themselves had got rid of the old order. Naturally the old order must have been partly responsible for the disaster and it was certainly a terrible failure of diplomacy to slide into a war that was obviously going to be fought on three fronts; for the defection of Italy from the Triple Alliance had been taken for granted for years. But in fact the politicians and those who wrote for them had got rid of nothing; nearly all the new rulers were put there by the victors. Not one of the new Succession States was voted upon by its people and elections were held only after the new order was established. Every one of the new states held within its borders large minorities of disaffected citizens, and in at least one of the new countries almost half the inhabitants were unwilling to belong to it from its foundation. One of the mysteries of the inter-war period was the belief that such 'nations' could maintain themselves; but the mystery was more apparent than real, for millions of the people concerned never believed that they could. The politicians and their foreign benefactors believed in them as long as all went well, but when the inevitable began to happen in the Danube vacuum of power those benefactors could not help their artificial creations.

These are openly expressed and unpopular views and the quick-witted reader will suppose that I chose the subjects in this collection in order to illustrate them. Not so; I was only one of several people who chose the personalities of these narrative essays by democratic discussion and they were chosen for one reason only. To make a varied and interesting gallery of portraits. The only subject chosen by myself without previous discussion was Gustav Mahler. I suggested him after accepting the commission and starting on the book because it struck me quite suddenly that there was no musician in the list of subjects.

Are the people here presented so out of the ordinary that they cannot be said to reflect the society of their time and place? Perhaps they are, since all but one of them achieved a good deal, albeit in one case in a distinctly negative sense. The only one who achieved nothing was Crown Prince Rudolf and, to be fair to him, he was unlikely to do that for he was born to one of the greatest inheritances in the world and there was little left for him to aspire to. The curious thing is that of the seven people chosen for their achievements – again the Crown Prince is the exception – no less than five of them came from the artisan lower-middle class and the other two from the educated middle class. The only aristocrat among them was a murderer and suicide, so that together with the super-spy Redl, Archduke Rudolf does present a picture of decadence. The other six rose to high honour in their various professions from small beginnings. All these examples were chosen because of what they did with their lives, but it is remarkable and quite unintentional that of the seven commoners five came from the most commonplace of families and the other two from prosperous but otherwise undistinguished parents. The confidante for thirty years of Emperor Franz Joseph was the daughter of a small shopkeeper. The absolute dictator of the Imperial Opera was the son of a disreputable pedlar and pot-house keeper. Anna Sacher came from the counter of a suburban butcher's shop as apprentice in the restaurant trade. These three people must have been of considerable talent and character and their careers would have been notable if they had gone to America to make their fortunes. But they did not emigrate; they stayed in their native place where their origins could not be hidden even if they wished to hide them. In fact none of them did wish to, for class differences, although strong, were not saturated by the bitterness which characterized British society at that time. Once again, this is true of other parts of Europe as well as Austria-Hungary; it may well have a good deal to do with competent teaching of the prevailing language in schools. As in France, it is very rare for native German speakers of normal intelligence not to be able to speak and write the language correctly although dialect may be normally spoken between themselves; neither do regional accents carry a class implication but are heard universally. The rancid inverted snobbery of inability or refusal to speak the native language correctly seems to be confined to English, and not only in Britain.

It is clear, then, that these people did not live in a rigidly stratified or closed society. It was classified but not caste-bound, difficult of access but not closed. Honours and success were not easy of attainment but they were not only attainable to the gifted and determined but were worth having when attained. The framework of life was clear and ordered and so generally agreed upon that to rise within it brought the reward of public respect and admiration. No aspect of society at any level was fluid enough to dilute the rewards of prowess into disappointment; achievement was real. Nor could prestige either be bought by money or expressed in its terms. Money was of course powerful, but there were many things it could not buy because the source of honours was outside and above wealth and resided in the Emperor, whose reputation was untouchable. This was not fear, as was sometimes said after 1918. Franz Joseph was universally respected for the simple reason that examples of injustice or even irregularity on his part could be counted on the fingers of one hand over a long lifetime of devotion to duty.

Consciousness of an ordered framework disappeared abruptly with an effect of silence created by the ending of the ceaseless battering of artillery that filled the foregoing four years.

That shocked silence was anything but peaceful and the pause to catch breath lasted for less than a generation. Then the quiet of exhaustion and recuperation was broken again by the renewal of the war and in 1945 a completely new order was established in the Danube basin. The old realm became a new Empire and the sons of those who had wanted the end of the Dual Monarchy were obliged to learn the ineluctable facts of power by losing all control of their own destinies.

The fate complained about in the past for many years overtook them in reality and if it had happened only to the politicians one might almost say that by inviting the 'Magician's Apprentice' into their homelands they got only what they deserved. Unfortunately the millions of ordinary people who had, then and now, no say in the matter, suffered the same fate but without having invited it. None of the people who figure in these stories lived to see the prophecies of the pan-slavists come true; the one among them who lived longest, Katharina Schratt, died in 1940 before the febrile hubris of Germany had done its worst.

1

Mayerling

IT is an oft-told tale and whenever it is told again it catches the imagination afresh with the completeness of its facets; power, sex, death and mystery. There are descendants of those nearby at the time who still believe that Archduke Rudolf was murdered but they never say by whom or for precisely what motive. They continue to quote persistent family hearsay but there is no substance in their beliefs. Rudolf was a murderer but he was not murdered. Yet we are never quite sure we know just what happened in that intensely personal drama that affected the fates of millions so that the two actors are reduced to miniatures by the huge and ancient frame that surrounds them. Was Mary Vetsera an archetypal figure, an Isolde of the very time of Wagner's *Tristan and Isolde* which was first produced only a year or so before her birth and was a major influence of her short lifetime? Or was she a frivolous little flirt who got into the usual mess and lost first her head and then her life? Is the story a political thriller with principalities and powers as the stakes of reckless and incompetent gamblers? Or is it the sordid end of a decadent weakling unworthy of his high destiny? Tragic drama, or society gossip? It is all and none of those. That is its fascination.

Everyone who contributed to the events or who told the story at the time lied at some point. Some for reasons of State, some for practical or personal reasons, not always dishonourable. Some felt the need to defend themselves against accusations or gossip and by their very defences prove at least the dubiety of their action or inaction. The only two actors who never lied were those who never spoke and they were Rudolf's parents, Franz Joseph, Emperor of Austria and King of Hungary and Bohemia and his wife Elisabeth. All contemporary published accounts of the tragedy but for that of Mary Vetsera's mother, were based on the two brief official announcements of Rudolf's death. On that narrow foundation huge edifices were raised running into millions of words. All those thousands of lies, rumours, intrigues, accusations and counter-accusations, defences and attacks, have been endlessly repeated, interpreted and judged in history, reportage, fiction and film to this day. Even the best of recent analyses treats factoids from newspapers by men who cannot possibly have been sure of what they wrote with the same weight as objective facts. Accounts which have been taken seriously by historians show deep flaws, on the one hand by repeating unproven statements as fact and on the other from lack of knowledge of the time and place; of the machinery of courts and governments; even of the language. Many accounts fall unwittingly into the universal human temptation to blame someone or something other than the people concerned. Many of these misinterpretations were, on the contrary, deliberate, either from personal animosity or by knowingly distorting facts for propaganda purposes throughout many years of preparations for wars and the justification of wars. This is so of the work of some otherwise serious historians whose academic reputations ensure acceptance of their accounts by the general public.

But in fact we know pretty well what happened at Mayerling, or we can know, and have done so since 1928 when a definitive biography of Crown Prince Rudolf was published by Oskar von Mitis whose account, based on State and private papers, has only been confirmed and enlarged by everything that has since then come to light. Further there are some objective facts and quite an amount of circumstantial evidence; police and other reports made at the time and just before it when the significance of times and places was not clear and therefore not tampered with. There are three sets of diaries known to be accurate in quite other matters, kept by persons close to the events. Police reports after Rudolf's death, the findings of the Crown Commission of Enquiry and the doctors who examined the bodies, must be treated with reservation as far as senior officials are concerned because as civil servants they were dominated by the need for secrecy; but they can be checked both for facts and for gaps against other evidence. There is the existence, but not necessarily the contents, of Rudolf's farewell letters and those of his mistress. Then with great caution it is possible to deduct and induct from the self-exculpation of Mary Vetsera's mother, and with greater confidence from the account written a few days after his death by Rudolf's friend, Count Hoyos, who was present at Mayerling. There is also light thrown on Rudolf's physical and psychic health by modern doctors from contemporary evidence, such as medical prescriptions.

The Memorandum privately published by Helene Baltazzi-Vetsera, who was Mary's mother, is a deeply interesting and marvellously feminine document in its mixture of worldly intelligence and naiveté. Its frankly-stated motive was to refute the accusation that Mary's mother was guilty of pandering to the affair of her not yet eighteen-year-old daughter with the Crown Prince. To be even faintly credible this involved making the love-affair as short as possible. It could not be denied that Baroness Vetsera knew that her daughter had a lover a few days before the end because one shattering scene, later described, was heard all over a large mansion full of people and a second hubbub took place partly in public view in a big hotel. But by the skilful use of letters from Mary to a confidante, called Hermine, the seduction was put at a fortnight before Mary's death. For some reason many commentators have accepted this timing although it conflicts both with known facts and with common sense; the Memorandum mixes quotations from these quite genuine letters with other phrases including some from Mary's diary and things said to her sister and her maid; above all the dating of the letters was quite simply omitted or changed.

For example, Mary complained of having to go on a journey with her family to England because it would prevent her seeing Rudolf; and that journey took place a whole year before the tragedy. By putting this accurate information together with still earlier remarks by Mary about seeing Rudolf from afar before she knew him, the impression is cleverly created that by seeing Rudolf Mary meant simply looking at him in public. However, the Memorandum is useful about events immediately before and after the tragedy because its story had to be in conformity with the knowledge of a number of other people who could and did talk. Moreover it was printed four months after the deaths and must therefore have been written in the weeks after them, allowing neither time nor hindsight for help in invention.

Everything after the tragedy happened at great speed while all the persons involved were disoriented by shock and in most cases, grief. Secrecy was imperative for reasons of state but was quite impossible to enforce. There was never any legal enquiry into the two deaths, neither by the police nor by the judiciary; nor were witnesses interrogated by competent lawyers who might have clarified their stories. Finally, an important factor which has caused much misunderstanding especially of the police: there was no access to imperial property by any authority except naturally to its owners and in the last resort to the Emperor himself.

Thus briefly prepared, 'let us sit upon the ground and tell sad stories of the death of kings'.

In June everyone went to the races. Mary's Baltazzi uncles were all four of them good judges of bloodstock, owners and riders of racing horses, riders to hounds when in England or Ireland, rich and reckless gamblers, lovers of women and all the pleasures of life. When in Vienna they went regularly to the meetings at Baden and the Freudenau, an extension of the great park of the Prater, and took their nieces Hanna and Mary with them. The brothers were all still in their thirties and their sister in her early forties; the two girls in their teens. The

Freudenau racecourse by the Danube – its name means 'pleasure meadow', was surrounded by the great poplars and willows of the Danube banks with their evocative scents, by the fresh green of lawns and the blossoming flower beds of May and June which showed up the pretty white grandstand. The Austrians are on the whole a good-looking lot and the Hungarians even more so; they were all well-off and well-born in the stands and in that society which never knew puritanism there was no inhibition about enjoying the good things of life so long as the proprieties were maintained. Hussars in splendid uniforms, their moustaches as sleek as the coats of the racers, senior officers in white tunics or the dark green of the General Staff, tall dragoons with their highly polished accoutrements paraded with fierce rivalry before the pretty women, as handsome as the horses and as proud. Vienna in those days was full of the atmosphere of intense sensuality which always attaches to centres of power and the smallness of the city and its society added the excitement of secrecy to a thousand intrigues. We, in an age of 'anything goes' cannot imagine the seductiveness of rigid convention and formal manners; then the realities of human nature were an open secret, a delightful joke which everyone conspired to pretend did not exist. The sun shone, the Danube wind fluttered everything that moved, the wine glinted green-yellow, laughter and chatter rose and fell in gusts like music and the beauty and spare lines of the thoroughbreds with their dashing speed aroused in everyone the delightful apprehension of physical grace and power.

It was a life that was never going to end; everything was settled for good and in the most charming way for those who inherited it all. The aristocrats had the self-confidence of absolute certainty and considerable ignorance and the few who may have been aware of the new industrial proletariat pressed close together in the back streets of Ottakring were sure that the age of inventions would solve any problems still existing. Medicine and engineering produced constant successes; the framework in which life was lived was stable. There was, there could be no threat; it was a time of euphoria in those circles. Only Rudolf himself, with his excellent education and understanding, was melancholy.

Mary had been watching the Crown Prince for some time. He was her 'crush' and together with a thousand other girls she adored him. Tripping about in the group of her family and friends she would manoeuvre so that she came face to face with him, in the enclosure leading in the winners, waiting for the light curricles and phaetons to go back to the city in the evening light. Once the Prince of Wales, always with an eye for a girl with looks and vitality, pointed her out to Crown Prince Rudolf who reacted with convincingly assumed disinterest. When Mary saw him she would tell her maid how wonderful he was, how his eyes admired her, she was sure he knew her feelings for him. Everyone knew that Mary was 'in love' with Rudolf; it was a family joke. They all knew too that she was to make a great marriage which would bring the whole clan into the highest circles. A Braganza prince was in love with Mary, and one of the Liechtensteins, too. Yes, Mary was to add great rank to the Baltazzi family to go with their looks and their money. With her small and graceful figure, her magnificent eyes and her sensuous vitality she was so desirable that she could pick and choose far greater prizes than the barony conferred on her father on his retirement from the diplomatic service. Mary's mother was sure of that. She had advanced her own rank by marriage but Mary would make a much greater spring upwards.

The Baltazzi family claimed to have come from Venice, but in that generation they came from Constantinople where they were bankers and held the concession to collect tolls on the Galata-Stamboul bridge which had made them immensely wealthy. In Vienna they were therefore looked upon as Levantines but they mixed informally with the highest families, including the imperial family when away from Court. But they were not part of the small group of courtier families and that was what Mary's mother had set her heart on. Helene Baltazzi-

Vetsera was a social climber and like many another before and since she used the weapons fortune had given her: money, horses, her own sexuality and for the future, her daughter. Her brothers were on familiar terms with the British Prince of Wales and stayed in the great houses of the hunting shires with him and his friends. They went to the Imperial studs and hunting lodges too and sometimes took their sister; at least once Helene was staying at a neighbouring house in Hungary and was taken to Gödöllö when the whole Imperial family was there – it was the favourite country house of the Empress – and flirted so outrageously with the then twenty-year-old Crown Prince that even the Emperor made cynical jokes about her attempts to ensnare the boy. Mary's mother was thirteen years older than Rudolf but there is nothing odd about that; no more odd than that Rudolf was thirteen years older than Mary herself.

At that house party or one just like it Helene Vetsera became close friends and allies with another Marie. Marie Wallersee-Larisch was one of those figures who occur throughout history and romance as shadowed by the bend sinister. The men of this kind are familiar to us from Renaissance literature as 'The Bastard' whose birth makes him aggressively ambitious, devious, even treacherous in its claims to royal blood while yet being unchangeably illicit, inferior. Marie's father was one of Empress Elisabeth's brothers, Duke Ludwig in Bavaria, who lived with a Jewish actress and the child was born six months before Duke Ludwig in Bavaria arranged to have her legitimized after marrying Henriette Mendel. They were accepted everywhere and the Empress and her family were always grateful to Countess Wallersee, as she became on her marriage, for her success in managing an eccentric husband. But the child always felt herself to be discriminated against. She was not, she was not only accepted at Court as the Empress's niece but was for some years a particular favourite and protegée of the Empress who took the trouble to cover one or two of the girl's juvenile indiscretions, including one with Rudolf, and arranged her marriage to Count Larisch. It was a marriage of convenience designed to establish the Empress's niece and in this it succeeded. Marie Larisch had the formal right to be at Court which Marie Wallersee could only have informally and she used this right to bring grief to those who gave it to her. Years later her own son committed suicide on discovering his mother's role in the Mayerling deaths.

It was Marie Larisch who introduced her cousin Rudolf to Mary Vetsera. Whenever she could get away from the boring round of a country landowner's wife Countess Larisch came to Vienna to the brilliant balls and receptions, to Court, to the races, to drive in the Prater and be seen at the Opera. This cost a lot of money which Georg Larisch was not prepared to allow her and Countess Larisch was always in debt. Still, she had rich friends and loyal relatives, among them the Baltazzi brothers and their sister, Baroness Vetsera. There is no doubt the wealthy 'Levantines' were generous. Nor is there much doubt that Marie Larisch took advantage of her envied position as a member of the Imperial family, on intimate terms with the fabled Empress and with the heir to the throne her cousin Rudolf, who was her own age and whom she had known all her life. She would not borrow from her friends, still less bargain favours or threaten to disclose secrets such as Helene Vetsera's affairs. No, no, that is not how such things are done. One sighs about the dressmaker's bill and in the next breath one says 'do come with me to the Palais Trauttmansdorff next week, I should hate to go alone.' And the bill just gets paid.

So one day at the races, either genuinely not noticed or carefully not taken note of, Marie Larisch presented the swooningly adoring Mary Vetsera to Crown Prince Rudolf. After that Rudolf came noticeably more often to the races and drove more often in the tree-lined avenues of the Prater where all the world went in its carriage to see and be seen. There one might stop the horses for a few moments and chat across the gleaming coachwork, the Countess and her charming young companion with this or that dashing young man, including His Imperial Highness with his romantic, melancholy eyes. At the time they met Rudolf was in his late twenties and Mary sixteen or seventeen; vagueness is inevitable because we do not know exactly when they first met, nor even whether their first public encounter was really the first meeting, for in illicit affairs social meetings are frequently used to cover other events. In a small and gossipy city containing an even smaller and more talkative Court, secret intrigues require overt excuses; the first rule of security, in whatever dimension the word is used, is never to do anything that offers only one explanation. There were something like half a million persons who would recognize the Crown Prince on sight, and a much smaller number but still several thousand who would know Mary Vetsera as a titled young lady who would never normally appear in the street or any public place alone. If she merely drove in her uncle's carriage from her mother's mansion to the hotel on the Ring where Countess Larisch stayed when in Vienna, she would be accompanied at least by her personal maid, if not by an uncle, her mother or her mother's companion. She would be escorted to Marie Larisch's suite and might be left there by a member of her family but the maid or companion would stay, waiting in another room. Alternatively Countess Larisch would drive the mile or so to Baroness Vetsera's house to pick Mary up; being a married woman, the Countess could and did go out alone but for a lady of the highest circle this informality was not entirely *comme il faut*, especially as Marie Larisch did not keep her own carriage in Vienna but used an 'unnumbered' cab. So Mary was a useful companion for Countess Larisch, just as the older woman was chaperone to the young girl.

In the 1880s prudence was not only necessary but was part of the excitement. In Baroness Vetsera's house with its family of five there would be twelve or fifteen servants and governesses and tutors coming every day. Dressmakers, jewellers, lacemakers, embroiderers, fanmakers, bonnet makers, market porters, coachmen and grooms, guests and their attendants, doctors and constant visitors as well as the four uncles who did not actually live there, were always in and out. Secrecy in such households was an art because all these people talked incessantly in the house amongst themselves and in all the other houses they went to. Friends covered each others' actions and were also in each others' hands and the maids and valets used for message carrying were frequently in positions of servile power that operated in both directions. While a dismissed servant could not get another reputable job and was therefore doubly dependent, he or she knew a great deal about the employer and relationships between them, sometimes affectionate relationships, were based for years, for a lifetime, on something approaching a state of continuous unspoken threat. Servants in aristocratic houses were, it must be borne in mind, much better off than their siblings, enjoyed higher standards of living and easier, more comfortable lives than unmarried countrywomen who were often practically enslaved by the head of the family; and the contrast with unmarried and unprotected townswomen of the poor was even greater. To say nothing of the state of married women; and these things were so not only in Austria but all over Europe.

Vienna was very much the Residence of the Emperor, and the services needed by the Court and foreign diplomats and all their officials still dominated the atmosphere of the inner city. Delayed and insufficient industrialization had by then produced a new proletariat whose leader, Dr Viktor Adler, succeeded in co-ordinating the various groups into one united Party at the beginning of the very month of Rudolf's death. A symbolic conjunction of past and future. At the time it was hardly noticed for politics like war are always conducted by the light of the past; in 1888 the old-fashioned among the ruling class still worried about the Freemasons and the modern discussed Karl Lueger and his 'mass' party of the lower middle class. If they discussed politics at all. Current real politics as distinct from theoretical ideas meant the continuous haggling between the two major nationalities of the Dual Monarchy, the Austrians and the Hungarians.

During the winter of 1888–9 the subject of the unending power-struggle was the Austro-Hungarian Army. The number of conscripts was to be raised; the Hungarians, official and oppositional – which meant almost all Hungarians for they are the eternal 'aginners' – wanted to refuse and many wanted Magyar as command language in all regiments officered by Hungarians. This would have meant separate armies in effect and that is why the Hungarian opposition wanted it. The legislative basis to raise more troops was being forced through the Budapest Parliament in a gunpowder atmosphere during the last few days of the Crown Prince's life. This time-conjunction has led to the suggestion that Rudolf committed suicide because he was involved in a plot with the extreme opposition in Hungary to depose his father. Well, it is just possible. The accession to the throne of Germany by Wilhelm II in 1888 increased his jealousy of Wilhelm, for Rudolf was unlikely to succeed quickly to the throne of Austria-Hungary. His father was still in his fifties and in perfect health. This made him dislike the Germans, and Wilhelm had been tactless in his comments on Rudolf's performance as Inspector-General of the Infantry. If there was any evidence of such a conspiracy, it disappeared in the general clearing up of papers after the tragedy. But it is unlikely. Rudolf certainly played with the comparatively moderate Hungarian opposition led by Count Stephan (Istvan) Karolyi, but there are no grounds for believing that he was involved with the extremists who wished to dissolve the Dual Monarchy. Moreover the apparent political cause, that is the final vote on the conscription question, was not taken before Rudolf's death; the voting then taking place in Budapest was an interim stage in the parliamentary process and although it *may* have been intended to be the signal for a coup d'état there is little sign of it in actual events. Nor does the figure of a desperate adventurer fit Rudolf's character; he was a man who went into projects, discussed them, looked at them from all sides and then backed down and was able to forget them. The political scheme Rudolf pursued longest of his various notions was that of increasing the weight of the southern Slavs in the Empire, an entirely anti-Hungarian idea, since what are now Slovenia and Croatia were governed by the Hungarians.

The whole idea of an Hungarian plot involving Rudolf hangs really upon the notorious telegram he received from Karolyi immediately before he left Vienna for Mayerling; but in the first place he constantly received telegrams from Karolyi; in the second, a message containing crucial conspiratorial news would hardly be sent by public telegraph; and in the third place, if the Crown Prince were really about to head a rising of the Magyars against his father he would have been somewhere in Hungary and not playing about with his mistresses in Vienna. The story just does not stand up in any real world. If Rudolf had been deeply involved with determined plotters they would have made sure of his presence in Hungary under their control. The last place he would have gone to is a small house in a walled courtyard in a heavily wooded area within instant striking distance of at least three major garrisons and without a single adjutant or staff officer belonging to the forces he is supposed to have been plotting with. What may just conceivably be the case, is that the flash-point for a conspiracy may have been set in the immediate future and that Rudolf killed himself rather than face it. But even that is quite unlikely for some evidence must have survived among the family papers of the Hungarian nobles concerned; and nothing has ever come to light. If anything, even hearsay, ever existed it would have been published from the archives of the Karolyi family – one of whom was a left-wing Socialist – after the Great War, or by the Communist Hungarian government when the property of every noble Hungarian family was sacked after the Second World War. The reason that nothing has ever come out is simply that there was nothing to come out.

The Hungarians were not the only people Rudolf dallied with. He had been for years in close and confidential contact with the publisher of the second in importance of the Vienna newspapers and sometimes supplied material for editorial articles to this friend, Moritz Szeps, occasionally writing articles himself. The newspaper was liberal and reformist, and the friendship between Rudolf and Szeps was based on their agreement that imperial policies were mistaken and reactionary. Just as the Hungarian opposition was diametrically contrary to Rudolf's own interests as the future Emperor, so were some of Szeps's views. The overriding and inevitable rival of the Dual Monarchy, the constant danger for the Habsburgs, was Russia. Habsburg foreign policy was therefore almost bound to depend on alliance with the other neighbour and rival of Russia, Germany. But Rudolf disliked the rulers of Germany, Wilhelm II and Prince Bismarck, as much as he feared and hated the Russians. Szeps on the other hand was in close contact both with Bismarck and with the French republican government through his daughter who married Georges Clemenceau's brother. Moreover the inside knowledge of state business given by Rudolf to Szeps was so intimate that its source was very limited and easily identified. Such contacts are necessary and proper to journalists, but for the Crown Prince to supply news to Szeps about his father and his father's government in secret takes on an aspect of personal disloyalty. It is not the case that Rudolf was excluded from all knowledge of government affairs; he was kept constantly informed by the Foreign Minister and others, with the Emperor's knowledge. If the Crown Prince felt that he was distrusted and spied upon it is only fair to point out that this lack of trust was not unjustified. That was not his only unrealism; neither personally nor publicly is it wise to quarrel with both one's neighbours at once and neither is it sensible to commit oneself to those who are undermining one's future – the Hungarians – while openly advocating at the same time an increase of influence to their vassals – the South Slavs.

Rudolf was watched. So were all the members of the Imperial family, about sixty persons, and so are all ruling families everywhere now as then, royal or republican. One of the major reasons for Empress Elisabeth's reputation for eccentricity was her refusal to be guarded when travelling: she was assassinated.

Before the telephone was in general use police agents were much more in evidence than they would be today but already in 1888 the telegraph was making their job easier and less conspicuous since one police station 'morsed' to the next as their illustrious charges moved about. It is an odd circumstance that the only two members of the Imperial family who are known to have complained constantly about this necessary protection are the same two who are also known to have been involved in political and not merely personal intrigues. That is, Rudolf himself and Archduke Johann Salvator.

The encounters with Mary at the Freudenau and on other social occasions may have amused the Crown Prince for a few weeks; hardly more than that. He was a young man of many opportunities and women of all kinds and from all stations flung themselves at his head. Heirs to thrones are, naturally, always handsome and charming but in fact Rudolf may well have been very attractive to women apart from the glamour of his rank. His mother was one of the most beautiful women of her time and his father a tall, well-built and impressive man. Rudolf is said to have inherited his mother's beguiling voice and that charm of which every witness spoke and that made Elisabeth the best-loved and most hated and envied woman in Europe. Over and over again in all the accounts of Rudolf's mother the warning occurs that neither words nor portraits could ever show her grace and beauty as they were in the living woman; all who did not adore her must jealously resent her and there is much evidence of that dichotomy. Such a man, in his late twenties, who had probably never been refused by a woman, would hardly have the patience to continue exchanging glances and light chat with any girl for long. Either the matter would be taken to its logical conclusion or he would drop it without even a shrug. As for Mary, her eagerness may be taken for granted; she knew she was desirable and was full of vitality. Her upbringing and the style of her family were entirely frivolous and self-indulgent; the conventional moralities of the time, whether of religion or prudence, meant as little to her as any girl alive although she used the phrases dutifully like everyone else. Any girl of Mary's age lacks the experience to be genuinely afraid of consequences and human beings with strong erotic urges will never keep the outward rules. And Mary was luxuriously rich, spoiled and indulged by a family undisciplined by duty or responsibility, devoted only to enjoyment; that includes Baroness Vetsera, who is known to have had a number of affairs herself. It was simply a matter of how to arrange things. The answer was simple: Countess Larisch.

Mary Vetsera wrote to her friend Hermine that Countess Larisch, in order to arrange meetings, had begun to 'borrow' Mary as companion to go shopping in the city. On one of these expeditions they went to a fashionable photographer and were taken together, the picture being intended for Rudolf; perhaps an unusual procedure for a girl madly in love to send her lover her own likeness accompanied by that of another pretty woman but that may have been a remnant of convention or a hint of another kind. After that, wrote Mary, they returned to the rear door of the Grand Hotel where Marie Larisch always stayed, changed cabs to Rudolf's personal fiacre and were driven off at speed the few yards that separated the hotel from a sloping cul-de-sac leading to the garden side of the Hofburg, the Imperial Palace. Here they were met at a postern gate by Rudolf's valet and led through corridors, across rooms and up and down dark stairs in the labyrinth of the old buildings, to the Crown Prince's apartments. Mary says that a large black bird, like a raven, flew past them as they entered his door. After some conversation the Crown Prince left Mary alone in his study and went into the next room with his cousin for a few minutes. Mary looked about her and picked up a skull that stood on Rudolf's desk, where she also saw a revolver lying. Rudolf returned to the room and took the skull from Mary's hand as if shocked at her holding it, whereupon Mary assured him she was not afraid of it, making him laugh.

Well, well, it may have happened just like that, just like a scene from a gothic novel of the time. If so it would be interesting to know whether Rudolf was simply seeing Countess Larisch out; or did they have something to discuss that Mary should not hear? They may have done. Rudolf quite frequently helped his cousin with her money affairs which are hinted at in the letters she wrote him, including one that survived from the very weekend of Mayerling. In the midst of a threatening scandal, which she must have known would ruin her, over the elopement aided by herself of the heir to one of the Great Powers of Europe with an unmarried girl, she did not forget to mention obliquely her need of money. Countess Larisch was clearly one of those women who keep an eye on what seems to them the main chance while lacking any sound concept of self-preservation.

The revolver on the desk is not surprising. Rudolf was the Inspector-General of the Infantry, an office newly created in 1888 in the course of an attempted reorganization of the armed forces. He was therefore professionally much involved in the design and provision of small arms, as well as being a serving officer. But the bird of ill-omen? The skull? It may have been so for Rudolf was very morbid as we shall see. In the custom of the time and place a first scene in a seduction would more typically be staged with music and flowers, but it may have been so.

Mary's description is alleged to have been written to Hermine in November 1888 and the actual seduction is said to have taken place on 13 January 1889, a fortnight before Mary's death. That date was used by Baroness Vetsera because Mary had it engraved on a present to Rudolf so that it was a crucial date, and one that could not be left unmentioned. Yet the previous November when Mary's mother was spending the evenings attending a Wagner cycle at the Opera, Mary made constant excuses not to go to Wagner and went instead secretly to see Rudolf. If he had been a boy of her own age this would be credible but even if the dating of Mary's letters were not false, it is hard to see an experienced philanderer keeping busy evenings free to sit holding hands for hours alone with a desirable and willing girl. It is very much more likely that they had been lovers since soon after they first met.

It may in general be said that the crucial moment in a love affair comes at some time after the first year. It varies a great deal with temperament and character and with the responsibilities and other people involved but to be a matter of life and death within weeks is very unusual indeed. Not only does a physical passion need time to become necessary to an experienced man, but people with busy lives and many formal duties, professional and social, do not become deeply involved until a love affair is so much part of themselves that they cannot support the remainder of life without it. This is especially so for a man whose marriage was from the first a matter of reason and has turned out badly – which is by no means always the case.

In this case it was so. Crown Princess Stephanie was graceless, stupid, aggressively self-righteous, and the intelligent and highly educated Rudolf would never have found her satisfying for long. They were married in 1881 when Stephanie was just sixteen and Rudolf twenty-three so the wife was hardly to blame; she was just not clever or attractive enough. Diary entries by someone in a position to know suggest that Rudolf did not want to marry and that the change in his personality towards gloominess dates from that time. They had one daughter born in 1883, the Archduchess Elisabeth.

Early in 1886 Rudolf was ill and to judge from the medical treatments prescribed and from subsequent ailments such as rheumatic pains and eye-trouble, it was almost certainly gonorrhoea. At the time it was called cystitis and peritonitis and Princess Stephanie was not told otherwise. Much later in her memoirs she wrote that Rudolf had infected her with the disease; she told this too to friends and complained that the secrecy practised at that time cost her years of ill-health and unhappiness. The worst after-effect of this infection is that it causes sterility, particularly in women, and in fact poor Stephanie never had another child. At that time venereal diseases were not only terrible in themselves but were attended by shame and self-disgust. When Stephanie discovered what was wrong and that the nature of her illness had been kept secret to protect her husband's reputation, one can imagine that her horror was deep enough to make her hate Rudolf; it would be hard to think of a more decisive way of wrecking any marriage.

Rudolf too showed the signs of despair, becoming very promiscuous, drinking too much and at any rate for a time, taking morphium to alleviate the pain and discomfort of the medical treatment. All this seriously undermined his general health. To remorse and illness was added an even deeper anxiety. King Ludwig of Bavaria was Empress Elisabeth's second cousin and by 1886 both he and his brother were incurably insane. Ludwig was deposed by a Council of State and incarcerated in a castle almost surrounded by the waters of Lake Starnberg. Barely twenty-four hours later he and his doctor were both found drowned in the lake. Altogether there were more than twenty marriages between the Bavarian royal family of Wittelsbach and the Habsburg family and there was mental illness too in the Baden family from which Elisabeth's grandmother came. Elisabeth and Franz Joseph themselves were first cousins (their mothers were sisters) and related in other ways several times over. Rudolf therefore had only half the normal number of grandparents. The rigid family custom as to the rank of possible marriage partners and the need for an heir to the greatest of the Catholic dynasties to marry only a born Catholic, made the choice very narrow. Fatally narrow.

Rudolf represented his father at poor King Ludwig's funeral and his mother was staying with her Bavarian family at the time. Rudolf was horrified by the effect on his mother; she swayed between fatalistic melancholy and an unappeasable restlessness and nervousness and it is not too much to say that these moods never left her again. Elisabeth should not be called neurotic for it was a justified fear that drove her; she was terrified of the mental illness in her family. Nothing is so catching as fear and Elisabeth's only son was infected by his mother's anxiety and by the whole sad, weary and frightened atmosphere of her family which was certainly not made lighter by the uncertainty as to how Ludwig had died. It was not clear then or now whether he threw himself into the lake and his doctor died trying to save him, or whether he tried to escape and was being restrained.

In the state of mind Rudolf was in this additional burden gnawed secretly at his stability, and as with all deep fears, the atavistic superstition that speaking of it might invite the very curse that is dreaded, kept him silent. He did not speak of it, but he began at various times and to different people, to speak darkly of death.

This serious self-distrust came into violent conflict with Rudolf's accepted vision of himself. He had been praised and flattered since he was a small boy. Apart from the first one his teachers flattered him; naturally the courtiers did so, and women did so. He was widely loved and highly praised by the general public. His mother, in one of the few dynamic actions of her life, had insisted on his having an education of the highest standards and half the best academic brains of Vienna were the boy's school masters. Rudolf possessed considerable natural intelligence and was able to profit by his learning so that the inevitably liberal tendencies of a comprehensive education were bound to contrast with the conservatism natural to one who was to inherit an ancient and powerful destiny. Cleverness and praise made him more arrogant than he was bound to be and an education far superior to most of his cousins and the other aristocrats he mixed with gave him the conviction that he could do everything better if only he were allowed to; he was frustrated only by the authority of his father, the machinery of Court and State and the idleness of high-born ministers. But the chance of being able to put his ideas into practice while he was still young was remote; his father was by no means old and had been reigning since he was eighteen. Rudolf felt the weighty shadow of his father even more than most boys do;

he was much in awe of the Emperor and admired him deeply but he was also deeply jealous. Objectively, the Crown Prince was not in nearly such a difficult position as his kinsman, the heir to the British Empire who was relegated to an inane unemployment for most of his life. At twenty-nine Rudolf was given a highly responsible and serious job, that of Inspector-General of the Infantry which was the most important arm of a great land-power's armed forces.

It was by no means entirely the Crown Prince's fault that he failed almost spectacularly at the beginning of this task. New weapons had been ordered before his appointment which examination – Rudolf's responsibility – showed to be unsuitable. Briefly, modern and more powerful rifles needed ammunition of a weight and size that made the infantryman's load too great for marching. Nobody noticed this until large orders had been manufactured. It was precisely to prevent that sort of thing that an Inspector-General of Infantry had been appointed, and if Rudolf had been giving his whole mind to his job it could and should have been corrected or cancelled in time. The new German Emperor, the same age as Rudolf and greatly envied by him, had been brutally frank about this failure. This was a public professional disaster to which not enough weight has been given in Rudolf's tragedy, but although blame attached to his staff it attached to Rudolf too. To put it mildly, nobody can do a job well if he spends half his nights drinking and whoring in low taverns, which is what Rudolf was doing for several years. His rackety life, often accompanied by Prince Philipp of Coburg, became notorious in the capital and some of his escapades took the machinery of Court and State to cover them up.

Thus within three years Rudolf suffered bitter humiliation in the two departments of life that make a man what he is, his profession and his sexual life. He was hag-ridden by the inescapable fear of insanity. He was under the Emperor's weighty displeasure and his wife was constantly complaining. There can be no wonder that he was morbid and reckless. All this time the Hungarians were trying and perhaps succeeding in wheedling him into their convoluted intrigues and his friendship with Moritz Szeps was near-public. On at least one occasion Rudolf was covertly attacked about Szeps in a small anti-semitic newspaper, on another the same kind of bullies beat up Szeps's editors in their office; it was an open secret where Szeps got his inside stories. No blame to the journalist, whose duties are always opposed to the established power, but the friendship was not good for Rudolf and not good for Szeps; nor was it in the long run good for the Jews in general.

With all these pressures increasing, both inwardly and from outside, the wonder is that Rudolf could have the energy, or could be bothered, to begin a new love affair at all. He might have been expected to make do with his other Maria, called Mitzi, who was what would nowadays be called a call-girl. Maria Kaspar was pretty and well-grown, a practical and sensible girl who worked hard at her trade, remained friendly with the lawyer who launched her on her career and who was a confidant of the police, was in touch with a high-class procuress called Wolf whose clients came from the very highest circles and went to bed with Crown Prince Rudolf whenever he wished. They spent the night together, drinking a lot of champagne, from 27 to 28 January, which was the day on which Rudolf took his last journey to Mayerling. According to the Palace Commander of the Guard, Mitzi was in the Hofburg in Rudolf's rooms; one of the letters he left for his Executor to deliver after his death was to Mitzi.

Rudolf, as far as a man in his psychic state was capable of affection, was probably genuinely fond of Mitzi and depended on her cheerful energy and simplicity for distraction from his gloomy moods. It is indirectly from Mitzi that we have the real key to Rudolf's death.

Some time before, Rudolf suggested to Mitzi Kaspar that they should go to a public garden and shoot themselves together. She laughed at him but did not fail to inform her lawyer-protector, knowing of course that he would take the story to the police in confidence. Earlier still Rudolf wrote that he tried to find opportunities to watch both human beings and animals in the moment of death, 'and I try to accustom my wife to the sight too'. In the last period of his life Rudolf often hinted at his own suicide, usually saying that his honour required it. He spoke of death, his own death, quite often too in a general way; there are several recorded memories of Rudolf indicating the Archduke next in succession to himself and saying that he and not Rudolf would inherit the throne of Austria-Hungary. He was wrong; the Archduke Franz Ferdinand was assassinated at Sarajevo a generation later. But the meaning of all these words and actions is quite clear. Rudolf suffered from an obsession with death and in particular with his own death in conjunction with sexual relations. There may have been other lovers to whom Rudolf made hints of death; he made them to each of the three women intimate with him of whom records have survived. This pathological state of mind is called necrophilia and is the cause of many sexual murders. If poor Rudolf was not a necrophilist he was very near it, and when he was in control of himself the thought must have terrified him. His fear of insanity must have been much sharper, much more immediate, than such fears usually are if he felt such impulses strongly enough for him to suggest to others that they should be translated into action.

In November 1888 Rudolf was thrown by a horse and suffered a concussion which caused severe headaches but, his vanity hurt by the misadventure, he pretended it had not happened and did not consult his doctors. This was not a serious accident but it improved neither his health nor his mood.

The rumours in Vienna and in the kernel of Vienna, the Court, grew with choking luxuriance. Gossip about the little Vetsera was hardly covert any longer; not that anyone minded injuring the girl's reputation but it was unwise to offend Rudolf who would one day have power. Princess Stephanie was going to separate from her husband or he was going to send her away. The Crown Prince was going to write to the Pope to ask for an annulment of his marriage; he had already written to the Pontiff who had returned the letter – but to the Emperor. There had been an open quarrel between father and son. The Emperor had cut his son dead in public. The Emperor was going to send Rudolf away as Governor of Bosnia. Some of these stories have a familiar ring but for the illustrious titles; all men with mistresses who cannot quite be abandoned without consequences tell them that they don't really live with their wives, that they are separating, getting divorces; that they will get other jobs in other places and will live together happily ever after. Sometimes the husband even means these things; sometimes he actually does them. But more often he does not, especially when he has great possessions and privileges to lose; and a dragon of a wife can be useful to a philanderer. Rudolf was no different from other men of the kind who must constantly test out their power to attract and when he said such things to Mary she proudly repeated them to her confidantes under seal of secrecy. When Hermine warned her in letters, she was sure she knew best. Her sister tried to warn her, even her maid who carried messages and watched that no one was about when Mary wanted to slip out, tried to warn her. 'I love him,' she cried, poor child, 'I can't live without him and he loves me. If only we could go and live in a cottage or the Governor's Palace outside Sarajevo, we should be so happy.'

But Rudolf was different from other men. When Mary said 'I can't live without you' his reply was not 'but you don't have to, darling'. He said then they would die, that death was better than loss, than growing old, better than life. Sometimes he was going to separate from his wife, sometimes they were going to die clasped in each others' arms, like Tristan and Isolde. For a girl of not quite eighteen these were almost interchangeable pictures of romance. Unfortunately Rudolf meant it.

Summer days at the races are now so far away that they might never have existed. Perhaps they never did exist, so like a remembered scene from an operetta do they seem in the dark of January. Confined in loose-boxes the horses hide their deli-

cate muscularity under monogrammed blankets, stepping rest-
lessly on narrow hooves. The grandstand is closed, the flower
beds sheeted with snow and when the sun shines it glitters on
frost. The handsome officers are back on duty; in winter-quarters
they do not need their parade uniforms. The ladies of Cernowitz,
of Krakow, of Varazdin are just as pleased with their escorts
in service tunics and heavy greatcoats. All those silk and muslin
dresses, like bouquets of flowers in themselves, are discarded
and given away to poor relations, to provincial dowdies like
Hermine, to servant girls who wear them at the balls of the
carnival season.

The scene was indeed changed and it was now deep winter.
Snow whirled, the great winds blew, the river swelled gun-
metal dark and cruelly swift. The spires and domes of Vienna
outlined in white showed against the looming sky and in the
hilly forests of the Wienerwald veils of icy fog drifted when
the wind dropped.

If it was still theatrical, certainly it was no longer operetta.
A tale of complicated trivialities, it had become a Wagnerian
tragedy. Tragedy is the conflict between the will of the gods
and the will of man. The will of the gods is what *must* be and
the fate of man is either to accept what must be or revolt and
take the consequences; all Wagner's later work is founded in
that ancient theme and it powerfully influenced the imagination of his time for a good reason: his work is prophetically
real. Wagner himself, unlike most artists, more than half understood what he was saying – he even wrote about it before he
wrote the great operas – and it is not necessary to go further
back than Wagner to disprove the absurd and widely accepted
claim that Freud 'discovered' the unconscious mind or soul.
All artists deal in the unconscious; that is one definition of art,
valid at least since the aesthetic expression of the Greek myths
and probably long before them.

And there lies the lasting fascination of Mayerling for it
expresses not one but two ancient mythical concepts. There
is the king and his son and there is eros and death. What

frightened and undermined the society, the polis, in which Rudolf lived and died was the reversal of the natural order where the king must die and his son survives him as embodiment of the polis. The son was killed by the weight of the crown and the father condemned to carry that burden into the future; the past unnaturally and damagingly lasting long beyond its time because the future had been removed.

The poetic conjunction of love and death had until the middle of the nineteenth century a perfectly practical basis throughout history. Until medicine, beginning with a Viennese doctor, Ignaz Semmelweis who found the cause of childbed fever, began to make childbirth safer the chance of survival of a woman with child was not much better than fifty-fifty. Up to about the same time there are no reliable records, but history is full of examples of the universal truth that the act of love might well condemn the woman to die. Driven to love the woman accepted that and driven to love the man was both the source of life and the killer of the source of life. Man was literally the surrogate of God or Nature on earth because he made both life and death. No wonder this tremendous power has always until our own day been surrounded by complex magic and regulated by the stern rules and sanctions of all civilized societies.

Richard Wagner died only five years before Mayerling, and *Tristan and Isolde* was first performed in 1865 and in Vienna in 1883. Its influence as music and theatre steadily increased and although most of its audiences were not aware of it, its theme of love and death was more powerful than it could have been at any other time precisely because for the first time in all history the meaning of the theme was changing. Or perhaps rather, the concept of eros and death was beginning to lose its meaning.

The doctors like Semmelweis and Lister who discovered antisepsis, to name only two among many, changed the whole fundament of human life; they removed the knowledge of ultimate responsibility from the minds of men. And medicine was only one part of knowledge that changed the whole view of mankind of itself and of nature or God; Darwin who feared he might undermine belief with his biological determinism had good reason to fear his own discoveries for the opposite reason. Instead of educated mankind feeling itself to be demoted to the company of plants and animals, it felt on the contrary that man was the survivor and dominator, the Superman who could challenge the eternal laws of nature. Nietzsche expressed the thought as 'The Man Who Killed God' and both of Wagner and Nietzsche it can be said that they are feared and hated because they prophesied the truth and not for the inverted reason that has been invented for a fear whose cause we cannot admit. The terrible hubris of the time was expressed naïvely by ordinary people in the gross arrogance and loss of proportion of their houses, their clothes, the painting they admired. Artists, half aware of the meaning and quite sure of the ugliness of contemporary fashions, were beginning impotently to warn.

Rudolf and his Maries lived out in an apparently meaningless charade in which love, power and death trickled away into vulgar gossip, the crucial dilemma that the nineteenth century was preparing for the twentieth. The dilemma of great power which has lost the constant reminder of unavoidable responsibility. It has issued in what a great Russian poet, Anna Akhmatova, called 'the true twentieth century'; that is, in a succession of unlimited horrors.

Now pay attention. If the story is complicated so far, it is about to become much more so.

As happens so often in illicit love affairs, after months of apparent calm everything went wrong at once. For lovers in such an exposed position, Rudolf and Mary were not particularly discreet. At least once Mary walked alone with Rudolf in the gardens of Schönbrunn Palace with its long rows of overlooking windows. At least once she drove home with him in his carriage. He left her at the door of the house next to her mother's mansion and was seen himself by someone who at once recognized him. Several times they met in the Prater, Mary accompanied by Countess Larisch, at times when to be seen there would at once arouse suspicion. At least once Rudolf got in touch with Mary by the public post. The last two circumstances prove an important point. Rudolf could no longer use his personal servants to carry messages although they were entirely loyal to him. In other words Rudolf had been ordered to end the affair with Mary and had given his word to do so to the only authority that could demand it of him, his father the Emperor. Princess Stephanie had requested a formal audience of the Emperor and complained of her husband's behaviour, at the same time warning him of Rudolf's worsening health and nervous state. Franz Joseph sent her off with a few words intended to be comforting but this complaint may have forced him to interfere with his son and he would be seriously annoyed at being forced to take open notice of Rudolf's indiscretions.

The Emperor was already displeased with Rudolf as a soldier. He was his only son's Commander in Chief as well as his father and the débâcle over the new small arms was a personal humiliation to himself. The Emperor almost certainly knew something both about the Hungarian intrigues and about Moritz Szeps as well as about Rudolf's frequent drunken evenings in the town; he may too have heard the ridiculous rumours about Rudolf asking the Pontiff to annul his marriage and Stephanie may have mentioned Mary Vetsera's name. Of course the letter to the Pope was never written; even in his melancholic and paranoic state Rudolf cannot have so lost touch with reality as to think he could get rid of his wife. We know he did not lose contact with ordinary facts because he continued with his public and official life. But he probably *told Mary* he would get a papal dispensation to separate formally from Stephanie; and Mary had repeated his assurances. The Vatican archives and the personal papers of the Pope were searched by an American scholar after the Second World War and neither a letter nor any tell-tale sign of something having been removed were found because, of course, there never was a letter. But the diaries of three ladies at Court, one of them Rudolf's younger sister, which are known to be reliable, mention a painful interview between the Emperor and Rudolf. It must indeed have been a painful occasion and the Emperor's natural reserve must have been stiffened to coldness and anger by embarrassment so that he spoke harshly. There was no alternative but for Rudolf to give his word to break off the affair as quickly and discreetly as possible, and to mend his ways in general.

On 26 January Baroness Vetsera's lady-companion went to her and told her that the day before, on their way back from skating, Mary had insisted on the companion going with her to a fortune teller. On coming out of the woman's 'consulting' room Mary was pale and upset. Thinking this over the companion had decided that Mary's mother ought to know of it. She then went further and recounted another incident. On 15 January the companion went shopping with Mary who took her to the jeweller Rodeck and ordered a gold cigarette case with an engraving; when ready it was to be picked up by Mary's personal maid. Mary begged the companion not to say anything about this purchase because it was intended as a surprise present. But now, after the visit to the 'fortune teller', the companion was so concerned that she felt she must tell Mary's mother about it.

This is the story told after the tragedy by Baroness Vetsera. It would be quite in character for a young girl at the crucial stage of a passionate love affair to consult the stars or have her hand read. It is clearly even more likely that the woman was a mid-wife who would indeed tell Mary her fortune. But that is a guess. Baroness Vetsera took the trouble in her memorandum to deny this possibility with as clear a hint as the conventions of the time allowed. That guess is not only the most likely and common-sense explanation of the sudden crisis, however. Many years later an old lady came forward and made an official statement about papers she had been shown in her youth. These were in the possession of the heirs of the Count Taafe who was Prime Minister at the time of Mayerling and were in fact part of those papers extracted from the Imperial archives after the tragedy, which had been kept by Count Taafe. When the descendants of the former Prime Minister intended to leave central Europe and go back to Ireland, their former homeland, these documents had been shown to the old lady, a connection by marriage, evidently with the feeling that some record of their existence ought to be made. As far as is known these documents were later destroyed by the Taafe family in accordance with the oath of secrecy sworn many years before to the Emperor Franz Joseph. But the old lady not only remembered quite clearly something of what she had read, but she was very careful not to claim more than she did know and cautious about details so that she was clearly a person to be trusted. And she said that among the documents was the report of the Court doctor who examined Mary Vetsera's dead body and she was pregnant.

Having heard the story related by her companion Baroness Vetsera sent for Mary. After a long and noisy scene heard by a number of members of the household, Mary admitted that she had ordered the gold cigarette case for Crown Prince Rudolf but maintained that she had sent it to him anonymously by a public messenger. It bore the inscription, translated, 'January 13th 1889. Thanks to good fortune.' Evidently something crucial had occurred on that date, and the existence of the cigarette case, which had been shown to several people by the Crown Prince, obliged Baroness Vetsera to account for it in her Memorandum, which she did by dating the seduction of her daughter on that day. But Mary did not mention the inscription and stubbornly denied any personal relationship with Rudolf. Helene Vetsera no longer trusted her daughter and insisted on Mary opening a small iron cassette where she kept her jewellery and other treasures. The expected love-letters were not there but there was a diary and an 'iron' cigarette case – it may have been gun-metal or polished steel – with a sapphire set in the cover and the inscription 'Rudolf'. There was also a will dated 18 January 1889; that is, just over a week before. Young girls restricted by convention and wealth to concerning themselves with nothing but their own persons and kept carefully in ignorance of the realities even of that very limited field of perception, always kept diaries and made wills, and Mary was no exception. To make a will leaving one's trinkets to one's friends was not the expectation of dying; it was the recognition of something of importance happening in one's own life, a small ceremonial act marking change. And diaries, except those of born diarists touched by the recording angel, for whom we should all be grateful for the minutiae of past times, usually show blanks just at the times when something is happening. Like over-emotional friendships between girls they have disappeared as young women are allowed to do something more active with their time.

But the 'iron' cigarette case was another matter altogether. Where did Mary get it? Countess Larisch had given it to her, Mary finally said. Rudolf gave it to his cousin and Mary had begged it off the Countess as a memento. Finding no love letters or other evidence of a personal acquaintance between Mary and the Crown Prince, Baroness Vetsera recounts that she felt reassured and although Mary looked pale and drawn after this scene, she recovered enough to go for the usual afternoon walk with her mother.

At six in the evening Mary was missing from her room and the servants said she had gone out alone. Baroness Vetsera at once assumed correctly that Mary had gone to the Grand Hotel on the Ring where Countess Larisch stayed in Vienna, and followed her there. She was told that the Countess had just left the hotel to take her young friend home. On her return the mother found her daughter in bed, deathly pale and shaking in a state of nervous collapse. Her sister Hanna reported that Mary had fallen in a faint to the floor and that she and Countess Larisch had put her to bed. The Countess was still there and asked Mary's mother what had been happening. Mary had sent to her to ask if she could come to see her. The Countess sent back a message that she must be with the Empress at seven in the evening. But Mary herself then rushed into the room, alone, threw the cigarette case at the Countess crying 'take it back! I'm going to throw myself in the Danube.' She then fell to the floor in a dead faint, just as she did on her return home. The Countess revived Mary and at once brought her back home.

The Baroness asked her friend about the steel cigarette case and received the answer that it was a present from herself to Mary; she knew nothing at all about a gold case. She added that she must rush off, she was already late for dinner with the Empress. But she would find out from her cousin whether he knew from whom the present of a gold cigarette case had come.

On the following morning, which was Sunday, Mary managed to get up and went to her mother looking pale and exhausted with weeping. The mother kissed her and begged her to be sensible and stop all this nonsense. What would people say if they knew that Mary was sending expensive presents to the Crown Prince? Then the Countess Larisch arrived with the news that Crown Prince Rudolf had been to see her, had laughed at her concern over the gold cigarette case and definitely had no idea who had sent it to him. It was then agreed that the Countess should collect Mary at 10.30 the next day and they would drive together to the jeweller and get him to change Mary's name in his order book to that of Countess Larisch, thus removing the evidence that Mary had been making valuable presents to a man. At the same time Mary was invited to drive with the Countess that afternoon, and the Baroness agreed that she could go.

Now, with all the events of this fateful weekend, the actual movements are more or less correct, with the usual mistimings from memory. They had to be because so many people heard and saw them. It is the purpose, the content, of the activities which is always suspect. The police reports in the files of the Police Chief of Vienna, Baron Krauss, conflict somewhat in timing. The police commissioner for the First District – the old city – reported that Rudolf visited the Grand Hotel by the servants' entrance on Sunday 27 January at 1.30 in the afternoon after a messenger had taken a letter and a packet to him that morning in the Palace from Countess Larisch. The report from the political or security police, however, says that Countess Larisch arrived from her home at the hotel on Saturday evening and at once sent a message to Rudolf who then came to see her in the hotel on Sunday morning at about ten o'clock. These differences are more apparent than important; both reports were written a week or so after the tragedy by the heads of the departments concerned and not by the actual policemen present at the time. The time of Countess Larisch's arrival at the hotel is not recorded, but even if she came as late as five o'clock, when in January it would be dark, Mary could still have visited her at about six. It is entirely possible that there were two messages to Rudolf and two reply visits by him to the hotel, on one of which he came secretly, as he thought, to the back door in the street parallel to the Ring and once openly by the main entrance, so that he would on each occasion be seen by a different policeman or other informant.

Certainly Mary Vetsera would want to let Marie Larisch know immediately that her relations with Rudolf were in danger of becoming known and Marie Larisch would equally want urgently to get this news to Rudolf. She wrote two letters to Police Chief Krauss immediately after Mary's disappearance and one at least, because it survived to cause her banishment from Court, to Rudolf during that weekend. All three letters are incoherent with panic, which is understandable enough after Mary's abduction. But why was Countess Larisch so upset in her letter to Rudolf when the crisis over the two cigarette cases was already resolved? After six in the evening of Saturday 26 January at least thirty people in the Vetsera household and the Grand Hotel knew that something was seriously wrong. There had been tears and uproar, wails and raised voices; at least one Baltazzi uncle had been called in, Mary had run out into the street alone, been seen distraught and weeping in the hotel hall and on the stairs, heard screaming at Countess Larisch in her suite. A little later the Countess, in full evening dress for dinner with the Empress in the Hofburg, had been seen helping the half-fainting girl into a cab and driving off with her when she should have been leaving for court – it may be taken for granted that hotel staff would know that Countess Larisch was dining at the palace. To arrive late for dinner with an Empress is no light matter; yet Marie Larisch did not dare leave Mary alone to create more disturbance. She was forced to make sure that Mary was taken back to her mother. The following day messages were passed to the Hofburg and Rudolf came at least once and probably twice to see his cousin at the Grand Hotel.

That the women might lose their heads over a problem of who had given a cigarette case to whom, even that they should be upset after this matter had been solved by Mary giving back to Countess Larisch her iron case and Baroness Vetsera believing that Rudolf did not know where the gold case came from; that is just possible. They were terrified of an open scandal. But can anyone believe that Mary's Baltazzi uncles or Rudolf himself would take such trifles so seriously? The surviving letter from Countess Larisch to Rudolf shows that the men were taking it all seriously. Literally translated, including the punctuation, it runs: 'you know I am totally committed to you and will obey you when ever you call on me. Of course I will come with her in these threatening circumstances, I can't let her face the difficulties alone – I will *definitely* come, no matter what happens! – I wanted to send her alone because I have an important meeting on which everything for me depends, if I get there later than twelve, because I have to catch the train at two; still, after the incident yesterday with A. I will come with her, he is capable of anything! Your devoted Marie.' She then added 'it will be better for me to use my own cab, we will be there about half past ten!'

Two of the four Baltazzi brothers had names beginning with A. There were Alexander and Aristide; between them came Hektor and the youngest was Heinrich. Heinrich was a professional soldier, the others were all tough sportsmen and reckless gamblers; one of them was criticized by the Stewards of the Jockey Club in England, one owned an English Derby winner (Kisber in 1876) so with the possible exception of Heinrich who was bound by the stern code imposed on army officers, none of them can have been exactly delicate in his feeling of honour. But the public reputation of their womenfolk, as distinct from their chastity, would be of great importance to them; of even more importance than to a contemporary Viennese of their kind because they came from a Moslem country. They were the fatherless Mary's natural protectors and would be extremely angry at the discovery that she was having an affair which threatened to become public, both with their niece and with their sister for failing to supervise the girl. The identity of Mary's lover removed any possibility of a duel or of threats; to threaten the heir to the throne was high treason and in any case for such social and personal troubles there were clear rules. The procedure would be to remove Mary from Vienna and if necessary to marry her off quickly; the lover would be requested through a mutual acquaintance or by one of the brothers, to return any letters or tokens in his possession and to promise discretion. But such extreme measures would only be needed in the case of either pregnancy or an open scandal or both; a little folly of exchanging cigarette cases would be covered up by removing any evidence of it, and this was already in train. Countess Larisch had already volunteered to take the responsibility for buying the gold cigarette case on herself; the recovery of any letters of Mary's was a foregone conclusion. They need only be asked for; the sanction of a complaint to the Emperor need never be mentioned.

Even after Mary's disappearance all the evidence shows that everyone concerned except Mary herself was dominated by the fear of scandal. So why the hubbub which produced the danger of scandal? Why did the highly experienced Helene Baltazzi get so upset herself and so upset Mary that the whole house heard them? Why was a family council called during that week-end of the whole family including their brother-in-law, Baron Stockau? Above all, why was Mary, after the noisy argument with her mother, so frantically upset that she ran out into the street alone – even to an adventurous girl then, that would be physically frightening – was seen weeping and certainly dishevelled in the public rooms of a large hotel, and fainted twice ? If the story offered by her mother is what happened, the cause of dissension had already been partly removed and she had the co-operation of mother and confidante-chaperone in removing the evidence of it.

It was in the days of tight lacing far more frequent than it is today for women to faint; but they fainted then for the same reasons that they still do. The causes are violent shock, the early stage of pregnancy and sometimes menstrual pain. Either Mary was pregnant or the reality of her position had been brought home to her with staggering suddenness. The likelihood is that both causes were present. When she was left alone in her room after the walk with her mother, the evidence she already possessed combined with what her mother had said to her to produce a state of anguish and despair. She no longer believed what Rudolf had been telling her, she saw Marie Larisch as a false friend whose loyalty, if it existed at all, was to Rudolf; and she assessed realistically the changes in her relationship with Rudolf of the last few weeks. It had become much more difficult for her to go to him in his apartments in the Hofburg. At least once he had been obliged to send her a message addressed to her maid by the ordinary post. Several times they had met after dark in the Prater, Mary being accompanied by Marie Larisch. Whereas previously they had been able to arrange meetings between themselves, Rudolf had recently been obliged to telegraph Countess Larisch who left her home and came to Vienna against the express wishes of her husband in order to cover their meetings. We know that Mary was an intelligent if uneducated girl, and of a practical nature; if she were not she could not have managed to get in and out of the family home at night as she had done without being caught.

Mary already knew that Rudolf had been ordered to end his illicit affair. He must, clearly, have had to explain the changed situation to her. Now her mother had certainly told her with horrifying clarity if not downright brutality, that any hope of a permanent relationhip with Rudolf was moonshine, that even if Stephanie were to die he could never marry Mary nor could he maintain a second household with the silent compliance of his family and public opinion as was the custom in other countries. If Rudolf had told Mary differently, he was lying to her. And this was conclusively proved by the cautious behaviour of the past few weeks. Because if he intended to acknowledge his relationship with Mary the crucial moment was the challenge by his father. At that moment Rudolf must either have defied his father or he must have agreed to obey him; there was no other alternative. The apparent third way, that of Rudolf saying to his father that he would give Mary up and continuing to see her, was not possible for more than a very short time, which had already elapsed, without the Emperor knowing of it. Rudolf was near-paranoic on the subject of being watched and was convinced that the Emperor always knew everything that went on in the whole of his realms, let alone in his own palace. Mary must have known this at least as clearly as all Rudolf's other friends; it was the subject of his almost obsessive talk.

The Emperor was in fact not a martinet as he is often depicted, and was as permissive in sexual matters as any of his subjects, being by no means averse to the occasional affair himself. But as with all serious people, for him the family came first; and these were Catholics and the holders of ancient rights and privileges which carried correspondingly heavy obligations. The heir to the Apostolic Crowns of Austria and Hungary could not possibly be publicly known as an adulterer, no matter what he did in private. There was no agreed custom, such as existed formerly in France, of royal mistresses once the succession had been secured and even if there were it would not come into being until Rudolf and Stephanie had at least one son.

There are two main categories of philanderers; those who say honestly that this is an affair and no more and make sure that the woman understands that; and those who delude themselves at the start of each adventure that this is the one and only love, and thus delude their lovers. Rudolf was of the second kind and there is much evidence from childhood on that when faced with a decision of any difficulty he would put it off and prevaricate about it in the hope that it would go away. By the time he was thirty this was a confirmed characteristic and in his privileged position complexities had so often gone away that Rudolf was sure they always would. That is why he was reduced to despair when, as with his illness, they did not. So when he heard from Marie Larisch what had happened he did not recognize that this was the end of the affair with a vengeance and that the only thing left to do was to see that Mary was married off before it was too late and never to see her again. He procrastinated. He agreed with his cousin that they must see Mary and persuade her that all would yet be well if only she would remain calm and keep her head. This would be the course advised by Marie Larisch whose vital interest it was to prevent a scandal which would – and did – ruin her. It was also on that particular day not only a temperamental necessity for Rudolf but a practical one as well.

Because he and Mary were bound to see each other that very evening in the presence of 'all Vienna'. The evening reception in honour of the birthday of Emperor William II of Germany was taking place at the residence of the German Ambassador Prince Reuss. If Mary was in the state described by Marie Larisch and if at least one of the Baltazzi uncles was 'capable of anything', it was essential to restore Mary's nerve at least long enough to get them through to the following day. Otherwise there would be a scene in front of the Emperor Franz Joseph, the Archduchess Stephanie, most of the other Archdukes and Archduchesses, every Ambassador and Ambassadress in the city, the whole of the high aristocracy, the Ministers of Court and State and the senior officers and General Staff of the Army. A prospect to make the stoutest quail.

Mary was to go driving on Sunday afternoon with Countess Larisch. A police report confirms that Crown Prince Rudolf crossed one of the city bridges near the Prater. But it is unlikely that an emotional discussion would be risked in so public a place, even in mid-winter. They met in Marie Larisch's suite in the Grand Hotel. Whatever was said or done that afternoon, Mary's desperation was changed not into self-control but into brilliant happiness; she was transformed within an hour or so from despair to the heights of triumph and the certainty of being loved. Count Hoyos, Rudolf's devoted friend who had no cause to love Mary, described her a few days after the tragedy as he saw her that evening, Sunday 27 January. She looked startlingly beautiful, he wrote, her eyes glowed almost uncannily and although they were scarcely acquainted she spoke twice to him. The second time she asked him if he ever went shooting with the Crown Prince, a question that surprised him and he hardly recalled what he replied. Mary was teasing poor Hoyos, the most loyal but not the brightest of men. She knew very well that he was going the next day to the Crown Prince's shooting box at Mayerling and that she too would be there.

We may discount the 'uncanny' brilliance of Mary's eyes. She was recklessly in love, transported by fulfilled and shared desire and on the verge of a great adventure. She was going to run away with her lover the very next day, and the first stage was to be Mayerling where she would 'disappear'.

Unlike almost everyone who has written of Mayerling, the present writer has one great advantage: she was once a wildly undisciplined and emotional girl of eighteen and clearly remembers that distant being. That experience makes it almost impossible to believe that Mary Vetsera ever actually envisaged her own death. All that is known of her from those who loved as well as those who despised and disliked her, is vitality, high spirits, frivolity and sensuality. The note of scorn in most of the memoirs that mention her skates suspiciously near to envy when written by women; those by men treat her either as an unimportant cypher, which she was poor child, or with a coarse censoriousness which would be funny if it were not rather disgusting. A somewhat surprising exception, almost unique in its kindness, was the British Prince of Wales who wrote what he knew of the tragedy for his royal Mother's information; he referred to Mary as 'the poor young lady' and this lenience is made more striking both by the fact that it was written by a man to his mother and by Queen Victoria's reputation of being not usually tolerant of feminine frailty. Perhaps Queen Victoria's reputation was as wide of the mark as Emperor Franz Joseph's? Those who uphold society get stiff-necked from the strain and it is easy to mistake the stiffness for lack of understanding.

The reception at the residence of Prince Reuss was the point, appropriately formal and inconsiderable in itself, on which the drama turns. No one invited could decline or not attend; that would be a direct insult to Austria's close ally and brother-in-arms. Nobody who must attend could risk the least sign of crisis. The only actor not present was Countess Larisch; the chance of her not being expected to be in Vienna excluded the intriguer without whom it could not have happened. A week later Vienna was full of stories of incidents supposed to have taken place there; none of them in fact occurred and nothing marred the urbanity of the occasion worse than that Mary, keyed up by anticipation, played so constantly with her bracelet, a present from Rudolf, that she loosened a jewel in it which fell and was found next day by the servants who returned it to her mother. This little detail of Mary wearing a bracelet given her by her lover makes the whole ignorance of Baroness Vetsera suspect, for a woman so devoted to self-adornment could hardly not notice the trinkets of her daughter on whom she had set all her hopes of social advancement; how could Mary have accounted for it?

On Monday morning, the 28th, Mary went with Countess Larisch to Rodeck the jeweller where the order for the gold cigarette case was to be altered to Marie Larisch's name. They went to the Kohlmarkt, the most fashionable shopping street in the old city; and Countess Larisch went into the shop, leaving Mary to wait for her in the cab. The less Mary was noticed in

Rodeck's, the better. As soon as she was alone Mary scribbled a note on a leaf torn from her notepad, alighted from the cab on the far side and walked away – or picked up another cab – to where Rudolf's personal cab-driver Bratfisch waited for her. There are several versions of this manoeuvre but they do not matter. She probably did take another cab because although the Hofburg is a stone's throw from the end of the Kohlmarkt, to get to the postern gate on the ramp where Bratfisch waited Mary would have had to walk alone up the street, round the Michaelerplatz, along the narrow way between the stable and the Spanish Riding School, cross the north side of Josefsplatz, past the Augustine Church and in front of Archduke Albrecht's Palace which is now the Albertina Gallery, turn sharp right opposite the Opera house and walk up the open slope. This is a walk of five minutes, but the chances of being seen would at that time of day be higher than fifty-fifty.

What matters is that Mary got into Bratfisch's cab and was driven out of the city, south towards Baden, to a coaching inn in the Vienna woods.

About the same time or a little later Crown Prince Rudolf also left the city from the Hofburg in a court carriage with a groom but driving himself. He drove to the same coaching inn and from there sent back his carriage with the groom. Bratfisch then drove Rudolf and Mary, by side roads, to Mayerling, taking for such a speedy driver rather a long time about it. It was a bright sunny day but cold and on the slopes of country roads there was a good deal of ice in patches and they had some trouble with the horses which kept slipping. Several times Rudolf alighted and helped Bratfisch with the nervous horses and in doing so he got overheated and caught a cold.

Countess Larisch finished her business at Rodeck and on coming back to her cab found Mary's note which ran 'I can't go on living. Today I am a jump ahead of you and by the time you read this I shall be in the Danube. Mary'. She drove at once to Baroness Vetsera, rushing into the house and crying out that Mary was gone. As to the note, she was sure it was not true,

Mary would never commit suicide. It must have something to
do with the Crown Prince. This mention of Rudolf, on which
the various accounts agree, was a serious slip of the tongue by
Marie Larisch and proves that she was not privy to Mary's disappearance and was upset by it. Only the previous day she had
assured Rudolf in her note that she would 'go with' Mary; now
Mary had gone off alone and Countess Larisch no longer knew
what was happening. Up to that moment she had denied to
Mary's mother any knowledge of a personal relationship between Rudolf and Mary. However, Marie Larisch recovered her
slip by offering to go herself to Baron Krauss the Police Chief
of Vienna, and ask his help in finding Mary. She knew him
personally, he would help her. If one of Mary's family went to
the Police Chief it would attract attention. Baroness Vetsera
suggested that it might be better to go direct to the Prime
Minister Count Taafe but Marie Larisch dissuaded her; Taafe
might talk. He knew everybody and was on intimate terms with
the Emperor himself while Krauss was not a social figure. Count
Taafe was not friendly towards Rudolf and might think it his
duty to go straight to the Emperor; and of course it would be his
duty. Countess Larisch would, she said, also try to discover
from the Palace exactly where Rudolf was.

The Police records show that Countess Larisch was in Krauss's
office at about noon. In the evening she was there again, accompanied by Alexander Baltazzi, the eldest of Mary's uncles.
On both occasions Krauss declined to interfere. By the second
interview, if not at the first, it was known where Rudolf was.
The hunting party had been planned several days in advance
and both Count Hoyos and Prince Philipp Coburg invited to
take part. They were to go out to Mayerling early on the 29th
by train and carriage. But Krauss reminded Marie Larisch that
the police had no jurisdiction on Imperial property. It was impossible for him to ask the Crown Prince if he had a lady with
him in his private house; supposing it turned out that Mary was
not there? Supposing she was there but refused to return to
her family? An appalling situation for a civil servant to put

himself into. The only possible way to discover Mary's where-abouts was for her family to make a formal 'missing person' report so that the police could and indeed must, search for her. That of course, would be the end of any hope of avoiding open scandal.

During all this running about and wringing of hands there is not the slightest hint, official or private, that anyone made an attempt to search the Danube banks. The river, feared for its tearing swiftness, lies outside and to the north of Vienna, while Mayerling is about two and a half hours' carriage drive to the south. Bodies that get into the swirling currents of the Danube are often never recovered and when they are it is some-times many miles downstream. If it is feared that anyone has fallen or swum out into the mainstream – unlikely for a poor swimmer in any case and impossible for a non-swimmer – speed is an urgent necessity in searching for them. Yet nobody asked and nobody searched. Clearly nobody took Mary's note seriously and equally clearly, no matter what was said then or later, everyone concerned was pretty sure if not where she was at least with whom. It is inconceivable that no search would be made if even the slightest suspicion existed of Mary having 'gone into the Danube'. But this fact not only indicates some knowledge on Mary's mother's part. It also shows how very unlikely a candidate Mary was for self-murder. Even when she had disappeared and announced her intention of killing her-self, she was not for a moment believed. Of course not: they all knew perfectly well what was going on.

By the second interview with Marie Larisch and Alexander Baltazzi the police chief would know where Bratfisch had gone that morning. His employer, the owner of the cab company, would certainly not lie to the police upon whose goodwill his business depended; nor would he have any reason to do so. The police chief may even have known from one of his agents that Bratfisch's passenger had been a young lady. But Krauss had his cynical joke; he suggested that Baltazzi should go himself to Mayerling and ask questions. He also suggested that Baroness

Vetsera should go personally to the Empress and ask for her daughter's return, on the ground that Rudolf could not lie to or refuse his mother.

Mary Vetsera and Crown Prince Rudolf were in his rooms at Mayerling where Mary remained, unseen by either Count Hoyos or Prince Philipp. Philipp Coburg was a rake and Rudolf's companion on many drunken nights and he may have known or suspected that his host had a girl in his rooms; Hoyos did not. The servants knew, if only because Bratfisch remained in the house. The two guests were lodged in the farm-house belonging to the estate and were out shooting all day Tuesday. At four in the afternoon when it was already dark Coburg left by train for Vienna where he was expected at an Imperial family dinner in the Hofburg to celebrate the engagement of Rudolf's younger sister Valerie. Rudolf excused himself from this family occasion by sending a message that he had a heavy cold. Hoyos and Rudolf dined alone together; they talked of the extraordinary perceptions of hunting dogs and Rudolf was in good spirits, eating heartily and praising the cook. After dinner Hoyos went to his own rooms outside the main house and at some time later in the evening Bratfisch entertained Mary and Rudolf with his singing and whistling of popular songs, a talent on which he prided himself. Mary mentioned this in one of her farewell letters. It is one of several details that make Mary's final letters so curiously devious in atmosphere. She wrote three notes for certain, possibly another, and a fifth was years later claimed by Countess Larisch. She remembered to ask her mother to take care of her personal maid who was suspected, rightly, of having helped Mary to deceive her family. She made a daring joke to the Duke of Braganza who was a suitor of Mary's – he was to have a boa of Mary's and to hang it over his bed. To her sister Hanna Mary mentioned the lifeline in her hand, a reference to hand-reading. 'Think of the lifeline in my hand'. Was that line very short or was it long and the allusion a hint? The third known note was to her younger brother; all of them mentioned death. Reading these short notes over and over a marked feeling of joking deception arises; there is neither desperate resolve nor finality about them. Did Mary believe to the last second of her short life that she was eloping with her prince and laying a trail for her disappearance? Rudolf was morbid and unstable but Mary was reckless, gay, self-confident, an instinctive yes-sayer to life.

Philipp Coburg returned to Mayerling early on the morning of Wednesday 30 January. It was a few minutes past eight o'clock. He was met by Hoyos. Rudolf's gun-bearer had just reported that the door of the Crown Prince's bedroom was locked and that he could not be roused. The valet had been knocking and calling for half an hour.

Hoyos explained that just before eight o'clock as he was about to go over to the main house for breakfast with Rudolf, he had been told that Rudolf was not up and could not be awakened. He had replied sensibly that perhaps the Crown Prince was sleeping heavily and should be allowed his sleep out. But no; His Highness came out of the bedroom at half-past six in a dressing gown and told his valet to call him at a quarter to eight. He returned to the room, whistling, said the man. This instruction fitted the breakfast time agreed the day before, at which Coburg on his arrival was to join Rudolf and Hoyos.

Years later the valet wrote his account from memory claiming variously to have heard a shot at about seven o'clock, and to have heard the lovers talking earnestly in the night. Rudolf's bedroom was the oldest part of the house with enormously thick walls and cross vaulting and although the valet slept nearby it is quite likely that even a revolver shot in the morning would not be heard outside the room. It is much less likely that the shot that killed Mary would not have been heard in the silence of the night; even muffled by the thick masonry it could be expected to wake anyone in that side of the quite small hunting box. After six in the morning servants would be bustling about and making their own noise, the clatter of pails, rattling of kitchen pots and such domestic sounds might cover the report but if the valet did not hear anything of a shot in the night it is very certain that he did not hear two voices talking quietly together in the closed room. Still, a small doubt remains as to why Hoyos and Coburg were so sure at once that something was wrong. It may simply have been the memory of Rudolf's moody talk of death and suicide, or it may, even more simply, have been the door locked on the inside for someone has to be inside a locked room by definition.

Philipp Coburg was Prince Rudolf's brother-in-law and as a member of the family decided on breaking open the door. The valet then told the two guests that Mary Vetsera was with the Crown Prince. An axe was fetched but the lock resisted it which by itself shows how massively built the place was. They then hacked open one of the panels of the door. The valet looked through the jagged hole and saw the two bodies; even in such circumstances the two gentlemen did not feel able to pry. The servant then unlocked the door by twisting his hand up through the broken panel and turning the key from the inside. The two friends remained outside while the valet went in to make sure both bodies were lifeless. From some half-understood tale that cyanide causes haemorrhage from the mouth he jumped to the conclusion in his state of shock that Rudolf had been poisoned, evidently not seeing the gun in his hand. He would not see much because shutters and curtains were closed. Mary Vetsera's body lay outstretched on the bed. Rudolf was half-sitting, half-lying on the edge of the bed. The revolver was clutched in his hand so that the doctor was obliged to force it out of his rigid grasp later that day. A hand mirror lay on the night-table; evidently Rudolf had used it to be sure of his target since he shot himself in the temple, the right temple, and not through the mouth.

Hoyos and Coburg agreed that Hoyos should take the appalling news to the Hofburg while Coburg would, almost literally, hold the fort until doctors and officials could get there with the Emperor's orders. The procedures for the death of a member of the Imperial family were strictly codified as were those for any ordinary citizen. The Crown Prince had told Bratfisch the previous day that he, Bratfisch, was to return to Vienna on Wednesday morning with a passenger, so the driver was ready with the horses harnessed. He got Hoyos to Baden station for the fast night train from Trieste due there at 9.18 and with enough time to spare for Hoyos to send a telegram to the Master of the Imperial Household to meet him at the Palace. At eleven minutes past ten by the courtyard clock Hoyos entered the Hofburg.

To get on to the express train Hoyos was obliged to tell the station master that he was on Imperial business for the train did not accept passengers so near its destination but only set them down at Baden. Trains were dead on time in those days and rules not so easy to bend as they later became; in fact it was the Mayerling tragedy that began the process of undermining the confidence of ordinary people in official integrity. Hoyos also left Bratfisch at Baden station to await the doctor who would be arriving in an hour or so. This long wait of the cab driver was certainly the start of the first rumours for Bratfisch was self-important and curious and had already tried to question Hoyos on the drive to Baden.

Hoyos conferred with Court officials on his arrival and it was decided that only Empress Elisabeth who was not travelling at the time, could take such news to Rudolf's father and she was interrupted in a Greek lesson to be told that her only son was dead. Princess Valerie, whose engagement party Rudolf had missed only the day before, was told, then the Emperor and then Crown Princess Stephanie. Hardly was this harrowing scene over when the Empress's reader told her that Baroness Vetsera was in the Palace and insisted, in spite of refusals, on speaking to her.

No one tells a bereaved mother at such a moment that an importunate visitor must be received without being sure that it is necessary. Ida von Ferenczy was Elisabeth's devoted friend as well as her reader and a woman of great intelligence and experience who was in the confidence of both Empress and Emperor in their private affairs. She must have recognized at once that the need to tell Mary's mother the truth was paramount. The nettle must be grasped, and at once.

Helene Vetsera had finally made up her mind to admit, by an official request to the police, that her daughter was missing. It was now the third day since Mary had last been seen. But to go to the Empress and the mother of her child's seducer, she must have been certain that Mary was at Mayerling. This is the only evidence, convincing if indirect, that at least one constant rumour of the time was correct: that two of Mary's uncles went out to Mayerling while she was there. The story was embroidered into some of the most luxuriant of the wild explanations of Crown Prince Rudolf's death, including a duel and a wild fight ending in Rudolf's skull being split open by a champagne bottle. These can all be dismissed as absurd. There were at least five armed men at Mayerling besides Rudolf; his two companions, their gun-bearers and a huntsman and several others who were not armed but were able-bodied and active. Any enemies who got inside the walled courtyard, not a difficult feat in itself, would have to imprison the whole staff and the two guests before they could penetrate the house to the Crown Prince's own room. They certainly did not enter by the window for the apartment was minutely examined and itemised by the investigating commission; so carefully that a crack in a coffee cup was noted. But one or more of the Baltazzi brothers could have driven out to Mayerling without arousing any notice and simply asked a few questions; for instance of Bratfisch whom they probably knew, or of one of the staff. With an air of authority and by implying that one knows in any case, much can be wheedled out of people who think they are being very discreet by anyone with the wit to do it. Helene Vetsera would hardly have dared to appeal to the Empress unless she knew the facts.

Elisabeth told the Baroness that both Rudolf and Mary were dead, and the Baroness is recorded as jumping at once to the conclusion that they had both taken poison, just as Rudolf's valet had thought and as the Court at that moment believed.

But since the Empress's Chamberlain spoke to the unfortunate woman before she was taken to Elisabeth, as well as Ida von Ferenczy, she may have suspected something already. The word poison seems to have been floating in the air and to depart from facts to speculation for a moment, it is difficult not to wonder whether everybody in Vienna had not been seeing a little too much of Wagner's *Tristan and Isolde* that winter.

It had already been agreed in the Imperial family that the cause of death was officially to be a heart attack and by the time the first investigator returned in the night of the 30th to the 31st January to make his interim report, this lie was already being printed for the official gazette. We know that this was agreed by the family with the approval of the Prime Minister Count Taafe, because Empress Elisabeth warned Mary's mother at the end of their interview, to stick to that story.

By the afternoon of the 30th doctors and a Court Commission of civil servants were at Mayerling. Mary Vetsera's body was removed to an attic where no outsider could see it. The body of Crown Prince Rudolf was laid out, his head bandaged, in a coffin which at about midnight was loaded on to a train at Baden and taken to Vienna.

The chief Court physician and the official investigator, a comparatively junior official called Slatin, came back with the truth. The doctor told the Emperor that Rudolf had shot himself and Mary Vetsera and that they had not been poisoned. This removed the possibility that Mary had poisoned Rudolf and herself and for a few minutes Franz Joseph collapsed with grief at this fresh shock; one of the very few recorded occasions on which he lost his self control. But he knew within minutes that the dreadful truth could never be hidden, at least as far as it concerned Rudolf. The following day's issue of the official newspaper carried in its unofficial section the announcement of Rudolf's suicide by revolver shot.

The first announcement had in any case been believed by no one; people seemed to know by instinct that there was more to the tragedy and a great number of ordinary Viennese knew that Rudolf could not have been living a life of constant activity in public and debauchery in private – a privacy far from complete – if he suffered from a weak heart. A huge, silent crowd stood all night round the Hofburg, awaiting the arrival of Rudolf's coffin.

On the following day an autopsy was carried out and the corpse was then laid in state without the head bandage but with a cosmetic wax cover over the brow to hide the wound in the right temple. The autopsy report was published, mentioning abnormalities of the brain to ease the permission of the Church for Christian burial. Whether the physical brain showed malformation or not it was certainly true in essence that Rudolf was in an abnormal state of mind. Several Churchmen did in fact make difficulties, or they tried to, for Rudolf was anticlerical and unpopular with the Viennese priesthood.

What was never mentioned officially then or later, was that Mary Vetsera was with Rudolf when he died, or rather, that her dead body was with him. Slatin's notes taken at the time for his report, state, precisely translated and with the original punctuation that 'in the extra-territorial building of Mayerling a female corpse was found, which . . .' The sentence was unfinished. This body lay supine and outstretched on the bed beside Rudolf's. It was taken to another room with its clothing piled over it to cover it, and lay there until the Crown Prince's personal physician was sent with Slatin to make some kind of autopsy, wash and clothe the corpse and lay it out. The bullet wound was in the *left* temple and must have caused instant death. There were already a number of discoloured patches on feet, hands and back. The condition of the body indicated that Mary had been dead hours before the time of Rudolf's suicide. While this horror-scene was taking place another civil servant was with the Abbot of Heiligenkreuz, a Cistercian monastery just outside a neighbouring village. Mary's perjured death certificate of suicide was signed by Rudolf's doctor, who was chosen for this task because his devotion to the dead Prince would overcome his reluctance to sign a false declaration. But the man sent to persuade the Abbot had to fall back partly on the truth. The Abbot refused to allow a burial to take place in Heiligen-kreuz cemetery if it was that of a suicide. For overriding reasons of State Mary must be declared a suicide; otherwise a legal investigation of her death must follow which would inevitably come to the only possible conclusion that Rudolf had shot her. The Abbot, when assured that Mary had in fact been shot and there was no evidence of her acquiescence in her own death, very reluctantly signed the interment order.

The steps necessary to remove a dead body from one administrative district to another were illegally juggled. Alexander Baltazzi and his brother-in-law Baron Stockau drove out late in the evening to the heavily guarded hunting box to collect the body of their niece. Slatin recounts that it was black dark and stormy and the hunting dogs howled. Well they might.

The whole district by then was full of journalists and agents of many of the foreign Embassies in Vienna; that was the reason for everything being done under cover of darkness. But why it was decided that the body must be removed in Baltazzi's carriage is a mystery. A farm cart in which it could at least have been laid down would have been no more conspicuous. But in the haste and panic over the possibility of the Crown Prince being known to be a murderer it was forbidden to take a coffin into Mayerling and poor Mary was carried out and propped up on the carriage seat between her uncles and so driven to Heiligenkreuz. There she was laid in a rough coffin and at nine the next morning, the ground so heavy with rain after frost that the two uncles had to help the gravediggers, she was buried and the prayers for the dead read over her grave.

Undoubtedly this macabre and revolting event was caused by the confusion and shock of the whole tragedy. That Baltazzi and von Stockau should have accepted their roles in it is almost unbelievable. But they did.

Rudolf was laid to rest in the Habsburg vault of the Capucin monks in the centre of Vienna.

Why? It is always the question left ringing in the silence of self-murder. Rudolf's letters give no real answer; the letters left in such tragedies rarely do. That is because the drive to death is irrational and not understood; sometimes it is not even known to the suicide. In the case of Rudolf Habsburg it was known to the victim; he had been aware of the longing for several years. Perhaps the real motive is always the same one; the inward sensation that the mind is going, that one is going mad.

There are rational suicides and irrational ones. If a human being knows with his reason that he is trapped and there is no way out, whether trapped by objective circumstances or by incurable physical illness, the decision to die is reasonable although sometimes such decisions are really sentences of death imposed from outside by others, as in cases like Colonel Redl's. In irrational suicides there is always an underlying motive and an immediate cause. Sometimes the immediate cause is quite inadequate to explain to a healthy mind the need to die. In Rudolf's death his overt motive was sufficient. Once he had shot Mary Vetsera there was no way out. He used poor Mary to force his own hand.

There is, however, one piece of objective if indirect evidence that may, but only may, indicate an involvement of Rudolf with Hungarian intrigues serious enough to have fateful consequences if it were exposed. His Will was written on 2 March 1887 and in it, among other quite conventional directions, Rudolf asked his executor to open his desk in his study in the presence of Crown Princess Stephanie, Rudolf's wife and next-of-kin. The papers in the desk were to be dealt with by the executor according to his own judgment, part to be destroyed and part to be kept. In Rudolf's last letter to this executor, written apparently before he left Vienna for Mayerling since it mentions specifically 'my desk in the Turkish room here in Vienna' (the Turkish room was Rudolf's study), this direction is changed. It runs that the executor should open the desk *at once and alone* and destroy the papers found there. It may not be significant for Rudolf was up half the night on his last night in Vienna, drinking a lot of champagne in the company of Mitzi Caspar and this heavy drinking was a confirmed habit. He was probably drunk then and on the following nights with Mary at Mayerling. He may have written the last letter to his executor when drunk and the words 'here in Vienna' were a mistake of his befuddled mind. Certainly that and the other letters, which he lists at the end of it, were found at Mayerling. Equally, 'at once and alone' may mean little or nothing. But it may have been important and it was carried out as Rudolf instructed, most of the papers being destroyed by the executor quite alone. He did not burn everything; but then he would not do that. He would preserve enough papers to convince the Emperor of the innocence of the desk's contents since it could not possibly be empty. Enough letters remained to be read by others, for instance, to expose Countess Larisch's role in Rudolf's tragedy and to ensure her permanent banishment from Court.

Now this executor was Ladislas von Szoegenyi-Marich, a departmental chief in the Foreign Office whose job it was officially to maintain the information-contact between the Budapest half of the Dual Monarchy and the Vienna half. This appointment was quite separate and distinct from the many other Hungarian diplomats in the joint Foreign Office, which was at times almost dominated by the Magyar element. The choice of an executor may therefore be significant in itself; moreover this last letter of Rudolf's was written in the Magyar language and referred to 'our dearly loved homeland' which in that language could only mean Hungary, thus by implication leaving out Austria. The postscript was written in German and included the list of letters to be delivered after Rudolf's death.

Against this possibility there is a considerable counterweight. After Rudolf's death, and after the immediate shock was over there was a complete and official overhaul of everything to do with Rudolf which ended in many papers being removed from the various Crown and State archives. It is impossible that such an investigation could be carried out without uncovering any secret activities in which Rudolf was concerned, whether political or private. If any evidence were found either of plotting or of the various theories that Rudolf was murdered it is quite inconceivable that revenge on the person or persons concerned would not have followed under some plausible pretext. Someone would have died in an accident or in a duel. That is as certain as anything can be. None of the Hungarian oppositionists came to a bad end, nor did any of those who might have hated Rudolf enough to kill him. This fact disposes alike of the Hungarian plot theory and of the murder theories. Rudolf Habsburg murdered his mistress and then shot himself.

Mystery was artificially bred by the attempts at secrecy but these in turn were not, as is usually supposed, frivolously motivated by fear of scandal although that fear is always present in such events. Secrecy was imposed, unsuccessfully in the long run, for two serious reasons. The first was the stability of the whole Empire; the shock of the heir's death could well have released unrest in the whole realm and it could just as well have encouraged foreign enemies to seize the opportunity of disorder to attack the Dual Monarchy from outside. In the event neither of these misfortunes took place. The malaise was much slower; it was the beginning of a deep loss of confidence in dynasty, State and administration which spread like a stain from the Court through Vienna and gradually through the whole Empire. It also changed the succession to the throne from a beloved Prince to one who, whatever his qualities good and bad, was always a controversial figure whose person never concentrated *all* the differing loyalties of the rival nations. The second reason for nothing being openly said was personal but equally serious. Rudolf killed himself while the balance of his mind was at least disturbed and probably broken; an inheritance of mental illness would have come through his mother. To admit that Rudolf was unhinged was to accuse his mother of tainting his reason and Rudolf's mother was the lifelong and unattainable love, the *princesse lointaine*, of his father Franz Joseph. The admission was bound to be made in order to allow the dead man Christian burial but that as in a million other cases was considered a pious fraud; it was afterwards denied and ignored until after the deaths of everyone concerned.

So died Rudolf Habsburg and his passing bell tolled the first warning of the end of a dynasty of over six hundred years and the passing of the necessary co-ordinating Power that held the eastern borders of civilized Europe for almost a thousand years. They were our enemies when that end came, but let us not be too sure that the end of the Habsburgs was progress. No one who is able to see 'the true twentieth century' as it is and no one who knows eastern Europe today can truthfully believe that.

2

Handsome Karl,
the Mayor of Vienna

In the 1870s Vienna was in something like the state of the city of New York a hundred years later. That is, it was sunk in apparently incurable confusion, inefficiency and corruption and the bank accounts were empty. It is to be understood that all large cities always are in a state of confusion, that being the condition of human affairs which are concentrated in human cities; what makes them civilized is the agreement of the citizens to order the natural and healthy confusion so that the city is a livable and workable community in its own terms. A port must take the sea into account, and a city built on a hill must live with its own ups and downs. Vienna must live with the river, an uncomfortable neighbour even today with the most efficient flood-controls and the harnessing of the flow to hydroelectric plants. Unlike most very old cities Vienna is quite easy to envisage. If one stands with one's back turned to the Danube in the north and – contrary to usual map-reading – faces south, then the city is shaped like an open fan. The straight line of the outer spines is the Danube. The semicircle formed by the inside edge of the fan cover is the modern Ring, its outer half-circumference the Gürtel, which means belt. The main streets roughly form the spines.

The decision to demolish the walls of the old fortified city was taken in 1859. In about ten years the fortifications were gone and the Ringstrasse was being built. The removal of the outer fortifications, where the Gürtel now runs, came about thirty years later and nine Districts became nineteen.

The first organized census was taken in 1859 together with a fairly comprehensive survey. The population was 490,000. At the inclusion of the outer districts into the city in 1890 the number was 1.34 million. That is, it more than doubled in forty years. It was always a city of many foreigners, and like all major European cities then its increase of people was largely by migration, by no means all permanent. But the proportion of citizens not born in Vienna was fairly constant during the growth at about half, including a changing garrison of something over 20,000 soldiers. With the additional information that Vienna held just over two million people before the Great War and something less than that today, we have enough figures to understand the problems. The doubling of the population presented enormous problems, social and hygienic, of transport and of control. The large cities of America, unlike European cities which all expanded about that time, faced a special problem during the expansions of the great wave of immigrants and this problem was shared by Vienna alone in Europe with America: that was language. There were at least seven different vernaculars with many splits into dialects and there was no system of German teaching for newcomers except in the Army where the essential words numbered eighty to ninety, mostly of course, command words. If it can be assumed that most immigrants and migrants could at first manage about a hundred words of German, it is still clear that a very great difficulty existed in communication, both in civil administration and personal intercourse.

The old and formerly efficient systems of administration and welfare were quite inadequate for such an increase in numbers. The physical urban structure of housing, roads, sewage, food distribution and police control were breaking up into near-chaos. Vienna was not and is not now a heavily industrialized city but a certain amount of growing industry added to the confusion of all forms of communication. Overcrowding, with all its attendant diseases and strains, was a growing threat to health and public order.

In some European cities these problems were greater than in Vienna; Berlin and London for instance were huge industrial complexes as well as government and international centres and they both grew fast. The difficulties in Vienna, apart from the already mentioned polyglot nature of the immigration which should not be underestimated – even the simplest transaction takes twice as long if one or both the parties does not really understand what is being said – lay in the essential character of the city. It was the capital and residence of the Emperor and that was its old function. Until its expansion nobody intended it to be anything else and the rulers intended nothing else until 1918. The city was to the Emperor and his ministers their residence, with the emphasis on the possessive; it was, being the centre of a huge Empire with entirely land boundaries except for a few miles of Adriatic coast, also and above all a strategic military problem. The expansion of the city was therefore looked upon as unnecessary, a misfortune and a threat to internal and external control. The unchanging aspect of the inner city made it easy to ignore the growing outskirts and as far as possible they were ignored.

The administration of Vienna, under an Imperial Governor, was in the hands of the city council and that was dominated for many years by the Liberals. These were not in any of the vague senses of 'liberal' any such thing, but a kind of Manchester Liberal supported by the expansive wealthy business classes in their own interests. This was not necessarily bad; the new business men founded and conducted what there was of modern industry and commerce in Austria-Hungary and from an historical standpoint their influence was not nearly great enough. The old and socially desirable structure of small family artisan and shop-keeping business was not capable of expanding into an industrial complex sufficient to maintain such a large State and more *laissez-faire* capitalism, however cruel its immediate effects, was much to be wished. Its lack was the largest single cause of the break-up of the co-ordinated control of the Danube basin by civilized Europe.

Such rapid and large changes of size in a fixed, conscious and old community are bound to change the nature of the community; quantity becomes quality. There was no question of an expansion of ambition and vigorous energy in the whole community which was the case in Berlin, where a new city was built with the enthusiastic support of the entire population. Nor was it an expansion and intensification in the tradition of the place and people, which was the case in London. It was something that simply happened, extraneous to the real life of the people and their rulers; it imposed itself on a polis which worked perfectly well in its old form and held the continuing acceptance of the citizens; and the old form was in fact so good and practical that it survived all the changes of the twentieth century and still deeply informs the polity of Austria today. This was the system codified by the reforms of Maria Theresia and her heir Josef in the eighteenth century.

If Vienna was to survive as itself and not as a quite new place, changes must be made, active and physical changes. Nobody wanted changes, which is proof positive that the old system worked. Changes were forced by outside circumstances. In all the circumstances, including the great European slump of the 1870s and including the considerable alterations in the internal balances of influence in the Habsburg Empire, the remarkable thing about Vienna from 1870 to 1913 is not that there was violence but that there was so little public violence.

Only a small group of men seems to have understood what was happening and only one of them had the insight and energy to see what was needed and how it could be achieved. This was Karl Lueger (pronounced Loo-ay-ger). It took him from the time of his first election to the Vienna Community Council as it was until very recently called, in 1875 until the Emperor ratified his fourth election as Mayor in 1897, to get the power to make the necessary changes. He then carried them out in an extraordinary forced march, as it were, in ten years. Lueger remained Mayor until his death in 1910 but the plans he had laid were in the last year or so of his life carried on by others.

Handsome Karl

Vienna today is the Vienna formed by Karl Lueger by adapting
the old to the new; there are at present extensions and adapta-
tions going on on a large scale, but they are almost all modifica-
tions to Karl Lueger's Vienna caused by modern prosperity:
that is the enlarging of individual housing-room and the motor
car. Karl Lueger not only designed and realized the renewal
of one of the most beautiful and practical of European cities;
he discovered quite empirically the means of doing it. He
organized an unrepresented mass of people into a unified party,
controlling them as the political development of the State
granted them the franchise under pressure from Lueger's friends
as well as the pressure of historical change in the whole State.

Probably one of the major causes of the troubled history of
the present century was the huge increase of city populations
everywhere in Europe in the nineteenth century and this factor
has never been given enough weight in the efforts to understand
what has happened in our time. It can be seen in an extreme
form in Vienna by the simple consideration that the number
of people living together in an already settled community rose
from half a million to 1.3 million in forty years, and that the
newcomers were almost all strangers. That is more than the
former total number of citizens. It happened in other cities but
the increases were of natives. To take London as an example,
the British population as a whole increased greatly in the nineteenth century and there was a massive and constant move
towards towns but it was almost entirely a move by native
British people who all thought, felt and spoke the same language.
In Vienna an increase of over one hundred per cent was almost
entirely foreign in language and therefore in thought. The old
native population did not greatly increase.

Karl Lueger was a native Viennese. His peasant father was
called up to the army and when invalided out of the service he
moved to Vienna, married and got a job as porter at the
Theresianum. This classical school was founded by the great
Maria Theresia to provide educated State servants. It was and
is one of the finest institutes of education in the civilized world,

of a stringency in intellectual as in behavioural standards that is second to none. It proved its ethical worth in accepting the porter into the school studies and he passed many of its examinations while continuing to do his own work. His son in turn was enrolled as a living-out scholar – it is a boarding school – and this good fortune of having such an intelligent and ambitious father and such enlightened patrons was the foundation of Karl Lueger's life. It was as if the groundsman and his son were students at Eton and a very good idea, too. His mother kept a tobacconist's shop, one of the many retail shops of the Imperial tobacco monopoly often granted to retired soldiers and civil servants. Until his mother's old age the family lived behind this shop and later, until Karl moved into the Mayor's apartment in the then new Rathaus, in the basic Viennese flat 'one room and kitchen', with water out on the landing. These were the narrow dwellings which became appallingly overcrowded in the poorer quarters during that time, but in themselves they were not entirely bad. They must surely be one of the social causes of the 'outwardness' of Viennese life, where people eat and sleep at home but go out for almost everything else. Coffee, wine, reading, card and chess playing, music and theatre, sports and friendships were then all activities pursued outside the home. This had the result that people lived much more with each other than they did elsewhere. This is a commonplace in countries where the climate encourages living out of doors, but Vienna and Budapest were exceptional in the bad climate of middle and northern Europe in that poor people were not shut in the box of the exclusive family and were not confined for companionship to their own relations.

From school Karl entered the University and became 'Doctor of Both Laws' by the time he was twenty-five. His family had no money at all so that this opportunity represented a great sacrifice by his parents and his two sisters. 'Both' laws does not mean civil and criminal law, but Roman and Canon Law. In the meantime the law itself relating to political association was liberalized and all kinds of parties and clubs began to be founded formally which previously existed either as coffee-house or tavern groups or as religious and theoretical clubs, many of which covered their discussions with other labels such as literary societies or mountain-climbing clubs. There were also a number of associations which were and remained secret, such as the Freemasons and some religious groups; these all now had a legal status, only the few anarchists and extreme revolutionaries retaining the conspiratorial secrecy with which they conduct their affairs to this day. All such groupings began to associate openly, from pietistic Catholics to Marxists, and naturally began to ally themselves into political parties. Up to then political parties had been confined to the middle and upper classes and had been effectually confined to the clerical-conservatives and the liberals both in national and communal politics. Liberal politics were those of the energetic and amoral expanding middle classes and dominated finance, industry and commerce while national administration and the Empire were still largely in the hands of the aristocratic land-owning class. Naturally the edges of these groupings flowed out into each other but they roughly expressed public political life and were minority activities. The vast majority of ordinary people did not think of politics and those who paid enough taxes or owned enough property to have the vote, voted by tradition. This voting system ranged according to property, small properties having less weight than large ones, was the last remnant of the feudal organization of society. It obtained all over Europe and was changing everywhere naturally and inevitably. It was these changes that Karl Lueger was able to use.

The watershed, the point of no return, in central Europe was 1866. The whole area was being unified, not by Bismarck but by the railways and the telegraph. Bismarck only made, among other decisions, the one to exclude the Habsburg possessions from the unification; that would have meant a rivalry of rulers. A boundary-fixing expedition concerning Schleswig-Holstein in the north-west of Germany was the cause of an Austrian claim to be included in decisions. This made the question clear and Bismarck took the opportunity to disagree with the Austrians and to make his disagreement plain by one of those short, sharp wars the success of which made him so unpopular outside Germany. The loss of real power at the battle of Königgrätz, at which the matter was decided, instantly affected the atmosphere inside the Habsburg realm. Those who feel a strong attachment to power always react to a loss of power instinctively with hatred and contempt for the loser. The Hungarian aristocracy took the chance to demand again, and this time to get, greatly increased powers within the Habsburg Empire which from that moment on were constantly used to undermine the authority of the Danube structure upon which their own safety depended. They continued to believe in this policy until they were forced to understand the realities of power by irretrievably losing it. A few years later their example was followed much more cautiously, first by the northern Slavs of the Empire and then by the South Slavs.

The effect of Königgrätz on the Austro-Germans themselves was to produce a new all-German nationalism. German nationalism in the Empire was up to then the expression, rarely needed, of the paramount role of the Austro-Germans within the Habsburg Empire. At once after 1866 there arose a movement demanding the secession of Austria to the German Reich which was the new power-focus. It was in the main confined to emotional power-lovers, feelers rather than thinkers. Those who reacted against it, since they now needed to argue, were more intellectual. Distinct from the inborn recognition of Germanness which had always been more a matter of language, culture and social organization than a spatial system of boundaries, Austrian patriotism was born specifically as a differentness within Germanness. It only gradually became a differentness from the Magyars and the two Slav groups that made up the rest of central Europe. These had supplied, almost incidentally, a supporting argument for Bismarck's exclusion of the Habsburgs from Germany. The intransigence of the Magyars which then encouraged the Bohemian Czechs to follow suit, caused the *assumption* of Austro-German paramountcy to become insistence upon it; insistence always being a sign of weakness. The exclusive nationalism sown into middle Europe by the Napoleonic invasions had at last begun to bear its crop from the dragons' teeth.

Within this national situation, the politics of Vienna were entirely in the hands of the Liberals. They were the representatives of the new and rich middle class whose interests were their own enrichment and aggrandisement, whose social sense was in practice non-existent and whose taste was unfortunately not non-existent but on the contrary was dynamically horrible. Only the last of these traits is intended as a reproach; their egotism produced wealth which filtered quite quickly downwards and it is always the case that those with power have to have the restraints of society imposed upon them and will not accept them freely. It was largely due to Karl Lueger that such restraints were imposed; if ever the time produced the man, Lueger was a case of it doing so.

Karl Lueger never had any money and never cared about it. At the time of the great slump he was a young lawyer with a growing practice which included a number of clients who would never be able to pay him. The state of the Viennese small service and commercial business people, pressed from above by growing large businesses and from below by the mass of immigrants, was pitiable. They supplied the skills and work that built the new Ringstrasse and filled the Vienna World Exposition of 1873 and the crash that followed these arrogant shows took their savings. The savers did not lose their livelihoods, only the profits of the boom but the loss of money which was their own work frightened them with the fear of future loss.

The Ring with its luxury and pride was still there; the economy recovered and the palaces were finished, with the symbolic exception of the extension to the Imperial Palace. People could see that the wealth was there but their own modest profits from it had disappeared. Many of the individual buildings were ugly and almost all were imitative of the various

forms of the Italian Renaissance. They had rejected the harmony
of the Austrian eighteenth century, proportion had become
pomp and dignity overbearingness. But the new and half finished
palaces were impressive and very foreign, they overpowered
minds accustomed to the reserve and restraint of inherited
tradition. The increased earnings from the building of them by
thousands of artisans which once looked like safety for the
future was lost, so that instead of pride people felt fear and an
uncomprehending resentment. In a sense they were right
because the slavish reliance on related designs from an Italian
past which cut out their own past and which were blown up
to a size that made them almost laughable, was aesthetically
bad enough to be a moral fault in the minds of those who
thought the results beautiful. Today, interspersed with Lueger's
lovely gardens, lined by great trees, the Ring is a handsome
whole, a splendid boulevard, but the affection that looks at its
single monstrosities as part of history was not then present. The
buildings were raw, the trees not grown and the gardens non-
existent. Many of Lueger's first clients had bought shares or
houses from the earnings of building the Ring and were then in
serious trouble.

Under the new freedom of association Lueger had joined the
Citizens' Club of his district, the Third, which was on the whole
a rich district in which his family were poor people. After
trying out a short membership with the small Democrat faction
he moved over to the Liberals and was elected by their influence
to the city council. Lueger never liked the Liberals, he simply
recognized that with them he could make a start. He was appointed – and how his enemies must have regretted the decision
– to the administrative department in the Rathaus which was
still the old and beautiful one. The new Rathaus, one of the
ugliest buildings in a lovely city, was opened in 1883. The corruption already known to Lueger from his work as an attorney
now became familiar from the inside. The city council was a
body of submissive toadies to Mayor Felder, who quickly became suspicious of the nerve and energy of his new assistant

who looked into everything with a shockingly intelligent and irreverent eye. Instead of covering up the profitable 'fixing' of contracts and the delivery of short measures and poor quality, the confusion and maladministration that had been going on cosily for years, Lueger and his friends began to issue writs. For months the courts were loud with scandals and at the next election the result could be seen in the severely curtailed majority of the Mayor.

Not content that Mayor Felder was obliged to dismiss or discipline some of his old friends, Lueger attacked the Mayor himself. He tabled a motion to divide the chairmanship of the city council from the executive chief of administration, both of these offices being held by Felder. Of course he did not succeed in pushing his motion through; the council was much too well packed. But he frightened the Mayor into panic. The dynamic young trouble-maker could have been transferred into a department where his energies would be tamed by over-work. Instead Felder dissolved the district committee of the Third District where Lueger had his friends and allies. Immediately Lueger resigned his seat on the city council, cunningly leaving his closest friend there as observer.

It looked like a defeat but it was far from that. It showed Lueger that he must have a power base and he saw where he could make one. Just at that time Bismarck in the German Reich was making his one major political mistake, the exclusion of the masses from politics which issued in the laws against the Socialists in 1878. In his much smaller field of influence, Lueger did the opposite. He quite empirically discovered the great weight that can be brought to bear in politics by harnessing a mass of unrepresented people. Throughout European history the mob, when aroused, has been the object of fear and therefore of suppression. Lueger was the first to turn a potential mob into a coherent mass-political organization. Since he published almost nothing and nothing at all as theory, it cannot now be said whether or not Lueger ever worked his plan out rationally. But if he was to get power he must have a following and one was there for the moulding. He was immensely ambitious but his ambitions were not personal.

Lueger seems to have been that rather rare type of human being who wants power in order to make people love him. Of this kind come the great doctors, priests and administrators who live their lives without privacy, without intimate relationships, in the service of their fellow men. They are often of a remote outward personality, not instantly and personally lovable, not able to appeal directly to others. But Karl Lueger was one of those who besides wanting power *as giving*, is able to get the giving back in love. He was more than universally popular; he was universally loved and towards the end of his life, revered.

His methods came to him quite naturally. He went to people and did not expect them to come to him. They were his own people, he knew how they felt and how they were because he was one of them; he did not need to understand their puzzlement, their anxiety, their sense of grievance because these things were in himself; he knew them. So he went to people; not to 'The People', but to individuals. Every evening he went with one or two friends to different public-houses, wineshops, coffeehouses all over Vienna and sat for hours talking and listening. He answered the worries and preoccupations of those he met with advice, suggestions, encouragement. It was no essay in 'public relations'. Everyone he listened to knew that Lueger really cared what happened to him. The manipulation of mass-audiences which came later and is now a major factor of political life everywhere was something quite different. The ability to stir crowds can be learned and requires a certain distance from the audience. In personal intercourse, sitting at the same table, the feeling must be authentic and informed, otherwise it does not work. For Lueger it worked with a whole new political class whom nobody had noticed. They were the lower middle class, the 'Five Gulden Men' who paid that sum in taxes and were just then enfranchised for national, but still not for local, elections.

The goal of all this activity was to get the vote for these men in communal affairs. The small radical groups were rapidly collected into the United Left and by using the same persuasive method on members of the city council Lueger managed to get the enfranchisement through but it failed in the larger provincial council for Lower Austria which was still, if no longer very safely, dominated by the Liberals. Lueger went back to the council and his influence rose at each election, almost at each council meeting. Discredited by scandals, Mayor Felder resigned and the new Mayor was more accessible to Lueger; or more sensible for by 1880 the United Left gained almost half the seats in the council. The scandalous maladministration of the city would have been a disgrace even if it were not now growing at such a frightening rate and had not been the object of public notice by then for five years.

In 1881 disaffection reached a new peak. A terrible fire in the Ringtheater exposed the incompetence of the fire department, the traffic police and the staff of the Imperial Governor with a shocking clarity. It cost the lives of five hundred people because the building was not properly protected against fire and the doors of the auditorium, just closed for the start of the performance, incredibly opened only inwards so that pressure from inside closed them only more immoveably. The uproar cost the Mayor his job and all the council factions were divided against each other in trying to push the blame away from themselves.

Just at this same time a project for the building of a new local rail line round the former outer defence wall (now the Gürtel, where the line still exists) was being discussed both in the city council and in the newspapers. The council favoured a tender from two British engineers to construct the new line. The opposition, vociferously led by Lueger, contended that the railway line would be pointless unless it connected with existing and future city transport; and that the contract should not go to foreigners. In the confusion of the city government after the theatre fire the project was slipped through against massive objection and by rather dubious methods.

British companies were not popular in Vienna. The gas for lighting the city was supplied by a British company and was both bad and expensive. It was equally bad in London itself but nobody knew or cared about that in Vienna; moreover as the panic in the Ringtheater started all the gas lighting was turned off so that darkness was added to the terrors of fire and claustrophobia.

Nor were railways popular. The argument as to whether the main line railway to the north should be nationalized or not exercised the public for years. This strategically important line was built by private capital but with large public subsidies which came, of course, from taxes. Military transport by rail was expensive on top of the subsidies and so was private travelling. The feeling against railways was focused on the North Railway, but was strong about all railways. Americans and British people do not understand the inborn consciousness of frontiers in peoples who have always had their being in the middle of a land mass and with land frontiers; frontiers on the far side of which may lie hostility. The ease of movement offered by the railway age was quite new and it produced a new fact of consciousness because the warning of the approach of strangers whether in friendship, indifference or enmity, was cut to hours and in enmity to minutes, instead of days or weeks. This made the whole idea of railways both seductive and threatening; one could go anywhere in these new trains with their powerful, snorting monsters of locomotives but other people could equally reach into one's life by them. The shining steel lines ran over frontiers, opened up valleys shut away from the outside world since before the dawn of history. Inanimate, they yet had a life of their own, they were changing everything much too fast. There is much sensual symbolism in railways, of power and ruthlessness and sexuality and people felt an ambivalent excitement about them that was half fear. It was to build the railways, among other changes, that many of the thousands of unskilled workers poured into Vienna. People knew that long-range bombardments had been made during the Franco-Prussian

War by huge guns mounted on railway cars. The Balkan railway cut through old boundaries which had always meant danger and they sliced through ancient defences, customs and beliefs into barbarian territories.

The educated and enlightened, those too intelligent to admit to primitive fears, thought of the Balkan railways as the opportunity to bring civilization to benighted tribes, as Crown Prince Rudolf did. But those were Turkish-dominated lands and the Turks were the ancient enemy, the fierce warlords who sacked Vienna in 1529 and nearly did it again in 1683.

Year-long controversy over the ownership of the northern line concentrated these feelings on to the financing of railways. People called the financier who built the Balkan lines 'Turkish' Hirsch and 'Railway Hirsch'. He was Baron Maurice Hirsch and his name, which means 'stag', took on with the nicknames an ambivalent dubiety. To mountain and forest dwellers the stag is a powerful symbol of untamed male force, as the horse is or was, until recently, to peoples of the plains. The Rothschild bank in Vienna was often called the Railway Bank.

In fact the telegraph changed life as much as the railways. But the railways could be seen and heard by everybody. There were not more Jewish financiers concerned than Christians. The great mansions of the Ring were owned by landowners and native new-rich more than by newly-arrived Jews. One of them was later owned by the object of the Emperor's infatuated affection and friendship, Katharina Schratt, but although everyone knew that Frau Schratt had been penniless a few years before, nobody minded her new riches. Nor was Jewish wealth more flamboyant than gentile money; no-one *could* have been more extravagantly vulgar than the major painter of the day, Makart. The advice of Chaim Weizmann to his fellow-Jews to be modest was unfair; it was a time of ostentation and Jews were no more heavily overcrowded in dress and accoutrements than anyone else. But they were visibly 'the Other'. Jews were both active and visible in the Stock Exchange, but the only profession in which they dominated was newspapers and unfortunately the press, of its nature, is also very visible. All the major news-papers were opposed to the widening of the franchise and to the New Left of Karl Lueger.

There can be no doubt that Karl Lueger was as much affected by this trend of the times as other Viennese of his background. It is true that Lueger used the prevailing climate of anxiety and dislike for foreigners in general and Jews in particular, but he was also quite simply influenced by it. Theodor Herzl was right in his view that economic change and strain were the cause of anti-Semitism all over Europe. But Herzl was a man of the mind while Lueger was a man of feeling and action, his brain dealt in plans and organization. What Lueger had in common with Herzl was that his loyalty and affection was given without reservation; Herzl's to an idea, and Lueger's to people.

His people were the small artisans and shop-keepers who felt their control over their own destinies slipping from them in the concrete form of limited companies and large manufacturing complexes manned by operatives who owned nothing and were dependent on the owners of the machines. They lived next door to these new 'workmen' and could see how ill-paid and ill-treated they often were. The fear of sliding down into that proletariat was a very real one. They also watched the hunger riots and strikes and joined in them because they feared the machines and hated those who owned them. It was a Rothschild who said that hatred of the Rothschilds was the focus of Parisian anti-Semitism; that was simplistic but simple people do simplify. Anti-Semitism grew and Karl Lueger both reflected and en-couraged it. It was countered by constant persuasion in the Press and by the known disapproval of the Emperor whose influence was strong enough to make Lueger look and sound sheepish at times but not strong enough to calm the widespread unease.

The extreme anti-Semites of Lueger's time were in fact the pan-German nationalists who despised the weakened Habsburg Empire and adored the expansive energy of unified Germany. They were a small group, but noisy. Their leader, a minor land-owner called Georg von Schoenerer, exposed himself several times to charges of treason. He finally got himself arrested after a drunken attack on the editorial offices of the *Neues Wiener Tagblatt*, which was the Jewish-owned newspaper whose publisher was a friend of Crown Prince Rudolf. Schoenerer was jailed, his title confiscated and his civil rights removed. No doubt this was an oblique revenge for his treasonable utterances but it also shows conclusively that authority disapproved of his anti-Semitism. No doubt, too, his covert attacks on the Crown Prince as a friend and confidant of the Jewish publisher of the *Tagblatt*, Moritz Szeps, did not make Schoenerer less disliked in Imperial circles although the sentence on him was a matter of law and not of private revenge. But, although he did not know it himself for some years, Schoenerer was finished as a public figure. Lueger, though in trouble, was far from finished.

The granting of the contract for the city rail project did not stop Lueger attacking it in and out of the council. Bribery was the customary means of disarming opposition, so bribery was tried. First Lueger was offered the lucrative post as law consultant to the contracting company with a retainer of 20,000 Gulden, then a small fortune. Then he was offered a directorship in the company. But Lueger did not care about money and enraged at the insult he named in public the two councillors who had approached him. They promptly sued for defamation of character. Lueger's able defence lawyer turned the tables on the plaintiffs with the argument that Lueger was the only man in communal politics who had refused to be bribed. For that he found himself accused of the dishonour which attached in reality to those who had tried to buy him. The court found for the defendant. It was a personal triumph and ensured Lueger for life the trust of the public. The Press continued to attack him on the extraordinary grounds that he was making himself the spokesman of the propertyless masses. Since the New Left was by now beginning to address itself to employed workers who later became a large wing of the movement, this was true.

Having been elected to the Imperial Parliament Lueger opposed the privately-owned railways in that larger forum. That would probably of itself not have made him unpopular with the government and the 'all-highest' ruler; but long before the term was up for renewal in 1887 of the trade and customs agreement with the Hungarian half of the Dual Monarchy, Lueger began to attack that too. He was already quite well known in parliament as a member of the Committee for Social Questions through which useful new laws clarified labour questions; safety regulations and working hours, female and juvenile labour, agricultural co-operatives and the like. His view on the trade and customs agreements was that a ten-year term allowed and encouraged the Magyars to blackmail the rest of the Empire by threatening to interrupt the passage of money and goods if they did not get what they wanted, including high agricultural prices which affected every citizen. He said that the agreements should be negotiated once and for all. Very sensible and an attractively simple idea in theory, a department of thought in which Lueger did not excel. The trouble with it was that the Hungarians would never agree and could paralyse the internal trade of the realm, not to mention the armed forces and, through their large presence in the Foreign Office, international diplomacy as well. Moreover the greatest fear of the Emperor was of trouble with the Hungarians, a fear that went back to the first days of his reign in the revolution of 1848. Then, when Franz Joseph was eighteen and Emperor for only a week or so, his advisers lost their heads and called in Russian help to quell Hungarian rebellion; neither the Hungarians nor the Emperor ever forgot that mistaken brutality. The Emperor's personal involvement was increased by his wife's strong attachment to the Hungarians and by the leaning of Crown Prince Rudolf, vacillating and emotional, towards them. But the major argument in the Emperor's mind was that the Hungarians could not be forced. That kind of far-reaching complication was new to Lueger; he did not understand, then or ever, that there exist problems without solutions. His interventions infuriated Budapest and alienated the Emperor, who thought of Lueger for some years as no patriot and certainly no 'patriot for me'.

That was unjust to Lueger who was a passionate lover of his country. And no doubt the tremendous popularity of this man of the people in the Emperor's own city of Vienna did nothing to lessen the monarch's suspicions.

Although he was a Member of Parliament Lueger's real interest remained his own city. With logical coolness and shrewdness he consolidated his position, picking up allies from the various radical factions, including the more moderate of the pan-Germans. To his left new groups of Socialists were now active, divided as everywhere roughly into the two main tendencies of those who envisaged evolution within the existing order, and Marxists, who were logically Republicans but whose logic remained theory. Lueger too adopted an ideology, in a curiously casual fashion. The ideas of Karl von Vogelsang happened to fit and although, naturally, there was a certain formality about the process itself, the emergence of a massive Centre or Christian Social block happened as it were organically, growing out of the old customs and social structure of the people.

Vogelsang preached that all property of any kind was held in trust from the Almighty and that the use of it in the world must take account of the needs and dignity of others according to Christian doctrine. This view must logically lead to the consolidation of commerce and industry into the larger units needed for modern economics (which was seen correctly as inevitable) through alliances of small undertakings in co-operatives and buying-and-marketing agreements. In agriculture this system was put into practice and works to this day efficiently and harmoniously. In industry it was not used on a large scale and the history of investment-capitalism, whether in private ownership or that of the State, has overtaken it. Be that as it may, and this is not the place to discuss it, the Christian Social Party became a power in all Austria and nowadays, under another name, shares political support almost equally in Austria with empirical socialism which is a modified State capitalism. If Karl Lueger had been a man who thought out theories, a workable alternative to both investment-capital and socialism might have arisen. But he was not such a man; his passionate concern was concentrated on a single city.

It was his only real passion, apparently. Women were fascinated by him but he never married and if he ever had an intimate life at all it escaped the searching notice of jealous friends and hopeful enemies alike. He lived to the end of his parents' lives with his family and, after his mother died, with his two unmarried sisters. His opponents and the Press watched him like hawks for any sign of financial interest, corruption or moral laxity; to no avail. Lueger was not interested in money for himself and when he did become Mayor his first act was to halve his own salary; his public dealings were an open book and nobody succeeded for more than one issue of a newspaper in coupling his name with that of any woman. He was devoted to everyone and in love with no one; perhaps he loved himself and projected his narcissism into a general benevolence.

He was so handsome that the Viennese quite rightly called him 'der schöne Karl'. A big man with a big head, a lot of square-growing hair and a curly beard, his features were regular with large eyes. The eyes in photographs have an eager appealing look, habitual smile-lines form them under a wide and candid brow and his mouth is constantly about to speak. He was talkative in private and in public, with a splendid speaking voice and an intimate, almost caressing manner. He went everywhere, was always out and about, and always had time to attend childrens' parties, golden weddings, equally at home in civic functions, the great ceremonials of the Church and the corner tables of grubby wineshops. Neither manner nor speech ever changed no matter to whom he spoke or where he was. Being an educated man he spoke correct German but spoke it with the strong Viennese accent and cadence, falling frequently into dialect terms. Viennese dialect would be a subject in itself, having many Magyar, Slav and Italian words and a casual attitude towards grammar and syntax which makes it both annoying and partially unintelligible even to native German-speakers not used to it. It was and is universal in the city, without differences of rank; it is the modulation of the voice that produces class differences and not so much the actual speech or words used. For formality or when writing, High German, as it is called, is used but still spoken with the unique cadence. Pure German without accent in Vienna is called 'Burgtheaterdeutsch' because the classic theatre is about the only place one hears it.

Throughout the decade of the 1880s while the New Left became the Christian Social Party and acquired its theoretical basis from Vogelsang, Lueger and his friends went from strength to strength and rose at the local elections from about a third of the seats on the council to over two-thirds. In 1887 an Hygienic Congress was opened by Crown Prince Rudolf with a speech written in collaboration with Moritz Szeps in which he said that the most valuable capital of a state was its human beings. Great alarm at this revolutionary notion was felt by Church and government. The aristocracy was naturally, and not only in Austria, against the widening of democracy and particularly against democracy allied to Vogelsang's strategy and Lueger's tactical use of it. In the next year or so the Cardinal-Archbishop of Prague tried twice to induce the Pope to condemn the new movement, but in fact the Pope committed himself both to the right of workers to a share in management and to the need to control the trend towards monopoly in finance and industry. It was not the new Social Democrats, unified by then, but the Christian Social Party, who gained new strength from the Pope's enlightenment. The socialists pretended atheism – at times – and there were many Jews among their leaders. Lueger was a convinced and sincere Christian and disliked Jewish capital and Jewish Marxism equally, in common with a large majority of his countrymen. Although in principle afraid of democracy, the Imperial Government gradually widened the franchise in national, provincial and local elections.

In 1895 Lueger was elected Mayor with a majority of five votes, and declined the post because he knew that to reform Vienna he needed a large majority. In the autumn elections for the council his party got exactly half the seats and Lueger was again chosen as Mayor, this time with a two-thirds majority. The Emperor refused to accept the result and dissolved the city council. The new election repeated Lueger's success with the same consequence. The following April the same thing happened again. There were large marches and demonstrations, the citizens wearing white carnations to show their loyalty and determination. The rich began to talk about moving to Budapest where democracy was in practice unknown and the Hungarians threatened to revoke the trade and customs agreements.

The Emperor was badly advised over Lueger by the Imperial Commandant of Vienna, but his rejection of the election results was also caused by his constant caution in any question on which Hungarian feelings ran high. It is probable, too, that Lueger's extraordinary popularity in the city made Franz Joseph nervous of him as a demagogue and rabble-rouser.

The Emperor sent for handsome Karl. It must have been an interesting conversation, that audience. It lasted for over an hour, a normal long audience being about twenty minutes, and a purely conventional one, three minutes. The two men were alone and neither of them divulged what was said; it is entirely likely that they swopped gossip. But Karl Lueger agreed 'for the time being' to abide by the imperial veto. 'The time being' became as much a joke as its cause, the Hungarian agreements which were an '*Ausgleich*'. This is usually translated as 'compromise' but is unfortunately the same word that is used for the compounding of debts by one who cannot pay and is therefore near to bankruptcy.

'The time being' did not last long. The substitute Mayor Strohbach, who was always called Strohmann ('dummy'), resigned after a further election. The Christian Social Party had soon won every seat in Vienna outside the First District, the old city full of grandees, government servants and the shopkeepers who depended upon their trade. A week later Franz Joseph ratified Lueger's position as Mayor. It had taken twenty-two years to reach his ambition. Much had been prepared in the last few years, when the outcome was no longer in doubt. Now

Lueger could go to work. Franz Joseph was Emperor of Austria and King of Hungary; Karl Lueger was King in Vienna. He was fifty-three years old and, almost as if he knew that time must have a stop, he tackled his chance as if the devil were after him.

Lueger had protested when the new Rathaus was built, at the waste of money involved. When he got the power to do so he showed that his dislike of the extravagantly neo-Gothic monster was not only financial. He now occupied the Mayor's official apartment there with his two sisters, but quite rightly continued to dislike it. It is unpractical for any purpose and particularly for administrative offices, being dark, the interior over-complicated and lacking suitable rooms for a large staff of clerks. Outwardly it belongs to the worst kind of romantic and wilful Middle Ages as they never were, recreated on a scale that only a cathedral could justify : that is, a building dedicated to superhuman power. For a place supposed to take care of the affairs of human beings in their civic aspects it lacks any proportion to the human frame, which is the foundation of all good architecture. This is not a question of size but of relationship, a quite different matter.

In the works undertaken in Vienna during Lueger's rule, one name among many stands out, that of Otto Wagner. He was the foremost of the new architects. Among many other things he designed the stations and viaducts of the new metropolitan railways, the flood-control works of the Danube Canal and a number of other buildings. His friends, followers and rivals contributed other works, including the handsome superstructure of the canalization of the river Wien (part of the flood controls) by Friedrich Ohmann which provides a perfect example of proportion to surroundings and practical efficiency to the job in hand. These townscape works not only enfold the regulation of the river water, they grow out of rather than fit into the gardens that surround them. And more than any other architectural design near the Ring they show the contrast between the confused sentimentalism and vainglory of the Ring and the coherence of the Lueger period.

That was the whole new idea; building should grow from its purpose and the surroundings in both a human and natural way. False history disappeared, and decoration too in the sense of bits and pieces stuck on to designs as if they had been flung at the building after it was finished. The new designs were not decorated, their fantasies arose from their designs and purposes and were of natural, living beings; plant and animal forms. This style is usually called in English by its French name, *art nouveau*. It was, however, not French; its creative origins lay in Richard Wagner's concept of the 'whole work of art'. In English it should, not quite fittingly but more correctly, be called Edwardian. Its German name is *Jugendstil* and derives from an artistically revolutionary magazine in Munich called *Youth*, or *Jugend*.

Most of the new designers and architects of Lueger's time won their contracts in open competition and not by patronage; probably Lueger wished to get away from the corrupt patronage of city contracts, but the results prove the worth of the method artistically as well as morally.

Much planning and design was already completed before Lueger came to power, and some projects had been started on. The city's own supply of gas, the extension and electrification of the tramlines, the city railways, were built as a coherent concept. A large new cemetery outside Vienna with gardens and new entrances and all the necessary installations were designed as a whole and are still in use. The legal limits of a green belt and the protection of the Vienna Woods were established. They still to a large extent exist although in recent years there has been some encroachment on them, disgracefully much of it by the present city government which has gone back to contracts by patronage and without public discussion, with unfortunate results. The laying out of the gardens round the Ring made it possible to walk almost round the old city through parks. Sanitary and sewage works were entirely redesigned. Schools shot up out of the ground, accompanied by trade and technical training schools and the extension and organization of the Academies of the Arts in co-operation with various imperial ministries. Health and youth centres and orphanages as well as housing for the old grew together with health services for working people and the control of employment. A large mental hospital and extensions to the eighteenth-century general hospital were built. The welfare laws for the poor were not forgotten; nor were savings banks.

A major need was clean water. The first water pipeline from the hills nearest Vienna existed since Mayor Felder's day, but even with various additions was quite insufficient. There were eight plans for a second mountain pipeline lying about with expert opinions and studies for several years until Lueger stopped them and went exploring himself. Finally he engaged the consent of the monastery of Admont which owned the land in Styria where enough pure water was to be found. He laid the agreement on the council table almost literally with the words 'this is where we are going to get our water, and talk as much as you like, that's that'. Lueger exploded the first dynamite for the hundred-mile aqueduct in 1901 after nearly thirty years of indecision. It was to be finished in ten years and was in fact ready in nine.

Lueger was always slipping off to inspect the engineering and, no doubt, to interfere. Not only at the water works but everywhere else, no contractor or engineer could ever be sure that the Mayor would not appear without warning and alone, his eyes and ears open.

Being Viennese, they did not forget their stomachs. A municipal slaughter-house was built next to the cattle market and an extra pig-slaughterhouse was added to it with a separate horseflesh abbatoir. The central open vegetable market was enlarged and a big complex of covered markets with refrigeration newly built near the Ring in the Third District with a fish market down near the canal.

It all cost millions of Gulden, but where did they get the money? First, they used what money there was instead of wasting it. Then the new city gas, electricity and transport were monopolies and made profits. This is usually considered to be a contradictory theory but is not if waste and corruption are ruthlessly cut out. Then came the savings bank which in its first year collected nearly fifteen million Gulden in small savings. Because everyone knew that Lueger's eye was on him, nobody found jobs for his wife's cousins and nobody could escape the public book-keeping. In fact, it was good housekeeping; not a farthing wasted and not a farthing unused.

New military barracks were founded, new prisons, funerals and undertaking were communalized with fixed prices. Lueger thought of everything. Much of the thinking was done in the years of waiting for power. The action took place in something over ten years. The first signs of the kidney trouble that killed him showed in 1902 and were ignored. Perhaps Lueger knew that for kidney diseases there was no cure but in any case he behaved as if he did. Gradually his eyes failed, he could hardly move without help and his old friend and servant Pumera went everywhere with him. By the end of 1907 his public life, and that was his whole life, was over. Now for the first time people had to come to him for he could no longer go to them.

It is a success story. He left as his monument one of the most beautiful, harmonious and workable cities of the world. Those who came after him have tried systematically to bury the work with the man and have claimed it tacitly as their own achievement. Aided by the only fact known of Lueger in the outside world, his incidental anti-Semitism, a sustained effort of propaganda for the last sixty years has taken over his methods and work, adapted and adopted it. But it was Lueger who made Vienna what it is.

3

Hotel Sacher

SHE worked in the hotel, the new hotel behind the new Imperial Opera. She was plump, fair, with a round face and curly hair, twenty-one years old. Since her father was a butcher it is likely that his daughter was apprenticed to the delicatessen side of Eduard Sacher's expanding business; normally she would expect to marry a man in the same trade as her father and carry on his business. Sacher was already a rich and successful restaurateur. In twelve years he made enough money in his exclusive dining rooms and delicatessen near the Opera to be able to buy the site and the new building on it that took the place of the old Kärntnertor Theatre. He gave up the restaurant and moved into the new building nearby to make it into an hotel. The name of the theatre, Carinthian Gate, meant that it stood beside the old city gate on the southward bound trunk road. The Gate was gone with the city walls twenty years before and now the magnificent new Opera House stood massively there; that was why Eduard Sacher's freehold from the administrator of imperial land contained a clause that his new building might never be used for theatrical purposes.

It was 1880, the start of the great age of European hotels. People travelled more than formerly and travelled for pleasure; it was the first tourist time. With railways running between all major cities the hotels ceased to be just posting-houses on the main roads. They moved into city centres and became larger and more luxurious. Those who only a few years before would never have thought of staying in a capital city anywhere but in a private house, enjoyed the freedom of living in a palace without either the responsibilities of a guest to friends or family, or the trouble of running a great house; their only duty was to pay the bills. It was no longer an admission that one had nowhere else to go if one stayed in such hotels; quite the contrary, it was the new thing to do, and immensely smart. And besides, in an hotel one could do as one liked provided the conventions were maintained.

Eduard Sacher was taken with Anna Fuchs. He knew she was capable and saw that she was nubile. He may not have noticed that the jaw under the soft young skin was as uncompromising as those dismantled military bastions or that the level eyes could have been looking over a duelling pistol. In any case he was the 'Patron' – everyone used French words and phrases in those days – and was sixteen years older than his employee. So Eduard Sacher married Anna or she married him, and he ceased to be boss while remaining the Patron.

What genius first invented the *chambre séparée*? Probably it just grew of itself from an old custom of private rooms. Certainly it was the secret of Eduard Sacher's success as a restaurateur. He furnished a whole row of them in his first city venture and carried the idea over into the hotel; they were private dining rooms taken for the evening, larger rooms for big dinners and small ones for intimate suppers. The twelve private rooms were along the far side of the ground floor of the hotel where the restaurant now is. The public restaurant was in the middle of the building and is now the inside hall. The immense difference between these *chambres séparées* and those of former times or those of other capital cities, was that they were highly respectable. Nothing dubious attached to them. Ministers of State talked policy after dinner, old friends could reminisce undisturbed, diplomats sounded out other diplomats, treaties between countries and persons could be discussed before reaching a stage where anything need publicly be said about them. They were both public and private. That was their value because in the years since the 1848 revolution newspapers had expanded, using every scrap of the freedom given by relaxed censorship, and the invasion of privacy was greater after the invention of the telegraph as well as much faster and more widespread. If an ambassador dined twice in the same house it might be known not only by his own report to his capital city but in every other foreign office too. But if he dined three times a week at Sacher no one need know with whom. The people who met in the *chambres séparées* were seen and known only inside the hotel; and since those who saw were also seen and known, discretion was a matter of mutual convenience. It was a self-regulating arrangement. This was no Maxim's; the lady who walked down the corridor was probably going to dine with her own husband in any case and it was very certain that no *demi-mondaine* would be there. On the other hand the lady walking down the corridor might not·be going to dine with her husband but with somebody else's husband. And if you met her she would not pretend not to see you or flush and turn her head away. She would smile and exchange greetings and hand-kisses, even or especially if it were you yourself she was dining with; because what happened in private and what was seen to happen in public were two different things. An immoral lot, the Viennese; they did not even have the grace to play the hypocrite. It was not the moralities that must be acted, but the form. As Hugo von Hofmannsthal, no stranger himself to private dining-rooms, said 'But in the *how*, there lies the whole difference.'

And as far as what was mercenary went, it was true that no woman of a certain type could conceivably be seen in Sacher, no matter how expensive or how highly protected. Yet the two young officers with the two slender young ladies were entertaining near-juveniles from the Imperial Ballet chorus who certainly did not expect to lose by their complicity. Nor did they expect to hear any coarse-fibred mention of influence, still less of money. The ballet girls were part of the accepted world, within the closed circle as protégées of the imperial household and strictly supervised. They were enjoying themselves and so was everybody else. When they were a little older they might well marry Barons or Counts; the Burgtheater and the Opera were full of hereditary titles. And the handsome young officers might be kept very short by their papas and not have enough money to pay their bill; it would get paid at some time. In the meantime the boys were indeed handsome and the girls young and lively. Not until forty years later when self-righteousness became the unlovely fashion did anyone find much wrong with this arrangement. As long as everyone confined themselves to those who were known to be 'all right' there was not much danger of unpleasant surprises and if occasionally a heart got a little cracked on one side or the other, that was not taken too seriously either. It was outside the circle where the real dangers lurked, of scandal, blackmail and disease.

Anna Fuchs, who became Anna Sacher, was born to be the operator of such a system. She had all the necessary qualities of prudence, discretion, energy, a shrewd eye for character and, of course, a profound and romantic snobbery. She was dominated by an intense love of power; a small power, but complete in its orbit, and maintained by an open severity not far from bullying. She possessed her world; everything in it was hers or existed by her permission, included or excluded by her decision. With her guests and their guests she quickly found her own manner and never lost it. She was cordial, even affectionate to those she knew well but she did not encroach upon anyone's dignity or allow them to encroach upon hers. To the first guest who ever stayed in Sacher's Hotel, who was the Hungarian grandee Count Apponyi, to the Crown Prince and to the newly commissioned lieutenant she used the same pleasant, almost familiar tone of a friend; it was a small triumph of applied snobbery. An easy courtesy is the most unpassable of frontiers; this Anna discovered early. When she found someone, not always someone obviously vulgar, upon whom she felt she could not rely to maintain the correct and understood 'form', he or she was eliminated without more ado. She had a sure instinct; secrets did not come out, and the one or two exceptions only prove the rule. Those level, smiling, cool eyes did not even challenge: what secret? There were no secrets.

To be sure of that as well as to maintain the highest of standards in housekeeping and food, she ran the hotel with a rod of iron. In the contemporary accounts of Anna Sacher in youth the phrase repeatedly crops up in one context or another of 'her little hand' doing this or arranging that. Knowing the Viennese habit of irony it may be assumed that it was in fact a heavy hand and was often felt physically by the junior staff. To the personnel she spoke in dialect and what was less usual, used vulgarisms of speech. German is not one of the languages used for swearing; it is rare today and was more so then to hear indecencies in public and unknown for women to use them. Anna used them but only to junior staff. They were afraid of her and probably they needed to be. She was everywhere from early morning to midnight and after if necessary. No cupboard or cubby-hole was safe from her prying, no chef in the kitchens could be sure she would not check ingredients without warning. No waiter would dare to lean on a doorpost or maid stand with folded arms gossiping in an upstairs corridor. *Die gnädige Frau* would be sure to come round the corner as if advised by an invisible antenna, of slackness. After a month or so, if the employee survived, the standards of behaviour were second nature under a training as stringent and as much a matter for pride in all concerned as the highest standards of private service. The first and absolute law was discretion. Cleanliness, adroitness, skill and courtesy were taken for granted; nobody would be there after a day or so if they were not competent. The prescribed sanction was always present but rarely needed. All Continental restaurant and hotel staff was then and is now registered with the professional association in Geneva. That is why in any good hotel, small or large, modest or magnificent, the guests never needed to worry about the honesty of the staff because anyone complained of to Geneva would never again get any respectable job. In good hotels things were locked up against the other guests and not against the staff. In Sacher in those days the rules, above all that of discretion, went past what was demanded by the professional association. Not a curious look or a raised eyebrow was permitted. If a *Geschichte* came out there would be a razzia that the political police could not better; but if a story did come out it was from another guest.

For instance, the notorious tale that an Archduke, who is never named, came out of his private dining-room late at night in a lively state of mind and stark naked. Unfortunately the British Ambassador and his wife were just leaving one of those diplomatic dinners in another *séparée* at the same moment and the lady found it shocking. She is said to have complained to the Hofburg but that is rather hard to believe. The whole story is not easy to believe. The head-waiter Wagner is said to have had trouble persuading the royal guest to go back inside his own door but by Sacher standards Wagner would, in such circumstances, have made sure that the door was secured unless the Archduke rang for him. Nobody knew better than Wagner how much champagne was drunk and how well the guest could carry it. What may have happened is a much milder version of the same story. The Archduke found the room too warm, unbuttoned his 'Attila' and loosened his neck-band and thus improperly dressed came out for a moment into the corridor. This, by the standards of the time, casual disorder of dress would be enough to shock a Victorian lady and no doubt, as always with funny stories – and it should not be completely discounted that the story may have been told in Vienna against the Ambassadress and not against the Archduke – it did not lose in the re-telling. One version has it that His Highness was attired in shako and sabre – a likely tale! If weapons were used they were certainly not military ones.

The young Grand Duke Nikolai Nikolaievitch of Russia who often stayed at Sacher, wept his slav soul out when Betty Stojan sang sentimental songs for him. The *séparées* must have been better insulated against sound than any modern hotel is likely to be. In the next room a bombast of generals – the group noun is by courtesy of Mr Cyril Ray – might well be pushing the heavy silver spoons and forks about in after-dinner contingency planning. One can almost see and hear them in their proud uniforms, with their fierce noses and sweeping moustaches . . .

Their talk was theory, manoeuvres. The last major battle was the lost one of 1866 against the Prussians unless the fighting in Bosnia in '78 was included which was the kind of prolonged skirmish that the English fought every other year in Africa and which they had objected to so much when another power did precisely what they did. By the late eighties the commanders of regiments at Königgrätz were retiring. Soon there would be no senior officers on the active list who had fought a war and by 1914 few who had seen shots fired in anger. But all Europe agreed on one thing, the Austro-Hungarian Army was the best dressed. It was a good deal more than that, in spite of the charming manners that Queen Victoria, among others, praised. But soldiers are made in battles and the Emperor risked no battles for as he got older he got more cautious and pacific, both of which he had always been. So the Austro-Hungarian Army went on manoeuvres and discussed the Balkans and the dangerous gap in power caused by the retreats of the Turks and the increase of influence to the Russians in Bulgaria and eternally divided Macedonia. They talked of the Serbs who meanwhile were collecting a good deal of battle experience in the dust and blood of the Balkans where the fighting, as everyone knew, could only break out again; where there is a gap in power there is always trouble. Belgrade was not much more than a village but the Serbs were becoming a formidable army by means of invaluable and immediate experience.

But in Sacher it all looked like an operetta. Johann Strauss, taking over from his father, had developed the earlier rage for Offenbach and Millöcker and written melodies that went round the world because he was a genius of light music, and musically by no means contemptible at that. He gave the world a picture of Austria which the Austrians then and ever since found it amusing to foster and which is about as real as if the French were to be judged by Feydeau's farces. The world of small

retail business that Anna Sacher came from was nothing like
an operetta. But like everyone who comes from the outside
into or near a great complex of power and prestige, she got it all
just slightly wrong. She took the form for the content. The
form was delightful and so were most of the people who upheld
it. The content was the endless squabbling of Czechs with
Germans over language questions; the oppression of the Croats
by the Hungarians who in spite of dominating more than half
of the Empire were always irritably worried lest they should
really be somehow in second place. These bitter and childish
angers were so complex, so boring, so repetitive that
Scheherezade herself could not make a story of them. The reality
was a balancing act of compromises that continued throughout
the whole sixty-eight years of Franz Joseph's reign.

Anna Sacher's view of the aristocrats who frequented her
hotel was that of a romantic adoration very similar to what
Evelyn Waugh so brilliantly, but in the end so sadly, expressed
in English. There was Nikolaus von Szemere, a Magyar million-
aire and racehorse owner who wore the Hungarian noble's
costume, reserved normally for great occasions, almost every
day. Not only the close-fitting frogged tunic and knee-breeches,
but the Attila or over-tunic too, which was usually slung over
one shoulder like a cape; with this the feathered cap and all
trimmed with leopard skin. For some reason best known to himself he always wore socks of different colours and he gave
magnificent parties in his suite over the main entrance to the
hotel. He was a skilful gambler, winning and losing large sums.
Everyone who was anyone went to his evenings at Sacher, the
kitchen there being as he said, the best. He once declined an
invitation to dinner from the Heir-Apparent Franz Ferdinand
on the ground that he could not trust the Archduke's wife to
provide a table such as he was used to. He got away with this
piece of impudence, too.

But Szemere was not typical even if it were possible to speak
of any human being as typical of his time and place. Most of
those who were entertained by him were taking a change from

arduous duties in the army or civil service or as members of the government. Conrad von Hötzendorf was frequently to be seen, but that was far from meaning that he devoted his energies to horse-racing and drinking. Conrad was in the midst of his steep career up through the ranks of the Army, a constant pleader for modernization in the armed forces. He said and wrote untiringly that the Serbs were becoming dangerous with their reckless intriguing, that it was ill-advised to say the least for the Hungarians to drive the South Slavs of the Empire into the arms of their Serb cousins outside by social discrimination and economic exploitation. That the protection of Hungarian farming by unfairly high tariffs against Serbian produce was a serious political mistake. His warnings went on for many years until people thought him a nagger and a bore; he was a worrier by nature, they said. Later Conrad warned that after the murder of King Alexander of Serbia and his wife and his replacement by one of the murderers, Prince Peter Karageorgjevic, the Russians were practically in control in Belgrade. He advised a preventive strike against the Serbs during the Russian-Japanese war when such a move was safe. He was always sure that the Italians would not hold to their allegiance to the Triple Alliance with Germany and Austria-Hungary, especially after the supposedly secret but well-known French-Italian Treaty of 1902. If it came to war with Russia, as at some moment in the constant shifting weaknesses of the Balkans it must surely do, Conrad was not sure that the Germans would put the interests of Austria-Hungary high enough to ensure effective intervention. This last could only be said privately, in consideration of the alliance with the German Empire which was the Habsburg Empire's only support against the expansive pressure of Russia towards the south-east.

It was known that Archduke Franz Ferdinand, after the death of Crown Prince Rudolf, the heir to the throne, not only agreed with Conrad but furthered his career in spite of many disagreements. But for people like Szemere Franz Ferdinand too was thought to be much too serious; all his and Conrad's warnings of doom were really only their wish to be in control, their personal ambition. But unfortunately Conrad's views of the Habsburg position were correct, both in diagnosis and prognosis. The Serbs were dangerous, the Italians were unreliable friends, the Russians were constantly intriguing, the three-front war did come. When Conrad was to be seen at Sacher he was merely relaxing from his constant anxiety, not escaping from it. And this was true equally for many senior officers and officials; the gaiety and good-living in Sacher were more frequently moments off from constant hard work than the result of frivolity.

Outsiders, and Anna Sacher among them, took the appearance for the reality and the legend of Austrian love of living, of wine, women and song was focused on Sacher. Years later, in 1914, Szemere gave what must have been the last party of its kind in three separate restaurants near the racecourse at Freudenau. He had a great win in a race at Whitsun and engaged Sacher's to cater for three hundred guests, all his friends, the whole of the Jockey Club, down to jockeys and grooms and their wives. The celebration took dozens of cooks and several gypsy groups to provide music. There was only one thing wrong about this dinner to end all dinners and that was nothing to do with the party. A few days later the shots fell at Sarajevo and a few months after that half the gallant men who ate and drank Szemere's health there, gentle and simple alike, were dead.

It was Szemere who introduced Anna Sacher to smoking cigars and this became a lifelong habit of hers; her other affectation she found for herself, the fondness for miniature pug-dogs, several of which were always to be seen with her. Her husband was seen less and less and after twelve years he died and Anna was in law what she had been in fact for years; as she would say when strangers asked for the owner of Sacher's Hotel: 'Sacher – that's me.'

The food at Sacher was the best in Vienna and it became almost an institution that those who were to dine in the evening at the Hofburg had a meal at Sacher first. It is a little-noticed fact that people who go to Court, and not only in Vienna, find it easier and less obvious to let others know of their eminence by complaining of it rather than bragging. One does not openly congratulate oneself but says instead what a bore it is, how dreadful the food, the etiquette, the conventionality of hosts and guests. Just the same, there really was something lacking in the hospitality in the Imperial palaces. It was worse when the Empress was away which was most of the time and, after her assassination, became still worse. The Emperor maintained a soldierly frugality and simplicity in his personal life, eating and drinking little. More serious than that, he ate rather fast. He was always served first and etiquette required that when the Emperor had finished his food everyone else stopped eating too. At a large dinner it sometimes happened that the last guests had not been served when the host put down his knife and fork. No doubt this rigour was not as bad as it was said to be, but it was enough for those who ate often with the monarch to feel the need of gastronomic insurance, just in case. This they found at Sacher and with a late midday meal of *Tafelspitz* and a bottle of claret inside them they found the effort of concentrating upon affairs of State easier than with a grumbling stomach.

Tafelspitz was and is a speciality of the Sacher kitchen. It is the hind corner of the upper rib of beef, boned to produce a flat triangle of meat edged on top with fat. This piece is boiled with root vegetables, notably leeks and celery root, and must be simmered plain starting with cold water so that the soup is strong and good. The soup is eaten first with one or other of a dozen different additions; small dumplings, chopped thin pancakes, stuffed pastry, all sorts of delicious things. Then the beef is served in thick slices with one of several sauces and pan-browned potatoes and spinach or the vegetables from the soup. The sauces are made with a light roux and the broth, flavoured with either fresh dill, chives or horseradish, the horseradish sometimes being mixed with apple. Nothing that either clouds the soup or is anything but beef may be added. The meat must always be served with the fat uppermost and carved with a very sharp knife straight downwards, otherwise the slices will be stringy if not cut across the grain. In Vienna this is a luncheon dish and not served for dinner. Like all the best food it is very simple, the excellence depending on the quality of the ingredients.

The food at Sacher must have been very good but it evidently had its ups and downs for Crown Prince Rudolf wrote to his wife that the kitchen had improved lately, which suggests that it was not always perfect or perhaps that Rudolf was a demanding guest. Certainly he took an interest in what was to be eaten and drunk when he was host, and a bill of fare still exists on which he changed the proposed wines. That was a few days before he went to Mayerling – where incidentally he is also recorded as commenting on the food – for the last time.

Viennese cooks have always been famous for sweetmeats so that it was almost inevitable that Sacher had its own particular cake. In fact *Sachertorte* is not a typically central European cake, being a dense, not very sweet and almost black chocolate cake with bitter-chocolate icing. The recipe is a secret of the house to this day and after long lawsuits it was forbidden for any example not made in the hotel kitchens to be called the original *Sachertorte*. It is supposed to have been invented by an apprentice-cook for Prince Metternich in about 1832. That was the first known Sacher who was a cook and who founded the fortunes of his son Eduard, whom he long outlived. In the great days of Sacher Anna often used to drive out to his house outside the city for advice and to try out new recipes. He may well have been the only person Anna Sacher ever turned to for advice.

The exclusiveness that attached to the *Sachertorte* was only one example of Anna Sacher's determination that everything to do with her hotel must be not only the best of its kind, which was taken for granted, but the only possible one of its kind. She was a very possessive woman; they were her guests and ate her food and drank her wines and all of them were of the highest excellence. To be favoured by Anna a guest, if he were not titled, had to be outstanding in his own way. Many of the greatest actors, singers and musicians of the day stayed at Sacher when they were in Vienna, writers and painters too. But they were all the foremost of their kind if they were friends of Anna's, famous or immensely fashionable. She was first and foremost a snob, but a clever snob. She never ran after anyone, the standards on which the hotel based its success were real and the highest of guests was not safe from a rebuke if he behaved improperly in public. Anna would tear up bills sometimes if her favourites could not pay them, especially if they were run up by the young sons of great houses, for they would one day inherit. She would listen to their problems and their love affairs in her own room while she stitched away at her famous tablecloth; she heard many secrets and gave much sound advice.

For years Anna embroidered the names of the rich, famous and titled on her tablecloth. Everyone she valued must sign his name on the damask and she then stitched over the signature. The cloth is a roll-call of famous names. The first is said to have been Archduke Otto, the younger brother of Franz Ferdinand and a man so good-looking – which is naturally a matter of taste and he was a lanky blond – that he was said to have been like a Greek god. Franz Ferdinand himself signed the cloth and indeed only one name was missing. The Emperor never went to Sacher, he rarely ate away from his own table except to eat at Katharina Schratt's and certainly not in a public place. Finally Anna asked Katharina to get the Emperor's signature on a table napkin, which she did and the linen was cut out and sewn into the centre of the tablecloth in a space clearly reserved for it. One would have liked to have heard those two conversations, that of Anna and Katharina and that of Katharina and Franz Joseph. It was often said of Anna Sacher that the diplomats could have learned from her; a pity they did not for it was the diplomats who got all their calculations wrong. She had the mental suppleness of a great diplomat backed by the shrewd, hard common-sense of women which men so often lack.

With these qualities, usually carefully hidden, Anna Sacher controlled nearly everyone who went to Sacher nearly all the time. Occasionally she failed and one of those she failed with was the Emperor's brother, Archduke Ludwig Viktor. He had that trick of the truly malicious, of going from one acquaintance to the next saying that each had said thus and thus of the other. Usually things he invented himself. His nickname was Luzi-Wuzi which may indicate that he was not taken seriously, but he caused a lot of ill-feeling. In their youth he and the Empress Elisabeth were friends but when everything she said to him in joke or confidence began to come back to her from others in forms that made trouble for her, she became at first cautious and then angry. Finally she refused to speak to him unless there was someone else present who could vouch for what she said. This fate, rather naturally, followed Ludwig Viktor throughout his life but he never learned from experience. Many of the stories about Empress Elisabeth that made her unpopular in her lifetime and after it came in the first place from Luzi-Wuzi after they ceased to be friends. As soon as Sacher became fashionable he became a constant guest and left scandalous gossip behind him wherever he could. Being a brother of the Emperor he could not be refused access to Court or family, or to Sacher's. On one occasion he hinted to his brother of having seen Princess Louise Coburg, Philipp Coburg's wife, in a private dining room at Sacher with Count Matachich. In that case it may have been fact and not fiction because Princess Louise afterwards ran off with the Count; on the other hand if Luzi-Wuzi had not divulged this delicate tidbit she might have carried on the affair without anyone being the worse for it. Louise was the sister of Crown Princess Stephanie and her husband was a notorious rake and towards the end of his life the late-night companion of Crown Prince Rudolf on some of his most dubious outings; there were all kinds of things to come out once Luzi-Wuzi started them. Louise Coburg who was a silly woman and absurdly conceited, became hysterically upset, lost her head, and caused a real scandal by running away. Once the family fuss began it was, as always, very hard to put a stop to it. Louise lost her rank and rights and finally accused the Emperor of having her imprisoned. So he did in a sense, but in a clinic after a breakdown and not in a Ruritanian dungeon; a house she walked away from one day as soon as she was well again. Finally, after causing Anna Sacher as well as the Emperor endless trouble, Ludwig Viktor was sent to the beautiful rococo palace of Klessheim near Salzburg, and not allowed back in Vienna.

Luzi-Wuzi was dangerous, a man to beware of in any society. When stories got into the newspapers they were less serious; Anna ignored them, sometimes was obliged to deny them and once offered a reward to anyone who could divulge the source of them. She kept journalists out of the house, which did not make her more popular with them, and added to the stories herself sometimes by being harshly dismissive as well as always being seen, eccentrically smoking large cigars and attended by her adored pugs. In this she copied rather than improving on the professional diplomats, who rarely seem able to deal with publicists.

The imperial family included over sixty persons, many of them having no continuous employment and some of them being, like Ludwig Viktor, unemployable. The Tuscan princes, disinherited in the gradual unification of Italy, together with their children, were particularly wild. One of the Italians as they were called, who was a frequent guest at Sacher and who caused himself and others a great deal of trouble, was Archduke Johann Salvator. While still in his twenties he published a pamphlet attacking the training of the Army in which he held a commission. It was, as in all European armies, forbidden for a serving officer to make any public statement or accept any public distinction without the permission of his superiors. For this indiscretion Johann Salvator was rebuked by the Emperor and transferred from the artillery to the infantry; another officer who replied to Johann's arguments lost his commission. This drastic punishment was often described as too stern but this view overlooked the fact that the officer in question had previously already broken the rule about publication and was also being used by Johann Salvator in even more dubious adventures.

Johann Salvator has told the story of his Bulgarian intrigues himself in letters and although he certainly did not recount all the details with complete candour, he wrote enough to make his subsequent loss of rank and titles understandable while himself apparently seeing nothing strange in his behaviour.

Prince Alexander of Bulgaria, originally a Battenberg, was deposed by Russian intrigues after Bulgaria became free of Turkey and some of the Bulgarian chieftains were looking for a replacement who would help them against the pro-Russian party. Only by risking war with Russia could a prince friendly to the Danube Empire be forced into Ferdinand's place. Archduke Johann Salvator, using the same cashiered officer as agent, proposed at first that Ferdinand Coburg should take the deposed Alexander's throne. He met the Bulgarian king-seekers in Venice where they offered the throne to himself, but he claimed not to want more than to fight for Bulgaria against Russia. Not content with this highly inflammable meeting in Venice, Johann Salvator was foolhardy enough to allow the Bulgarian conspirators to visit him within the borders of the Dual Monarchy, at Linz where he was stationed and in Vienna itself. At about the same time, as if he were determined to get into trouble, Johann accepted the freedom of the city of Linz without asking permission, and was then obliged to let it drop again. Even after this he seems to have believed that he could hope for command of an Army Corps in Bosnia, which shows a lack of realism bordering on idiocy. The last lieutenant to be commissioned was more likely to get a Balkan command than the man who had shown himself so disloyal over Bulgaria. There was quite enough unappeasable unrest all over the peninsula without appointing a known conspirator to command troops which he might, judging by past form, think of using to interfere once more in the infinitely delicate relations between the half-freed Balkan peoples, the Russians and the Austrians.

Thus in the course of about ten years Johann Salvator had earned the undying hatred of the Inspector-General of the Army, Archduke Albrecht, who was noted for his unforgiving memory as well as for being a reactionary martinet; he was disliked by the Foreign Office which was hard put to it to repair the damage done to relations with the Russians over Bulgaria; he had finally lost the boyhood friendship of Crown Prince Rudolf, whose own position had been made more difficult by Johann's follies; he had involved in his plots fellow-officers who were far more vulnerable than himself; and worst of all he had earned the weighty displeasure and distrust of the Emperor.

Having lost all hope of a career in the Army, the play-boy rebel then decided that he would rather be a sailor in any case. The Emperor decided, on the other hand, that Johann had gone far enough and ordered him to abdicate his rank and titles. In the meantime Johann achieved his master's ticket as a seaman and bought a merchant vessel. All this time he was to be seen about Vienna, including Sacher's, giving his version of his misfortunes to anyone who would listen. As a final *coup de théatre*, in 1889, Johann married his mistress Milly Stubel and took her with him when he set off on his maiden voyage as Captain Johann Orth, a name that came from his mother's home. Orth was also the name of the hunting district in which Mayerling was situated and this detail no doubt added to both the inspirations and the confusions of the gossips once Mayerling became notorious. Johann's first voyage took him to the worst sea passage on the globe and his ship disappeared with all hands off Cape Horn. The Viennese are hardly a sea-going people and did not know that Cape Horn was the grave of many highly competent sea-captains, a voyage feared by all sailors and not to be undertaken by the inexperienced. So for a long time there were stories that somehow – one wonders how – the ship had been caused to disappear or alternatively, that Johann Orth had been rescued and was living in South America. Poor Milly Stubel, poor Johann Orth, they might with a little sense have lived long and happy as an earlier namesake of his did, who also loved a postmaster's daughter.

Some time after Johann's departure and after Crown Prince Rudolf's suicide, Countess Marie Larisch told a strange tale of how Rudolf just before his death had given her a black metal box and detailed instructions of how and to whom she was to deliver it. She was to take it at dead of night to the Schwarzenbergplatz, and would be met there by a man to whom she should give the box which contained details of Rudolf's alleged plots with Hungarian separatists. Marie Larisch claimed to have carried out this instruction and to have recognized in the cloaked figure, its hat pulled down over the brow, not a stranger but Johann Orth. Years later she published this farrago in her 'memoirs' and incredible though it seems, many otherwise sensible people believed her. It was to a great extent on stories such as hers and Louise Coburg's that Emperor Franz Joseph's reputation as a brutally unfeeling tyrant was built up abroad.

Those were great scandals. There were many smaller ones but those left trails of talk for years after them. The death of Crown Prince Rudolf a few days after entertaining a party to dinner at Sacher does not come into the category of scandals; that was a dynastic and imperial tragedy which altered history.

Just the same, scandal and the invention of stories does form a factor in the aftermath of Johann Salvator's sad tale and his connection with Crown Prince Rudolf as kinsman and former friend. There is not here any firm ground of fact, not even as justifiable deduction from firm facts. We move into a nebulous region of psychological guessing founded on other actions and known habits of those concerned, which is permissible only so long as it is understood to be exploratory and speculative.

Archduke Johann Salvator was a proven intriguer in politics. He used others, including serving officers like himself who could not defend themselves, as agents in his version of the 'great game' in Bulgaria. When unavoidable trouble ensued he tried to defend these agents from the wrath of authority, and did so in a general tone of injury and indignation which is ludicrously at variance with the known facts. This, combined with Johann's considerable intelligence, shows a complete lack of judgement, which is a quality of character rather than of brain and one not infrequently lacking in clever people.

Much of this intriguing and the subsequent discussion went on in the *chambres séparées* of Sacher as far as it took place in Vienna. Archduke Ludwig Viktor was constantly in Sacher and Louise Coburg by no means unknown there, while her husband was an intimate of the Crown Prince's and often accompanied him on night-time excursions which were supposed to be secret. Much of Louise Coburg's self-justification for her love-affair with Count Matachich in speech and later in print, consisted of complaints about her husband's profligacy which reflected on Crown Prince Rudolf. Philipp Coburg stood on the one hand of the figure of Crown Prince Rudolf, and on the other, the two arrayed like Tarot cards for interpretation, stood Marie Larisch. She too was an incurable intriguer who later insinuated many wild tales deliberately invented to discredit the Emperor and Empress who had banned her from Court. No doubt in his complex fears and uncertainties Rudolf picked out such dubious confidants as these two, as people in mental turmoil do choose the very companions who can do them most harm; but they equally picked him. Philipp Coburg did not talk afterwards, but Marie Larisch did and as with Ludwig Viktor and Louise Coburg, the more she was discredited the wilder her stories became. Witness the supposed black box of documents carried by her from Crown Prince Rudolf after his death to Johann Salvator; she would pick on Johann Salvator because he was already the centre of a great scandal and the improbability of her story is complete when it is examined. Supposing that such a box ever existed, which it almost certainly did not, why should Rudolf confide dangerous evidence of a military and political plot to an undefended woman? And to be handed over to an unknown at dead of

night in one of the widest and more overseeable squares in
Vienna; but – one visible from the front windows of the hotel
at which Marie Larisch always stayed in Vienna. And one she
had frequently traversed in a cab going to and from the Vetsera
mansion. The sources of the fantasy are fairly obvious. If such
a box existed Rudolf would have given it directly to Johann
Salvator if he wanted to, but he was estranged from his cousin
in any case; or he would have given the papers even more
directly to one of his unnamed Hungarian fellow-conspirators.

The two members of the imperial family who complained of
police protection or surveillance were precisely those two involved in different ways, in secrets and plots. But not only the
police kept an eye on Rudolf as on Johann Salvator; all the
gossips did so too, among them Ludwig Viktor, Louise Coburg
and Marie Larisch. Whether there was any connection between
Johann Salvator and Rudolf in the last days of his life is quite
unknown. Rudolf ostentatiously disavowed Johann Salvator, but
it is just possible that this was a blind; there is no evidence at all
either way. After the official disgrace of the Bulgarian affair it
is highly unlikely that Johann Salvator would be considered a
reliable conspirator by any Hungarian, but it is not known.
But he was certainly about in Vienna and in Sacher, trying to
convince everyone he met that he was a much misunderstood
man. Just as Rudolf was seen going in and out of the Grand
Hotel on the Ring on visits to Marie Larisch and Mary Vetsera,
so he was seen at Sacher, five minutes' walk away. Police agents,
hotel servants, the drivers of private carriages who talk as they
sit waiting alongside other carriages, the drivers of 'unnumbered'
or quasi-private horse cabs, all saw the actors in the several
dramas, speculated on their movements and drew their own
conclusions as soon as Rudolf was dead.

If inside Sacher a barrier of determined silence was raised,
nothing could stop the guests talking and particularly those of
the inner circle of intimacy. Indeed, the non-speaking of management and staff must considerably have increased the effect
of the talk of those who did, in undertones, spin their specula-

tions. The whole structure of gossip can be apprehended as a web of threads sliding through the fingers of people like Luzi-Wuzi, Louise Coburg and Marie Larisch while those about them, both those who upheld the impenetrable discretion of Sacher's and those who, as it were two minutes away, pledged their word to the Emperor in the Hofburg, remained dumb.

It may well be from this web of undertones that the rumours first came of a plot by Rudolf to get the Crown of Hungary for himself and split the Dual Monarchy into two. That was just what Johann Salvator actually did in the case of Bulgaria although naturally he denied that he had ever wanted that throne for himself. What more likely than that this knowledge of political plots seeped over into the mystery of Rudolf's suicide? It seemed a much more likely reason for suicide to worldly people than an unhappy love-affair, especially to those people who knew that Rudolf was by no means exclusively committed to Mary Vetsera but was sexually promiscuous. This story of the Hungarian plot arose not because it existed, but because the internal evidence of Rudolf's physical illness and mental instability did not then exist. Between the known disgrace of Johann Salvator over Bulgaria and the known proposal to have Rudolf crowned King of Hungary as a guarantee for the future during his father's lifetime, the combination must have seemed obvious, but only to persons fairly near the centre of knowledge while not being quite inside it.

Such stories and many others began to appear in the newspapers of neighbouring countries within days of Rudolf's death. They did not get printed in Vienna or Budapest, where closer knowledge of the various factors might have discredited them, because inside the Empire they would have been censored. But such stories do not normally start with journalists who have to vouch to their editors for some source of their reports. They start with people nearer to Court and aristocracy than reporters, those who think to do their own interests some service, or their enemies some disservice, by divulging them. The reporter, perhaps sincerely, would cover his news by saying truthfully that he learned it from a lady of the highest rank who dined the evening before with an Archduke. What better source? If the lady was Louise Coburg and the Archduke Luzi-Wuzi, the matter looked less credible, but an editor in Berlin or Paris could not know their reputations, and probably a foreign correspondent did not either. It was at this moment that such things were just beginning to come out in a nexus of scurrility and confused loss of repute.

In themselves these stories were not more numerous than may be thought normal in such a large family, nor more frequent than, for instance, in contemporary London. But London was a single coherent society, the rulers of which have never lost control over their own secrets, whereas the Habsburg family did lose that control, in part at the time and completely in 1918. The cause of the partial contemporary lack of control was the same as for most of the other difficulties of the Habsburg Empire; the diversity, mutual animosity and complexity of the multi-national State, which can be seen so clearly in the old guest books of Sacher's Hotel. Here is the Russian Grand Duke who was later the Commander in Chief of the Tsarist armies against the central powers. Here English and French entries. Polish names are next to Ruthenian ones whose holders were almost certainly mortal enemies of the Polish landowner in the next room. Here are the titles of Magyar nobles with long records of conspiracy against their Habsburg king. And next to them a Ban of Croatia, an Hungarian vassal whose neighbour in turn is a Serb, or a Croatian politician probably quarrelling with both Serbs and Hungarians. An Italian name follows that of a German title in South Tyrol, long coveted by the recently unified Italian Crown. A Rothschild sleeps next door to a Pan-German nationalist, a Transylvanian of mixed Hungarian and Rumanian family next to the provincial Governor from Cernowitz. High officers of the Imperial General Staff live on the same corridor with Czech politicians engaged in secretly suborning Bohemian recruits to desert the colours. They all come to Vienna as to the centre of the world and they are all

intriguing against each other or the Empire or both in the inter-
vals of enjoying the luxury and protection of the ancient and
stable order that they all without exception take for granted.

All these people and thousands like them, talk incessantly,
they are squabbling with each other and the state at the same
moment as they petition for some honour or privilege, lobby for
an advancement, claim some appointment of court or government given for generations to the same family which is married
into every other family. The unbreakable silence of Anna Sacher
about her guests' affairs is the reverse of the coin of ceaseless
talk; there can be no middle way. Either one belongs to the
talkers or one is silent altogether. From this ceaseless chatter
derives the secrecy of government; from it on a higher level of
both morality and rank comes the absolute nature of a promise
of silence made to the Emperor.

It was this pervasive climate of intimately connected gossip
and intrigue combined with the impalpable presence of power
that gave Vienna at that time its unique atmosphere. The concentration of power provided, as it always must, a strongly
sensual, including sexually sensual, muscularity and force to
the ambience. Its subtlety was contributed by complicated
diversity of interests together with the overriding need to maintain the always precarious balance of compromise, which in
turn produced an obliqueness of speech and manner; no one was
for a moment unconscious of the need not to offend one or
other of an eternally mixed company. And no one therefore,
ever said precisely what was meant; words always carried and
were meant to carry undertones and overtones apart from what
was said. And this constant necessary subtlety was universal
both in individuals and between persons and groups, for the
whole of the upper and middle classes of officialdom both civil
and military was inextricably intermarried and allied across
the language and ethnic divisions. The added fact that ethnic
differences were – and are – largely imaginary but strongly upheld, intensified the ironical and equivocal social atmosphere.
It might be felt, for instance, that the claim to be 'Czech' or

'German' when at home in Bohemia was absurd, but it was impossible to betray that feeling of absurdity to one's Czech brother-in-law; or even to one's Hungarian other brother-in-law for the childishness of Czech 'difference' would seep over into the equal childishness of Hungarian separateness. It was not by chance that Vienna was the predestined and only possible breeding ground of the deep if often wayward insights of Sigmund Freud.

The distilled intensity was most to be experienced, naturally, in the private houses of the great and influential. The place where it could most pervasively be felt in public was Hotel Sacher. There were other meeting places but at Sacher it had been deliberately and successfully cultivated by Anna Sacher. She had made a needed focus; a nucleus for informed talk which in London during the same period would be represented by the major London Clubs and in Paris by the salons. There were indeed salons in Vienna but they were either condemned to superficiality by their diversity, were closely exclusive to certain circles or were intellectual and artistic groups without contact to the structure of the State. Sacher was outside the official world of Court, government and Army, but was touched upon by it at a hundred points. There one could choose one's company so that a candour never possible otherwise could be risked on the unbreakable agreement that it would not be betrayed. The cultivated complicity of civilized intercourse between diverse interests which had over generations become an inborn habit of irony and obliquity was there channelled into small points at which plain speaking made a startling exception to the social rule without losing its pleasant amenity. Such a meeting place was a necessity in that society, more even for those who were burdened with real responsibility than for those on the periphery, who chatted.

One of the means of keeping Sacher exclusive, together with its high prices, of course, was its smallness. At times during the near fifty years of her career Anna Sacher must have been tempted to enlarge her empire, but she never did so. The hotel had about ninety rooms, some of which would always be occupied by the personal servants of the guests. Others were occupied or reserved for constant visitors, singly or in suites. So it was never easy to find room there and almost impossible for a complete stranger unless he carried a famous name from abroad. In Anna's days the rooms were heated by wood fed into the closed fireplaces by little doors in the corridors, and water was carried by servants in copper jugs as in private houses. There was a bathroom on each floor which until after the turn of the century was considered modern. But some of the suites must from the start have had private bathrooms, because the first time I ever stayed at Sacher was also the first time I ever saw a bathroom with bath, bidet, handbasins and closet all surrounded and panelled in mahogany. The walls and floors were of black and white marble. It was then a British Officers' Hotel but since the Russians had camped out in it only two summers before, the staff and management were not anti-British as might have been expected. I am sure such a bathroom cannot have been installed in the poverty-stricken days between the wars. Perhaps I was occupying the bed often slept in by Milan of Serbia in the great days of Sacher. It was a richly carved monster of the very worst period of late Victorian taste, exuberant enough for that colourful prince. How foolish of me not to have asked questions at the time . . . like Anna Sacher's guests of forty years before, I was too busy living then to interest myself in such historical matters, but how I should like to know, now.

One of the chief rooms was said to have been furnished with the furniture from Crown Prince Rudolf's bedroom at Mayerling, dispersed after the tragedy. This is a rather typical apocryphal story of the kind that Sacher always attracted, for nothing is less likely than that such objects would have been allowed to go on the market. One bed-story that is true, however, is that the bed in the room named after the old Emperor had really been slept in by Franz Joseph. Not in Hotel Sacher, where he never went, but in Schwarzau castle, where he stayed overnight for the wedding of his great-nephew Karl and Princess Zita of Bourbon-Parma. That was the last Habsburg Emperor and his Empress is still alive as this is written.

With the Habsburgs ended the era during which Anna Sacher made her little empire a small but important part of the larger Empire. There is nothing left of it now in what is today a good, smallish, hotel of the luxury class behind the Vienna Opera, except for Anna's tablecloth and a side hall whose walls are covered by signed photographs of former guests. Anna Sacher lived until 1930. But the great days ended in the summer of 1914.

Emperor Franz Joseph.

right
Empress Elisabeth.

The Hofburg from Michaelerplatz.

One of the elaborate fountains decorating
the entrance to the Hofburg.

Inside the Hofburg.

The clipped and formal avenue of trees leading to Schönbrunn Palace, residence of the Emperor.

Crown Prince Rudolf.

right
Baroness Mary Vetsera.

Crown Princess
Stephanie, Rudolf's
wife, and their
daughter, the
Archduchess Elisabeth.

right
Baroness Helene
Baltazzi-Vetsera,
Mary's mother.

Countess Marie Wallersee-Larisch.

The hunting lodge at Mayerling.

Karl Lueger,
Mayor of Vienna.

right
The tower of the new
Rathaus, built between
1873 and 1883.

19th-century Vienna: am Graben

below Kärntnerstrasse

4

Katharina Schratt

WHEN an actor or actress was engaged by the Court theatre he or she was formally congratulated on this achievement by the reigning monarch and in return thanked him for the appointment. So this must have been the first occasion on which Katharina Schratt and Emperor Franz Joseph met personally, although accounts vary. The audience would last for perhaps three minutes and was completely formal. Sometimes the Emperor had more than a hundred such audiences in a day and could hardly be expected to recall much about the individuals coming from all over the realm and of every kind and profession who were thus introduced to him. Nor did he, although the actress had the good sense to ask advice as to court procedures before she went to the palace and no doubt the three minutes meant a good deal more to Katharina Kiss von Itebbe than it could to Franz Joseph. That was in 1883 and she was about thirty.

When he saw her on the stage he did notice her; in fact he was enthusiastic. Franz Joseph was a theatre-goer; he did not care for music much but he loved plays and liked to be amused. He knew all the great classical dramas and admired many of their performers but his personal choice leaned towards entertainment which is hardly to be wondered at since he worked like a slave at his complicated and often boring profession of ruling. He saw her in comedies in which she often played the parts of innocent and direct girls such as the heroine of her first play at the Burgtheater, Lorli, in a long-forgotten play called

Village and Town by an equally forgotten playwright whose name was Birch-Pfeifer. Her first major part in 1873 had been in Kleist's *Käthchen von Heilbronn* in which both she and the production were sensational successes, and she followed it with *The Taming of the Shrew* in which she again played her namesake. The stock exchange crash of that year ended her success and for the time being, the City Theatre itself when its financial backers lost their money.

Katharina Schratt then went to the German Court Theatre in St Petersburg until Heinrich Laube managed to open his theatre again. Laube was one of the great theatrical talents of the time and taught Katharina Schratt a great deal. Franz Joseph did not go to the two successes at the Stadttheater, or he would hardly have been so struck with Katharina when he first saw her at the Palace Theatre, the full name of which was Hof und Burgtheater or Court and Palace Theatre. He was quite infatuated with her and his daughters teased him about his adoration.

It must have been at the end of that year, 1883, that the Emperor gave his admired actress another audience. Katharina was married to an Hungarian Baron and was already separated from him. His family lands and fortune had been sequestered after the revolution of 1848 and his grandfather hanged for treason. The Kiss family persuaded Katharina to try to get what was left of their wealth returned to them. Neither this petition, nor one for compensation, was successful; the Emperor as always did his duty and left the law to the law.

It was over a year before he talked to Katharina again. That was at the most elegant of the public balls of the carnival season from New Year to Lent, the Industrialists' Ball which the Emperor usually attended. As always many of the members of the Imperial theatres were present, including Katharina Schratt, and they had a noticeably long conversation. It may well have been the first time in his life, and he was then over fifty, that the Emperor discovered one of the great pleasures of life, that of chatting naturally with an amusing woman. With his own family he was father as well as Emperor and to the whole enormous Habsburg clan he was the head of the family. However fond he was of his relations, with them he could not leave his own role. With the courtiers and their families he was always obliged to be cautious for they were certainly no less concerned to engage his sympathies for their own interests than courtiers always are. At the least sign of favouritism gossip, intrigue and counter-intrigue started up. Everyone wanted something of him or wanted to prevent favours going to another, or both. This had been so since Franz Joseph was eighteen when the strict upbringing of a strong-minded mother gave place overnight to the power and responsibility of being Emperor over vast realms and millions of people. That power, usually described and thought of as 'absolute' was never even in theory absolute. The Apostolic King of Hungary and Bohemia and Emperor of Austria was bound by the teaching of the Catholic Church, by the rule of Law, by old traditions, by customs inherited by his peoples for many generations which could not be radically and above all not suddenly altered. Franz Joseph inherited not power so much as duty and if he ever felt inclined to forget his duties he was not allowed to do so; he rarely even felt like doing so and never once rebelled against his burdens. There are two major characteristics needed by any human being who is to wield power; the first is a powerful and inborn sense of responsibility and the second the talent for picking men to whom some parts of responsibility may be delegated. The first of these rare gifts was the major part of Franz Joseph's personal character; for much of his long reign it was the only characteristic that was allowed and forced to dominate his mind and his actions. There are only one or two actions during the sixty-eight years of his rule in which he can be shown as behaving with personal rancour or favour to any individual and he was almost as ruled by duty in his personal as in his official life. Not even in his relationship with his wife Elisabeth, whom he adored from the first moment he saw her to her death forty-five years later, did he ever put his own wishes or hers before his responsibility to his people and Empire.

The charm of talking to Katharina Schratt, then and later, was that she was outside this duty; she was a professional woman in a position of high respect who had her own life and disciplines and could and did confront everyone she met with the confidence of success in a demanding career.

On the stage what was always commented upon about Katharina Schratt was her naturalness; in an age of sometimes overwhelming histrionics, she behaved when acting as if she were in her own home and in fact that was how she behaved everywhere. And except for the titles and the marks of respect he received from everyone, that was how she behaved with the Emperor; pointing out to him what was going on about her, commenting upon the dresses and dancing, telling him who that was and where the other lived. She did not flutter her eyelashes or languish at him or preen herself; she just chatted on and laughed at his comments or simply answered them. And Franz Joseph must have found out quite quickly that she did not repeat to others afterwards the things he had said. The lesson of discretion can be learned in the theatre as well as at Court and Katharina Schratt had learned it; it is an even more essential quality in actors who belong to settled companies than to those of the commercial theatre where groupings change every few months.

Later that year the Tsar of Russia returned a visit to the Emperor. It took place at the palace of the Bishop of Olmütz, far away in the countryside and easy to guard because the Russian Tsar was in continuous danger from terrorists who had assassinated his father only a year or so before. The guests could not be taken to gala performances at the theatre, so the theatre went to them and among those who went was Katharina. After the performances the actors took tea with the Emperors and their suites and Tsar Alexander III who was a very taciturn man and lived in terror of the nihilists, came out of his shell and talked to Katharina with lively interest of her time in St Petersburg where he recalled seeing her act. There is a story that he arranged to walk in the gardens with her in the evening; she went, as if it were a matter of course, to the rendezvous and ignored his advances so skilfully that he hardly noticed the refusal because she never allowed it to reach the point where she must refuse.

Either by the Burgtheater or by Empress Elisabeth, a portrait was ordered of Katharina which formed the next step in her acquaintance with the Emperor. The Empress quite deliberately encouraged her husband's interest in the actress. If he had someone to talk to and relax with, she need not feel so guilty when she left him alone for months on end while she was travelling. Elisabeth thought it over for some time and no doubt watched Katharina carefully before she made up her mind that here was the companion for Franz Joseph. He was not only infatuated with her; she was just the kind of woman he needed to provide a refuge both from the ever-present State affairs and the Court itself, where any possible friend was connected by blood or marriage with half a dozen ministers and officials, and could hardly help becoming the centre of intrigue even if she did not wish to.

There was no danger of that with Katharina. Like many actresses of the Burgtheater she had married an aristocrat but she came of sound middle-class people in Baden a few miles south of Vienna. Her grandfather was a doctor who was decorated for his devoted care of the wounded in the French invasions. Her father went into business and was a prosperous draper in Baden where the house he bought still belongs to the family. Anton Schratt and his wife Katharina were by no means pleased when their daughter announced at the age of ten that she proposed to become an actress. A school playmate whose father was an actor took her to the local theatre where the play happened to need a child to say a few words. No doubt small Katharina begged to be allowed to take this walk-on part and did so with verve. Unfortunately that was also the day on which her father decided to go to the play and the aftermath was a spanking. When she was fifteen she still wanted to go on the stage so her parents sent her to two stern pedagogic ladies who kept a school in distant Cologne. After months of her writing pleading letters home and behaving so badly at school that the teachers could do nothing with her, the older Schratts gave in. She came home and was sent to a teacher of acting in Vienna. Through this well-known teacher she came to the notice of Heinrich Laube who had retired from a dazzling career as Director of the Burgtheater after nearly twenty years because he objected to the new system of management just introduced. Laube took over the new Stadttheater and wanted the young Katharina Schratt to join his company. At the same time the new Burgtheater Director was interested in engaging her and when a third producer made her an offer she cleverly told each of them about the other offers so that all three were in competition for her services. However, the three offers were the subject of so much discussion between her father, her teacher and the three producers that none of them came to anything. Katharina, typically, drew her own conclusions from this confusion and over-organization and went off to Berlin to the Court Theatre there for a year. Somewhat to her father's disgust she managed very well on her own and had a considerable success; when she returned to Vienna he recognized that she could and would manage her own affairs and ceased to interfere. At Laube's Stadttheater came the first major parts and a great success until the slump and her marriage ended the engagement.

The marriage did not last. All the Kiss Family – it is pronounced Kish – seem to have been spendthrifts and gamblers and after the birth of a son, Anton, the young people separated by agreement and never lived together again. Katharina was a forceful young woman who knew both what she wanted and what she did not want and she did not want Kiss and his debts. He became a diplomat and spent most of the rest of his life abroad in the service of the Habsburg Empire, an improvement

on the career of his grandfather who was flattered by conspirators into joining the rebel Hungarians in 1848, gave them
his fortune, was created a 'General' by them and executed for
his pains as a traitor.

By the time, in the spring of 1886, that a portrait of Katharina
Schratt was commissioned from a painter called von Angeli,
she was famous in Vienna for her playing of comedy and naïve
roles in plays labelled 'peoples' theatre' to distinguish them from
the classical repertoire. It is not by chance that three French
words appear in the foregoing sentence, for until Josef II in 1776
gave the title of Court and National Theatre to an already existing house just outside the Imperial palace, the theatre was a
European institution and not a local one. Hence the word
national in the new title, which quickly disappeared as the
concept of theatre became taken for granted as that of the
German-language theatre. Until the late eighteenth century a
large theatre anywhere in Europe produced both speech and
music plays in which the text was sung; during the reign of
Josef II the division of the two kinds of theatre was made which
has remained to this day. This was a much lesser change than
the revolutionary one connected in the history of the theatre
with the name of Gottfried Ephraim Lessing who in north
Germany wrote plays and insisted on their being performed
strictly according to his text. The same change was coming
about in France at that time and the protection and financing
of major theatres by ruling princes furthered the change. Fixed
texts made censorship easier and the time of the Enlightenment
was essentially a time of deliberate educational intent in government, of which censorship of the old 'peoples' theatre' and its
refinement towards great art was almost as much a matter of
eliminating vulgarity as subversion. The older and more spon-
taneous forms of acting where even written texts such as
Shakespeare's were changed according to the whims of the
owners and actors in theatres were often coarse and included
many sly jokes against authority and religion. The attempt to
remove the old clowns and butts of popular dislike or ridicule

was never successful, naturally, since it is a fundamental human need. But it was so much modified that when the realist trend of the middle nineteenth century began to make itself felt, it started what was then, and is to some extent still, considered a somewhat lesser branch of theatre; that is plays about ordinary people and not historical or archaic-mythical figures. This major European movement of culture produced a great body of wonderful literature in all the languages of the civilized world, fixing the work of Shakespeare and Cervantes and introducing that of Molière and the French classical repertoire, Goethe and Schiller, to name only one or two writers familiar to everyone. The music theatre was not behind this movement of the speech theatre and with Mozart it may be said that the change of opera from Italy to central Europe was not begun but established, which opened the German language to the singing theatre to which we owe the German, Slav and French opera of the modern world.

In the late nineteenth century the inclusion of 'peoples' plays' seemed to be a concession to popular taste in the Vienna Burgtheater which hardly reached to the great Nestroy, whose brilliant and delightful plays are largely unknown outside the German language and in spite of recent revivals, not nearly as well-known as they deserve within it. This was partly no doubt due to Nestroy's critical and ironical view of the world about him, but it was also an indication of the deep and inhibiting intellectual snobbery which has been for many years the curse of German literature.

Since Katharina Schratt's talent was distinctly in the direction of portraying ordinary women in ordinary circumstances, she was often considered a lesser artist than the classic and tragic actresses of her time, the various types of acting being then more decisively divided than they are today. It is said of her that she was more a personality of the theatre than a fine actress. Although it is no longer possible to form a judgement on this view because to do that one must have seen her act, it is probably more a matter of the lesser prestige of 'ordinary' plays than of her own talents. Certainly she was very popular with the public as well as with the Emperor and must have been one of the first naturalistic performers who showed that the trend of the time was towards the realist theatre just then being written by Ibsen and others.

At any rate, her portrait by Angeli was the occasion of her first personal meeting with Franz Joseph, in the studio of the painter. The picture shows a young woman with humorous and shrewd eyes, a mouth set sweetly but definitely set, and a determined, perhaps slightly heavy jaw. In later photographs the shrewdness rather dominates over the laughter in the eyes. It is a face of character, open, eager and forceful and while pretty and graceful not particularly striking. It was, of course, her normality and straightness that at first attracted and then held the attention of Franz Joseph. She must have had, to be a Burgtheater actress at all, a charming speaking voice well-modulated and one imagines her speaking quickly and with animation. A photograph of the same period as von Angeli's portrait is so typical of a certain kind of Austrian charm, fair, rounded, self-confident that it is quite difficult to see her as a person she is so much a type.

The Emperor did not himself commission this portrait, and we know that because he said in the first letter he wrote to Katharina Schratt that he would not have ventured himself to ask her to take the trouble of the sittings. It was at one of these sittings that the Empress and her husband paid a visit to the artist and talked to the subject. As thanks for her having given up her time for the picture, Franz Joseph sent her an emerald ring with a modest little note, and a few days later a further letter. In this he asked Katharina to let him know when she would be going to St Wolfgang for the summer as she had said in the studio. St Wolfgang on the lake of the same name in the Salzburg mountains is quite near Bad Ischl where the imperial family had a summer home and the Emperor proposed to visit her there. The reply to this letter informed him that Frau Schratt would be going for a cure to Karlsbad before going to the mountains, and to this Franz Joseph answered with further arrangements. In fact, she did not have time to get her trunks unpacked on arrival at St Wolfgang before a messenger came from the Emperor proposing himself to call on her on the next day but one at 8.30 in the morning. As he writes, this is an impossible hour to call on a lady and excuses himself by explaining that his 'business' fills most of the day. He went, sometimes with the Empress, to see Katharina a number of times during that summer when, as always, the theatres in Vienna were closed and the actors all in their summer residences. It is clear from the letters that follow that the friendship had progressed to what in those days would be called intimacy and that the Emperor's affection and admiration for his friend were now established.

The correspondence, as far as it has been published, together with Franz Joseph's letters to his wife, are the major sources of a judgement of Franz Joseph's private character. The letters cover many years to both his correspondents and since they were, of course, never intended for publication (an idea that would have been not even horrifying to the Emperor because he would not have been able to take it seriously) they show the man Franz Joseph as he was to his few intimates. Any editing that has been done to these letters has been intended to lessen their intimacy if anything, so that they seem less informal at times than they were. The man who appears through these letters disposes once and for all to anyone who reads them of the legendary monolith of the cold, humourless, inhumanly unemotional ruler.

From first to last, the last known note being dated in 1915, the letters are couched in the formal mode of address and with the courtesies normal at the time between well-bred people. They never addressed each other in writing, and probably never at all, in the intimate form unknown in modern English but used in all other languages. They were friends and not lovers.

There was a time when this relationship was very hard for Franz Joseph to maintain and although we have few letters of

Katharina Schratt's it is clear from some of his replies to her unknown letters that it was not easy for her either. But they both accepted the necessity of keeping the friendship as it was if it was to last. When the correspondence began the man was fifty-six and the woman thirty-four, and because of the absurd 'youth-cult' of the last generation the question of physical love may seem to some readers not to be a problem at all. This is certainly not the case in real life and was not then any more than now. Such things can rarely be established with certainty where the persons concerned maintain the outward forms of society; but as certainly as can be ventured, this was a friendship only; a loving friendship but one with no physical expression.

One of the curious details of the long friendship between Katharina Schratt and the Emperor Franz Joseph is the insight into the mind of Empress Elisabeth it affords. It is not, naturally, known whether Elisabeth envisaged her encouragement of the relationship as that of a love-affair, either consciously or not quite facing the thought. As long as she lived Elisabeth showed public and private affection and gratitude to Katharina and often went out of her way to protect both the friends from gossip by her own open acceptance of their intimacy. If she introduced these two people to each other and encouraged them to maintain their constant intercourse in the supposition that Katharina Schratt would take her own place as a substitute wife, that would seem to be a humanly understandable ruse in a woman to whom it is almost certain physical love never became real. But from her own letters and recorded remarks, it seems likely that Elisabeth did not consider that possibility. This throws a light on Elisabeth's ignorance of reality and on her psychological immaturity that illumines not only her life but her husband's. In 1886 she was forty-nine years old, the mother of four children and a grandmother. Her first departure on a long journey, years before, was probably caused by the discovery that Franz Joseph had a fleeting affair and this made her both jealous and unhappy; she is reported by members of her travelling suite, including her doctor, to have shut herself in her room for days on end, weeping. Yet her husband loved her passionately from the first time he laid eyes on her to the day of her death and beyond it. She seems never to have understood why a man who adored and desired her could ever have needed other women. This is not an easy thing for any protected woman to grasp, but it is a fact of ordinary observation that the vast majority of women, whether queens or washerwomen, do grasp it. That Elisabeth failed to content her husband was partly due to her astonishing beauty which made her seem to herself and others the only possible object of desire to anyone who knew her, but she never felt that any participation of her own was needed or even possible. Elisabeth was always an *object* to herself and she evidently never understood that a woman is more than a physical object; obsessively concerned with the maintenance of her own loveliness, she never became real. She lived outside her own person and expected others to share that objective stance, even where the objective was one of passionate love.

Poor Franz Joseph. He was not the man by temperament, upbringing or experience to dismantle such barriers. Inarticulate by nature, he was no different from most men always and everywhere, who confidently expect satisfactory love to arrive by the light of nature. But that he was unfeeling or inconsiderate is put quite out of question by his letters, both to his wife and to Katharina. On the contrary, if anything he was too constantly concerned for their comfort, health and happiness and worried about the smallest cold or over-exertion as if he had nothing more to do than any of his private subjects. In the midst of complex and threatening political affairs he found time to write his loving and often anxious letters, showing jealousy when Katharina was in the company of rivals, interested in her theatrical business and her son and servants. He was always aware of the restrictions his position put upon her and feared her impatience with them.

The detailed interest he took in her professional and domestic life shows with heart-breaking clearness how lonely he was and how he longed for commonplace domestic interests; something to fuss over. Those indications are understandable and are shared by almost all of us. People who live in magnificent palaces still live their own lives and Franz Joseph in fact lived very simply in the midst of all his grandeur which, of course, he took for granted. What was truly astonishing was his own shyness and uncertainty. The customs of the time required courtesies that seem today to be elaborate, but his asking of permission, his apologies for troubling Katharina with letters and questions, his self-denigration, would seem more natural to a boy of twenty with his first adult love than to a man who for forty years had ruled half Europe. He is often funny, recounting jokes against himself, admitting his boredom or lack of understanding with some, indeed many, of the public duties he carried out so patiently. Often he explains a gap between letters with accounts of the business that has filled his days, which would be enough for three men at times. He goes on manoeuvres in the autumn and tells her of the military details and how he found the troops in whose welfare he takes a constant interest which the soldiers did not fail, simple souls like himself, to appreciate.

The public man, the Emperor, was not easy to approach. His position aroused awe even in his youth in men as full of power and self-confidence as Bismarck. He himself was so used to his eminence that sometimes when his own questions produced answers that did not fit his view of any given situation, he would greet the honest argument with a silence that looked like rebuke but was often astonishment. He had, after all, been a ruler since he was eighteen, and one who knew from unremitting application the affairs and implications of his realm in great detail. He found it difficult to believe that others, when he consulted them, could know every aspect of a question as clearly as he knew it and very often he was right. He spent his whole life confronting problems that of their nature had no answers; the balance of interests between the nations of the Empire; the recurring demands for language autonomy in regions where the wish for the vernacular to be used officially was, seen locally, entirely natural, but which created huge administrative difficulties; the need to reform government and administration towards more active participation of both regions and classes; and within the government and the Court the need for neutrality and impartiality. It is far too little known in the outside world that the middle of Franz Joseph's long reign was a period of continuous reform and liberalization, in many cases pushed through by his own quiet and stubborn determination against the wishes of ministers, officials and his own family. There were many things wrong in Austria-Hungary as in all human arrangements, but the lack of understanding of them in their ruler was not one of them. Most of the history of that time has been written either by enemies of the Habsburgs or by those who inherited the chaos of disintegration after their disappearance; and it is consequently slanted at best and made the scapegoat for later follies and failures at the worst. The western world has always assumed that the breakup of the Dual Monarchy was beneficial to all concerned. This is an illusion and the life-long concern of Franz Joseph to balance the conflicting forces within the Danube basin was not only in his own interest. It was historically of the highest necessity. He was, of course, not the only man of his time who understood that; but whether he or his enemies liked it or not, *he* was unavoidably responsible for carrying out the understanding.

So he was inevitably a lonely man from his position which his uncommunicative temperament made still more lonely. The two factors reacted on each other and a large and jealous tribe of relations watched to see that no outsider penetrated the Emperor's isolation. Their guard was aided with unremitting zest by the courtiers and aristocracy who defended their privileges with a tenacity they might better have used on the real problems of the State they depended upon. It was the time in all Europe when the old aristocracies who were all closely allied with each other, and the diplomacies largely manned by them, failed completely to understand what was happening in the world and what needed to be done about it.

That anyone penetrated the Emperor's high solitude was extraordinary and the very thing that made it seem impossible at the time was just what made it possible. Katharina Schratt was not of high birth and her marriage into a landowning family which could have brought her into aristocratic circles was nullified by its failure. She was not a social climber but a professional woman with her own high standards and ambitions. She had achieved the height of ambition in her own art before the Emperor knew her; she neither wanted anything from the courtiers nor did she fear them. Any intrigue, and they were not lacking, against her came up against the wishes of the theatre public; for with the public she was popular.

In 1888 an important event in theatrical life in Vienna which caused great controversy was the closing of the old Burgtheater on one side of the open space before the main gate of the Hofburg. It closed on 12 October amid scenes of emotional leave-taking and the first performance took place in the huge new theatre on the then new Ring, opposite the equally new Rathaus on the 14th. Public and actors alike were reluctant to leave the old building for the much larger and more magnificent one. The public felt the auditorium to be unfriendly and too large. The acoustics were poor in parts of the house. The Viennese are on the whole phenomenally conservative and it is difficult to judge whether the grumbling was not simply bad temper at any change or whether it was justified; that is, it is hard to judge for one who never saw the old house and who has passed many unforgettable evenings in the 'new' one. I myself never saw the Burgtheater except as a ruin until its rebuilding was finished in the middle fifties after the Second World War, when the acoustic difficulties were certainly not there any longer. My own first memories of the Burgtheater company belong to the late forties when they played in the Ronacher theatre which was originally a variety stage and where one could literally hear the bang of the voices against the back of the auditorium which was much too small for the delivery developed in the great house on the Ring.

The voice-production of the Burgtheater is the result of stringent training in youth and has nothing in common with the 'stagey' voices and mannered tones of the western stage. The special training in speech was begun like so much else, by Josef II who disliked the variety of regional accents to be heard in his Court theatre and instituted a standard accent and tone in German which quickly became and remained the acknow-ledged correct speech as the 'King's English' used to be in England. The voices are so well trained that one may hear actors murmuring in intimate scenes so that they sound almost like undertones and yet can be heard all over the huge auditorium. When the company first began to use the new Burg they must have felt some strain at first in the much larger and higher space and this may have accounted for the complaints about bad acoustics. But another complaint was certainly justified and was not corrected in the post-war rebuilding, and that is the strong draught across the stage which can be distinctly felt in the front stalls. Stages are always draughty for the lofts act as air funnels, but the Burgtheater has its own characteristic blast. It has many other characteristics and one of them sometimes bewilders strangers who go there for the first time. After an especially fine performance the audience does not applaud but stands in silence before leaving. This custom, like that of not applauding sacred music, may well go back to the strongly religious strands in the Jesuit and later the eighteenth-century theatres. It is less often observed today than formerly because of the large numbers of German and other visitors who feel it discourteous not to express their appreciation in clapping. But when it does occur it is curiously impressive, much more so than loud acclamation.

Members of the Burgtheater company and the Opera held then and still do, a position in Vienna which, although one sees something like it in other central European cities, is both in structure and intensity of feeling peculiarly Viennese. It comes

partly from the historical place of the theatre in Austrian life
and partly from the hold on public imagination of music and
drama in Vienna itself. The history of the theatre goes back,
everywhere, to archaic times and there are still traces in the
circus and in carnival processions of figures whose ancestry is
pre-Christian. All the local seasonal masked ceremonies long
since adopted into the Church have heathen roots. From these
fertility and propitiatory rites comes the theatre as we know it
and its development can still be seen in Austria in villages
enough cut off from modern transport for them to have survived. The line can be followed in various places – not, of course,
in one place alone – from primitive devil-exorcism through
bucolic Passion and other religious pantomimes and plays,
Moralities where the words have been fixed since about the end
of the seventeenth century, into popular amusements which
have been recently and somewhat self-consciously revived. Some
of these are serious in intent and performance, the most famous
being Hofmannsthal's *Jedermann*, played every year in front
of the Cathedral at Salzburg. Some attempt to revive old profane
and populist spectacles with partially improvised words. The
deliberately educational reform of public performances of all
kinds was crystallized in the eighteenth century by Maria
Theresia and her son Josef ii with the double intention of raising
cultural and moral standards and of censoring scurrilous or
subversive contents.

Together with this movement the establishment took root of
fixed companies of players and musicians in their local theatres
which is today so much a part of European life that it survives
all other changes in societies. This structure of the theatre requires considerable capital and constant subsidy from public
authorities but one never hears – I think I have never once
heard in thirty years – complaints about the investment of taxes
in repertory theatres whether of world-wide fame or of the
houses of small towns. Every town of any size in central Europe
has its own theatre, and the most influential and most brilliant
without any question in all Europe, including Paris (although

recent reforms may be changing that) are the two great theatres in Vienna, the Burgtheater and the State Opera. There is a certain amount of debate on the rival values of the commercial theatre and the subsidised repertory theatre in most theatre centres of the world, but the results are so strikingly on the side of the subsidized theatre that to any objective observer with varied experience, there cannot be any real question. The faults of ensemble theatres are bureaucracy and internal intrigue. The faults of the commercial theatre are uncertainty and commercialism which inevitably lower standards. Standards in many provincial German towns are as high as at Covent Garden and the standards in Vienna are so high that one may often hear productions and performances that would be heralded as supreme achievements of insight and understanding in the American theatre torn to shreds by both critics and public in Vienna. They start from a standard rarely reached by western theatres and the acceptance of this standard is inborn in the public.

The theatre in central Europe is intensely serious, partly thanks to its eighteenth-century tradition of didacticism. Drama is an illumination of life and is taken as such, entertainment being a by-product although it should not be thought that such theatre fails to entertain; quite the contrary. The houses are always full; any production that does not fill its house falls by the wayside and since the public is highly educated in theatrical matters many plays which in New York could be labelled hopelessly unpopular and only interesting to minorities enjoy many performances and are carried over from year to year in programme planning. In the Opera houses the audiences are swelled by many foreign visitors, but in the speech theatres the public is confined to those who understand the language, so that the approval of the public is largely that of the local people.

Such an atmosphere results in enormous prestige for the performers and producers of all forms of theatre in their native cities. This was very much so in the latter part of the nineteenth century and in spite of the constant grumbling and nagging that is part of the Viennese character it was a time of great public interest and enjoyment in all kinds of theatre.

Katharina Schratt both came from this whole complex of feelings and attitudes towards drama and opera and profited by it. She could not be attacked without the public being aware of it; nor did she after one intervention, soon after her friendship with Franz Joseph began, need to use the Emperor's influence directly. In spite of the fact that 'everyone' knew she was a friend of the imperial family she was never particularly favoured by the direction of the Burg and was saved both by the fierce rivalries inside the theatre which prevented her encroaching into other styles of acting and by the restriction of her own talent. This was always for comedy and light drama; the 'heavies' were not for her. No doubt being an intimate of the Emperor's did her no harm in the selection of roles and plays when programmes were made up, but her colleagues and her own discretion kept the tendency to favour her within bounds.

This discretion was a major characteristic of Katharina's and she could not have maintained a thirty years' friendship even with a private person without it. She never repeated what was said to her and she never intervened in political matters; the few occasions on which she is known to have asked Franz Joseph for favours were in family affairs or matters of theatrical policy; but then, she did not need to ask. Their relationship was essentially one of small-talk and chat and everything she needed to say could be said without emphasis and had its influence without notice. They chatted about everything, from tiny details of costumes to international diplomacy and she was for the Emperor one of the very few voices from the people that could reach him spontaneously.

When they first knew each other Katharina was quite poor. Her salary was not mean, but she had a son to educate by herself and all contemporary costumes on the stage were the property of the actors and paid for by them. Only historical and peasant costumes were provided by the wardrobe department of the Burg. This was a great expense to an actress whose speciality was social and popular comedy. The Emperor arranged with great tact, almost with nervousness of any possible offence on Katharina's part, to take over her wardrobe expenses. He also on several occasions assured her that his Will would provide for her in her old age; there was no mention of Katharina in fact in the Will of Franz Joseph. He had obviously taken care of the problem privately. He was always a very generous man with money although frugal himself and he was so with **Katharina.**

Often they met to walk in the gardens of Schönbrunn Palace, only parts of which were then open to the public. These walks took place in all weathers, the Emperor driving out from the city in winter when he could find time. When he could he went to breakfast in her house near Schönbrunn, or to luncheon. Sometimes she went to which ever of the palaces the imperial family were living in. She was by a fortunate chance in the Hofburg on the dreadful day when the news of Crown Prince Rudolf's suicide reached his parents. She had that gift of friendship that seems like luck but is not: that of being there at the right moment.

It all sounds too agreeable to be quite true, and it was not always as easy as it looked. She was a forceful and outspoken woman and not easy to influence. Sometimes she would have her own way over things that Franz Joseph disapproved of; sometimes she made him jealous, especially when she went on climbing tours in the high Alps with mountaineers which both scared him for her safety and made him uneasy about other friends. On one notorious occasion she risked her neck by going up in a balloon, which was not only dangerous but much publicised and poor Franz Joseph was much upset. She gambled when she was in France on holiday and lost sums she could not afford. Franz Joseph lectured her lovingly but she did not stop. Often in the letters containing such reproaches one sees through the words how much he would have liked to be able to go off with her on such adventures; he could not move a step without being recognized himself. But in the thirty years of their friendship they had only one serious quarrel.

On 10 September 1898, Franz Joseph had just got back from the autumn manoeuvres in Hungary, and intended to rejoin them after clearing up urgent business in Vienna. He wrote to his wife and to Frau Schratt who was on a climbing tour. Empress Elisabeth was as usual travelling, this time near Geneva. She always travelled without professional protection from the police and on this occasion left her hotel with one of her ladies to take the steamer across the lake, the servant with the luggage having gone on in advance. The Countess Sztaray remarked in Hungarian that the horse-chestnuts were in bloom for the second time that year and Elisabeth answered that Franz Joseph had written that they were blooming again in Schönbrunn and the Prater. It was the time of the midday meal, hardly anyone was about on the quay. A man ran across the street towards the two women. They moved apart to avoid a collision as he passed but as he reached them he raised his right fist and struck the Empress a blow in the breast which felled her. She was helped to her feet, her dress brushed off, she straightened her dishevelled hair. The man dressed in working clothes had run on, out of sight. Elisabeth was sure she was not hurt, only shocked, but the Countess put an arm round her as they mounted the gangway of the steamer. A moment later, on the ship, Elisabeth slid to the deck dying from the stab of a sharpened file. A half-crazy building worker who called himself an anarchist but was in fact a pathological no-good seeking to make himself interesting, had put an end to Elisabeth's wanderings. The police arrested Luigi Lucheni a few minutes later as Elisabeth was carried back into the hotel, the management of which had given away her pseudonym to the press to publicise the place.

When Franz Joseph was told the news he cried out 'Nothing is spared me in this world'. Katharina Schratt arrived back in Vienna, recalled from the mountains, at the same time as the Emperor's two daughters.

Katharina was then almost fifty and that unfriendly date with its lowering implication of time for a woman, of time gone and perhaps lost, may account for her want of judgement in the next month or so. The Emperor's grief certainly accounts for the same unbalance in him.

For the fiftieth year of his reign an Order of Elisabeth had been founded and the Empress had promised Katharina the first class of this honour. When she recalled this to Franz Joseph he replied, in accordance with their old habit of caution with public opinion, that what from Elisabeth would have been a distinction and a continuing protection to her reputation, would become the opposite if he now awarded it after his wife's death. Katharina did not agree, she felt that the honour was not only due to her but that it was well enough known that the Empress had chosen the list herself for it to be accounted a sign of friendship from the grave. She was deeply offended and hurt and she said so without choosing her words.

Soon after that Princess Valerie, who had always been friendly to Katharina but whose husband was less well-disposed, invited her to visit her in the country. This was the very welcome proof of continuing protection from the Emperor's family. And a distinct change in the tone of colleagues and public towards her after Elisabeth's death showed Katharina how much she needed just that. Especially highly-placed persons allowed themselves to show their jealousy and dislike of Frau Schratt as soon as her shield was gone. But the Emperor again intervened; for reasons not easy to see he felt it better for Katharina not to go to stay with his daughter. There was a sharp scene and they both lost their tempers.

Katharina decided at once to leave Vienna for a long journey. She asked the Burgtheater director, a new man from Berlin who had new ideas for the theatre and who perhaps did not know the ins and outs of the matter being a stranger to Vienna, for leave. She wanted long leave, more than she was entitled to and probably asked for it in a way that took for granted its being agreed. The head of the imperial household, who was foremost among those who now felt able to show their dislike of her, was concerned in the renewing of her contract soon after she left Vienna. His letters to Katharina on the subject were cold and unfriendly and her wishes as to future roles were not taken account of. She threatened her resignation from the Burg. Instead of retreating, the Chamberlain hastened to put the request for retirement before the Emperor, and probably did so implying that Frau Schratt really wished for it.

Whether he believed this or whether he thought a more private life would be easier for both of them, the Emperor signed the retirement permission which meant the end of Katharina's career. She was of course, very much upset over this, forgot her own unwise move which had made it possible, and blamed Franz Joseph. She felt that although his friendship had advanced her professionally, socially and materially, that she on her side had given up much to their friendship; it had tied her down in many ways and made her, sociable as she was by nature, isolated among the colleagues who would otherwise have been her natural friends. And it is clear, although this was, of course, never mentioned, that it had prevented any other close personal relationship from being formed.

Katharina was at this time for months on end half-ill and never quite well and no doubt her bitterness added to her ailments. She refused to see the Emperor and a short letter he wrote at this time is at once so typical and so touching that it deserves to be quoted in full, if only to show Franz Joseph as he really was.

My dear, kind friend,

I have just got your letter which has depressed me all the more because I feel that it is my fault your nerves are in the state they are and yet I want only to be good to you and am so unspeakably fond of you. I hope you will soon feel calm so that I can see you again quickly, for the hours I spend with you are my only distraction, my only comfort in my sad and careworn mood. With the deep (sincere) wish that you can still care for me a little and that you are not too cross with me, I am always your most devoted Franz Joseph.

Katharina caught influenza, another member of his family died, and of the funeral he writes that 'the constant repetition makes one quite apathetic' while not neglecting to urge Katharina to obey her doctor and be a good patient. He also reassures her that a court conspiracy to come between them will have no effect on him.

While she is away, not quite ill, not quite well, he counts the days until her return. He always did do that, the words recur throughout the letters. But after Elisabeth's death Katharina was his only confidante and his longing for her company, her light-hearted chatter and practical good sense are very touching. He is so modest, so lacking in any arrogance and so far from ex-pecting his rank – he clearly never thinks of it at all, taking it for granted as he was bound to do – to carry weight in personal relations, that nobody who has ever been alone and neglected could read these letters without the heart quailing.

'I am a little afraid of seeing you again, not knowing whether you are cross with me. . . .'

'Perhaps you will write to me some time and tell me how you are. . . . ?'

On 24 September he wrote 'in the long time that I have had the good fortune to be corresponding with you there has not been so long a gap as between this and my last letter of the 14th, but then I have seldom been so rushed as just now. . . .'

Those who cannot find time to keep in touch with friends because they are busy might note that this man who was by then sixty-nine years old was not a business executive or a civil servant who can close his desk at five o'clock but the ruler of a vast empire of mutually discordant peoples who depended on him to remain the one constant point of their lives, the one source of authority, the one maker of decisions. And Franz

Joseph did not propose himself as ruler as a modern politician does; he had it forced upon him at the age of eighteen and carried the burden for sixty-eight years. The only person he could complain to of his task was for many years Katharina Schratt.

Gradually Katharina forgot her anger and they returned to something like their old relations. There must always afterwards have been some caution towards each other, but they were excellent friends again and Katharina was apart from visits to grandchildren, quite literally his only comfort in his old age.

As everyone knows, Franz Joseph died in the middle of the frightful war which destroyed Europe and from which Europe has not recovered to the present day. He died at Schönbrunn of an inflammation of the lungs which he did not allow to stop him trying to work until his last day. It was just after nine o'clock on the evening of 21 November 1916.

Frau Schratt was waiting and when they called her she carried two red roses which she put into the folded hands of her dead friend and they were buried with him.

Red roses in central Europe are a declaration of love, and that makes one wonder. . . .

Katharina outlived her friend many years. She died in Vienna in 1940. So neither Franz Joseph nor she herself lived to know the worst.

5

Caught in his own Trap - Alfred Redl

EXCEPT for the beautiful temptress this is the classic spy story but the part of the seductive and unknown lady is played by a handsome young man. Stephan was no longer the appealing, half-grown lad in an infantry cadet school, but the hungry and jealous passion for that boy still dominated the older man. Stephan was the son of a servant, lucky to be a cadet at all and with no influence. His lover arranged for a transfer to a cavalry training school and bought him the necessary horses, uniforms and equipment. He provided pocket money and watched over the boy's progress into an Uhlan regiment; he took his lovely lad about with him to social and military occasions which the boy could never have aspired to by himself and did it quite openly, introducing Stephan Horinka as his nephew. And now the foolish youngster had got it into his head that he was in love with some girl and wanted to marry her. That would cost money for an army officer must make a deposit of ten thousand Kronen to get permission to marry and still keep up the stand-ards of his class and profession. He could have the money, anything he wanted quite apart from his regular allowance of nine hundred Kronen a month from his 'uncle'; but not to make it possible to leave his protector.

Three times the threatened lover began letters to Stephan, but they came out all wrong. He was more used to writing staff reports than pleading love-letters, and one after the other the attempts were crumpled in a desperate hand and thrown into the waste paper basket. No, a letter would do no good. The thing to do was to go to Vienna and send for Stephan who could easily get to the capital from his garrison at Stockerau over the Danube. Made in person the appeal would surely succeed and too, the gift of a touring car that Stephan so much wanted would not look like a calculated bribe as it somehow did on paper. He would arrange for leave and Stephan would not be able to resist the thought of driving them both to Davos in his own Daimler. Yes, that was the answer; the boy could never withstand either his lover's undisguised passion nor the gift of love.

It was May 1913. The writer of love-letters was Alfred Redl, the son of a senior official in the Advocate-General's Branch, a Colonel of the General Staff, Chief of Staff to the Commander of the 8th Corps, stationed in Prague. His present post was one more step in a distinguished career which would take him higher yet, especially if the constantly threatening war should come. Redl was for years stationed in Vienna itself and had made a name for himself as a specialist in counter-intelligence and security. In the Austro-Hungarian Army passive and active espionage were not, as in some armies, clearly divided but were two sections of the same department of which Redl had been a capable and successful officer. He had helped to introduce modern criminological methods into his department, bringing it up to date, with cameras mounted behind paintings on the walls of interviewing rooms, listening and recording apparatus, systematized finger-printing of all visitors without their know-ledge and other refinements which made the Vienna centre one of the best-equipped in the world.

His chief there had been General of the Infantry Baron Giesl von Gieslingen who was transferred in the course of time to command the garrison at Prague. About the same time Redl went back on a routine tour of duty to his regiment and also left Vienna. That lasted only a year for he was a valuable expert and General Giesl asked for him as Chief of Staff. A specialist was needed in Prague to deal with the constant subversive activity of the Czech nationalists who openly invited military attachés from other Slav countries to attend the athletic tournaments of the Sokol clubs which were suspected of being the hardly disguised model for a future Czech Army. Spies and propagandists were everywhere, provoking anti-Habsburg demonstrations, encouraging desertions, spreading the panslav doctrine of brotherhood with the Russians. So Redl was promoted to full colonel and transferred to Prague. There he continued as the merciless hunter and prosecutor of subversives and foreign agents he had proved himself in Vienna, preparing cases for the Courts both military and civil with meticulous detail and fierce determination. He was known as an investigator who provided water-tight cases for the prosecution and always insisted on the maximum penalties being demanded; some of the most brilliant successes against spies in the last years were his achievement, including the round up of a whole ring in the Lemberg District which had been a sensation ten years before.

But he was not then thinking of his work; he must do something about Stephan before it was too late, before the silly boy committed himself to this wretched girl. He must act with his accustomed skill and speed. On Friday evening Redl ordered his soldier-servant to take the train from Prague next morning and meet him in the Hotel Klomser in the centre of Vienna. The chauffeur was instructed to get the big open Daimler ready and early on Saturday morning, in civilian clothes, Redl drove in his car from his quarters in the garrison Staff Building at Prague to the capital. He was in his hotel by the early afternoon where Stephan kept the appointment already made and was duly persuaded, after a long discussion and with the aid of the promise of his own sports car, that a powerful protector was a better bet for the future than marriage.

If he was to buy the motor on the following Monday, Redl needed money straight away and he knew where to get it. It had been waiting since March to be picked up from the Poste Restante office in the General Post Office in the Fleischmarkt. So late in the afternoon of Saturday 24 May, just before the office closed, Redl took a taxi for the short journey of perhaps ten minutes from the hotel, told the driver to wait and keep his motor running, and walked into the dusty little office with its separate entrance and its bare board floor. There he wrote on a slip of paper the code to identify his letters: 'Opera Ball 13'. The clerk was slow, he fumbled about; the typed envelopes had been lying there for two months and had been pushed to the back of the slot. But he was no slower than post-office clerks always are and finally produced the two letters and slid them across the counter to the tall, dignified gentleman in well-cut tweeds who took them impatiently and at once left the office. The taxi door slammed shut just as two men emerged by another exit from the post office; they were in time to note its number but not to stop it.

Alfred Redl had evidently not kept up with friends in his former department, because he did not know that the reforms introduced by himself had been further developed in the last year or so. There was a room upstairs in the Post Office where clerks who thought they worked for the Customs and Excise opened letters coming from border towns, from some foreign towns known to be active in espionage and from senders or addressees who had aroused suspicion. This interference with the mails was quite illegal but the public was unaware that it went on and those who scrutinized the letters were taxpayers themselves and thought it quite right that smugglers should not exempt themselves from tolls that everyone else was obliged to pay.

The two letters with their typed addresses had been posted in Eydkuhnen, a Russian-Prussian border town and had there-fore been inspected. Both contained Austrian bank notes, one six thousand Kronen and the other eight thousand. These were large sums – the entire yearly budget of the military intelligence department was 150,000 Kronen – and there were no letters enclosed. Clearly there must be something illicit about unex-plained payments of that size coming from the Russian border; the postal censorship was justified. Two plain-clothes policemen were posted in a side room where the clerk in the Poste Restante office could call them by ringing a bell when the suspicious letters were collected. After two months of pointless waiting the men on duty were half asleep when the bell finally rang and in spite of the clerk sensibly taking as long as he could to 'find' the letters they got out on to the pavement too late to clap that terrifying hand on the shoulder. The taxi was off.

They stood on the pavement, considering. From the number they could perhaps still find the driver that evening and concoct some dashing tale that would excuse their failure. If they couldn't, they were in for trouble. One can just see them there in the narrow street, gesticulating, growling at each other in their nasal dialect. They must have been short men, rather thick-set, in the well-worn dark suits of lower civil servants who afforded a new suit once in ten years, if that. They had money for their job but of their own salaries they would turn over every halfpenny. And every farthing of expenses must be accounted for.

As they stood there one of those coincidences that happen in real life but are too fanciful to be used in fiction, came to their aid. A taxi came by. It carried the same number they had impotently watched disappearing a few minutes before, but now it was empty. The two detectives rushed after it, shouting and waving until it stopped. Where had the driver taken his fare, the gentleman who went into the Post Office? To the Café Herrenhof. They bundled into the cab, and while they were being driven to the coffee house they found in the car's interior a small cloth cover for a pocket knife which had been left behind.

The driver went with them into the café to identify his fare, but he was no longer there and had probably walked in at one door and out at the other. At the taxi rank outside they asked the horse-waterer, left over from the days of fiacres who polished up the cars and held doors for fares. He recalled the man they described. He had told the driver to go to the Hotel Klomser, only a few steps away.

At the hotel the hall porter answered them; yes, two gentlemen had just arrived, business men from Bulgaria. No, not
them; a real gentleman, alone, who came in a taxi? Oh, he said
considering, I don't know about a taxi. The only gentleman who
came in in the last few minutes was Colonel Redl. In civilian
clothes, he was. I know him, of course, but there wasn't anybody
else.

The two detectives knew Colonel Redl too and their anxiety
rose to panic. The famous spy-catcher here in the hotel and
they were making a hash of just the kind of case he was so
stern about! But there was no time to waste; by now their
superior in the State Police must have heard from the Post
Office that the two letters had been picked up and they must
report back. They would ask if further enquiries at the Hotel
Klomser should not be referred to Colonel Redl who was by
the purest chance staying there. One of them went to the telephone to report, while the other stood chatting to the hall
porter. Laying the little grey cover on the counter he asked
the man to find out which of the guests had lost it.

At that moment a tall and elegantly uniformed officer came
down the stairs in the dark green tunic of the General Staff and
pushed his key towards the porter. Had Colonel Redl perhaps
lost the cover to his pocket knife, the man asked him innocently,
with no idea of what he was saying.

'Yes, I have,' replied Redl abstractedly and pushed the thing
carelessly into a pocket. 'Now, where did I leave . . . ?' The sentence was never finished for he recalled where he last used his
pocket knife; in that taxi, to slit open the envelopes from
Eydkuhnen. Had he dropped it? How did it get here, in the
hotel?

It must have been a moment of silent and violent shock for
two of the three men standing there at the porter's desk. The
policeman cannot have believed his ears. Redl must have tried
frantically to relive his movements in the cab as he pushed
envelopes, bank notes and the folding knife back into his poc-
kets. If he had left the cover lying on his knee it would have

dropped into the street as he left the car at the Herrenhof. If he had dropped it inside the taxi someone had almost immediately found it and he had therefore been followed from the Post Office. He must have left it in the car because nobody picking it up in the street would have connected it with himself. Unless he had been so closely followed that the watcher saw it fall by the cab door? Was there another taxi just behind his as he went into the Café? But if he left it inside the taxi, then how . . . ?

Redl could not guess at the coincidence that had betrayed him. What must have struck him for perhaps the first time, was the incredible folly of allowing money to be sent to him at the main Post Office in Vienna at all. Vienna was so small; he had been stationed here for years, he was a well-known and instantly recognizable figure to hundreds of policemen, soldiers, civil servants. Why had he not used an accommodation address? He must have been mad.

With the self-command of training and long experience Redl turned on his heel and went out into the street, turning right. He walked quickly down to the corner by the Café Central where a certain Bronstein often sat among the journalists and artists who frequented the place, playing chess or listening to that subversive type Karl Kraus reading his amusing skits aloud. Looking back Redl saw two men emerge from the street door of the hotel restaurant and look about them. Redl turned the corner and by the time the two reached it, had disappeared. He was not in the short connecting alley nor in the parallel street. He must have gone into the old Stock Exchange with its three entrances, two by the Café Central and another into a passage that ran down into the Freyung, a triangular open space with a number of exit streets.

In the hotel hall the two policemen waited only long enough to write down the secret number of the security police, give it to the porter and tell him to ring it and report 'everything is in order. The knife cover was Colonel Redl's.' This he did at once, still unaware of the import of his words, and the message exploded like a hand grenade at the other end of the line. The

Frau Anna Sacher with two of her beloved pugs.
below Anna Sacher's boudoir in the Hotel Sacher.

above The Sacher garden in the Prater.
below Katharina Schratt, friend of Franz Joseph. Photograph by Raoul Korty.

above The Schratt villa at Bad Ischl.
below The Burgtheater in Vienna, where Katharina Schratt performed many times.

Colonel Alfred Redl.

right
Field-Marshal
Conrad von Hötzendorf,
Chief of the
Imperial General Staff.

above Gustav Mahler with his sister, Justine.

below Gustav Klimt and friends: Klimt is seated second from the left,
Kolo Moser sits in front of him. Karl Moll is on the right, reclining.

Max Klinger's statue of
Beethoven in the
Secession building –
frieze by Klimt.

right
The Kiss by Gustav Klimt.

Austrian Jews in Vienna at the turn of the century.

Theodor Herzl.

The second Zionist Congress at Basle in 1898.

The aged Emperor Franz Joseph.

shock was even greater when it was passed to military intelligence, to the very office of which Colonel Redl had been chief. His name was a byword for efficiency, keenness. He had reformed the intelligence service. Junior officers were trained by his methods and his name was constantly used as authority for the most modern and efficacious system of gathering intelligence or discovering foreign agents. No need to ask in hushed voices what Redl knew. Redl knew everything.

His successor, Captain Ronge, went himself to the Post Office to check the description of the collector of the two letters and the slip of paper on which he had written 'Opera Ball 13'. There were plenty of reports and drafts in Ronge's files in Redl's handwriting, but in any case his colleagues recognized his hand. They could not even doubt any longer. One typed envelope from the Russian border with no letter in it, nothing but bank notes, might conceivably be the payment of a debt; but not two.

Meanwhile Colonel Redl looked back as he reached the end of the passage into the Freyung. The detectives were good guessers; he saw them as they emerged from the Stock Exchange into the inner end of the passage. To have any chance of escape Redl must hold up at least one of his shadowers. He pulled some papers from his pocket and tore them up, scattering them on the ground like confetti for the followers to pick up. He cannot have thought what he was throwing away for they were a receipt signed by Stephan for a money transfer and two registered letter slips with the addresses on them. One was a house in Brussels known as a French espionage centre where the Russians swopped their intelligence with the French. The other was in Lausanne, equally well known as an Italian safe house; so Redl had been betraying secrets to the Italians as well as the Russians.

This action of Redl's showed that his nerve was gone. The scraps of paper meant to delay his captors were the very proofs needed to make his guilt certain. Moreover the two policemen had learned their lesson. They were making no more mistakes that day. They let the confetti lie for a moment, stopped a cab in the Freyung and one man drove off slowly after their quarry while the other went back to collect the torn paper. Redl himself walked rapidly down to the quay of the Danube Canal. His motor car was in a workshop just outside the city along the canal bank. He must have intended to collect the car and drive off, to escape. The only frontier that offered a hope of safety was a day's journey away, between Vorarlberg and Switzerland. The Italian frontier was even further and very mountainous. But he had changed back into uniform. And his own system ensured that telephone calls would be made at once to all border crossings, to the towns he must pass through on his route and to troops and border guards to prevent an escape on foot through the Alps. Redl was trapped. He might have thought of buying or stealing other clothes that would disguise him, of taking a local train out of Vienna and gradually approaching that distant frontier by changing trains half a dozen times. But he did not try that way out. He was lamed by the feeling of the closing ring about him, by the recognition of his own appalling carelessness, by the knowledge of his guilt. He may have thought that the police would already be in the carriage-builder's workshop waiting for him to try and reach his car.

His chauffeur had delivered the car, an open Austro-Daimler, to the coach-builder on their arrival in the city. The outside coach-work was to be changed for gleaming patent leather, the interior to be lined with dark red silk. On the doors of this stately automobile were Redl's initials, A.R. The cross bar of the A was not the normal straight line but two diagonal lines that looked like a lower-case 'v', and over the letters was a coronet, carefully not a forgery but to a casual glance it looked like a nobleman's emblem. Anyone who did not examine the device would think it read A v. R. Alfred von Redl. This childish piece of snobbish vanity was the key to Redl's extraordinary lack of caution as a spy. The same vanity that made him dye his fair hair and moustache blond because it was going grey, made him unable to see the need for extreme caution and foresight – *he* would not get caught. Did he not know all the tricks of the trade from both sides? How could he be trapped when he himself was the inventor of traps for spies?

But he was trapped. Caught in his own net. Long before he reached the suburban workshop he turned back to his hotel. Somewhere on the walk back he thought of another way out. It was evening now and in the hotel waited an old acquaintance with whom Redl was to dine. It was Dr Viktor Pollak, whose name makes him almost certainly Jewish, an illustration of the extreme complexity of Jewish relations in Vienna. For Dr Pollak was a Prosecutor-General whose job was bringing into court the agents uncovered by Colonel Redl and, frequently on Redl's instructions, demanding and getting the stiffest possible sentences; in other words a servant of the State in its most minatory aspect.

The lawyer did not notice that they were watched in the restaurant; clearly such a thing could not even occur to him and if he had seen a plainclothes policeman his reaction would have been to wonder at a minor official being able to afford to eat at the Riedhof. What he did notice was that his companion was frantically nervous and upset. After a glass or two of wine Redl began to talk mysteriously and wildly. Half confessing his sexual deviations, hinting at vague crimes, asking Pollak for help without saying against what or whom he needed it. At last he managed to get out the request that Pollak should telephone the Chief of Security Police and ensure that Redl could return to Prague the following day where he would confess all to his commanding officer and throw himself on General Giesl's mercy. It must have been clear to an experienced lawyer that Redl was either on the edge of a complete breakdown or that he actually had committed some serious crime or folly. But espionage did not enter his mind for if it had he must have realized that once in possession of a safe conduct, Redl would not stop at Prague but would go much further, across Ruthenia into Russia. The two friends finished their meal and went on to the Café Herrenhof near Redl's hotel; the same café he used unsuccessfully in the afternoon to lose his 'tail'. From there Pollak telephoned once more, this time suggesting that Colonel Redl should be taken in an ambulance to a neurological clinic, at the patient's own request. (If he were mentally ill, he was unfit to plead.) To both of these proposals Pollak got the same answer. Colonel Redl should get in touch with the Security Chief on the next day, Sunday, and he would do what he could to help; so late on a Saturday evening it was impossible to arrange anything, and so on.

But in reality sentence was already pronounced, and pronounced at another dinner taking place that evening. In the Grand Hotel on the Ring the Chief of the Imperial General Staff, Conrad von Hötzendorf, sat with a large party. The band was playing operetta tunes, the luxurious restaurant was filled with the noble and fashionable, when the director of military intelligence was announced and asked for a few moments alone with His Excellency the 'Chief'. They went into a side room, one of those private dining rooms so often met with in Viennese stories, and Conrad was told the news. At first thunderstruck, he passed from unbelief into a towering rage. He could hardly be blamed for that but he made in his haste and anger a serious mistake. Redl himself would certainly have spirited the traitor away to a safe military prison and would have dragged out of him every last detail of his treason and his confederates.

But Conrad was proud of being a plain soldier incapable of deviousness. He proved it then by ordering that Redl must be arrested, forced to confess and then condemned to die by his own hand. That very night. The slightest chance of rumours which could damage army morale must be ended by removing their source. The results of this unconsidered haste were serious. Redl had betrayed Austrian secrets to his masters, including details of fortifications at Przemysl and Lemberg. But he also gave them the names of Austrian spies in Russia, so that some were captured and replaced by Russian agents and some were 'turned' to pass on fabricated information. The gaps and errors in Austrian intelligence were to cost them very dear in the following two years both on the Galician-Russian front and against Belgrade; there is reason to believe that machinations aided by Redl concealed the existence of a whole Russian army of 75,000 men. The whole extent of Redl's treachery was never assessed but it is certain that he cost the lives of thousands of soldiers. He is also one of the explanations of the extraordinary confusion in Austro-Hungarian knowledge of what was going on, both diplomatically and militarily, in Serbia. If the Imperial General Staff had known what they ought to have forced out of Redl after his arrest, they might well never have risked the outbreak of the threatening war with Russia a year later. That war was bound to come for all the powers, without exception, wanted it. But it need not have come in circumstances so hopelessly disadvantageous for the Habsburgs. And Conrad by a fantastic chance did not even achieve his immediate aim, to hide the extent of the damage from the army and the public, which is always the first thought of authority in such cases.

Four officers were deputed to acquaint Redl with the sentence against him. It was against hotel rules to allow visitors in guests' rooms so late, but these midnight arrivals were so stern and serious that the night porter felt no doubt of the official nature of their business. They mounted the stairs to room No. 1 where Redl sat in a dressing gown, writing letters. They addressed him bleakly as Mr Redl, for he had forfeited the right to be called by an officer's title.

He knew why they were there. They asked him, coldly and distantly for the names of his accomplices. He denied having any. They asked questions about the extent of his treachery. He replied that they would find all the evidence in his rooms in the garrison command building in Prague. That was the extent of the orders from the Chief of the Imperial General Staff. One of the officers asked if 'Mr' Redl possessed a weapon. No, he was unarmed. He might ask for a gun if he wished. None of the four was armed and one of them drove quickly to his home to fetch a Browning. The other three waited in dead silence by the door of the room, their backs to Redl. The gun was laid without a word on the table. Then they left to wait a few steps away at the corner of the narrow street so that Redl could not make an attempt to get away. One after another they went into the Café Central to drink black coffee. One after another they drove home to change into civilian suits so that four staff officers standing on the street corner should not attract attention. The last coffee house closed, the city was silent in the spring night. The hours passed slowly until it was five o'clock in the morning; it was light and still they could hear no sound of a shot or any other activity in the Hotel Klomser. Two of the officers must catch the fast train to Prague at six-fifteen to search Redl's room, and they had instructions to report to Conrad first thing in the morning. Finally they telephoned one of the two police-men already involved in the case and told him to come to the hotel as if to bring Redl a message. The policeman explained to the night porter that Colonel Redl had ordered a letter to be brought to him at five-thirty; he was allowed up. Two minutes later he emerged again and reported that Redl's door was un-locked and on entering he had found Redl's body, dead, lying by the sofa. All that was left to do was to ring up the hotel and ask for the Colonel to be called to the telephone. The servant would then find the body and it could be removed from the hotel before people were about in the streets. And a few minutes after that the hotel telephoned the local police and reported a suicide in Room No. 1. A police officer and the police surgeon appeared and confirmed suicide by shooting through the mouth. There were sealed letters to the dead man's brother and to his commanding officer and an open sheet of paper on which they read the words 'Folly and passion have destroyed me. Pray for me. I pay for my mistakes with my life. Alfred.' As a postscript, 'It is a quarter to two. I am going to die now. Please don't make a post-mortem. Pray for me.'

This note was unaddressed and there was no greeting, but it was probably meant for Stephan. Did Redl remember the receipt he had thrown away, which must implicate his lover? Stephan got three years hard labour for unnatural sexual practices, but it was clear that he knew nothing of Redl's treasonable activities.

The hotel management and the local police knew nothing of them either; they were concerned solely to get the corpse out of the way as quickly as possible. Redl's batman almost succeeded in causing a delay. He was quite sure his officer was not thinking of suicide and he knew the Browning did not belong to his Colonel, so it must have been murder and the Browning belonged to the murderer. The hotel manager and the police listened unwillingly, but who was the unknown man who called at five-thirty and left again without another word? If Redl was already dead then, which he was, why had this messenger not said anything? And the four officers who came at midnight? To silence the obstinate batman the members of the Commission of Enquiry already set up and including the four staff officers and a fifth from Vienna Military Command thought of a neutral explanation. The soldier was told that his Colonel had committed the military crime of abusing his authority over men under his command. At once the poor batman was silent; he knew what none of the others yet knew, that Redl was homosexual. So he accepted what he thought was a hint and the argument ceased. Redl's body was removed to the garrison mortuary.

When the Chief of Intelligence lunched with General Giesl on arrival in Prague and told him the truth, the unfortunate General was shattered. Giesl and his brother, the Minister of Legation at Belgrade, corresponded continually about the military and diplomatic situation there. This was an immediate concern of General Giesl's for the Corps he commanded was destined for the Serbian front if war came. He knew then that everything known between his brother and himself and known too to his confidant and friend Redl, had been making a fatal circuit through himself to Redl, on to Russian Intelligence and back to Belgrade. No wonder the Serbs had been leading the Austro-Hungarian foreign office by the nose; the news explained some extraordinary mistakes and failures in the last few years.

After this unhappy luncheon Redl's apartment was forced

open and his desk and cupboards examined. Their first impression was the womanish atmosphere. The place was full of scents, embroidered underclothes, feminine decorations in execrable taste. There were piles of love-letters from men with accompanying photographs of their actions, and the crumpled attempts of Redl's persuasions to Stephan. How was it possible that this almost open decadence had never become known, not even suspected? Redl's self-centred vanity led him to insane imprudences; evidently he had been unable to destroy anything to do with himself and even receipts for his payments from the Russians were found, not to mention photographic plates of his latest 'work'. The entire structure and organization of the 8th Corps down to the troops' rations were in the hands of the Russians.

The extent of the recent damage was now known, leaving the crucial question that must always dominate such affairs: how long? When part of the scandal broke it was officially maintained, again as it always is in such cases, that the spying was restricted to Redl's latest posting in Prague. But once the tip of the iceberg was recognized it became clear that Redl's extravagant life reached back at least ten years under cover of his having private means from an inheritance. He was stationed during two postings to troops, as is usual for Staff Officers, once at the fortress of Przemysl and once at Lemberg, both on the eastern frontiers. He could not then have known nearly as much as in later years, but enough to do a great deal of harm. And what he betrayed during his years of service in Vienna at the centre of Military Intelligence, did not bear thinking of.

They remembered then the notorious case of Colonel Hekailo of the accountancy branch. Hekailo was accused of embezzlement; he jumped bail and escaped to Brazil. Then a month or so later Captain Redl told the Advocate-General's office that his investigations showed that Hekailo was also a Russian spy who had probably betrayed the Austrian order of battle to the Russians. Redl knew where this was done: at Thorn on the Russian border. He also knew Hekailo's assumed name and his address in Brazil. Extradition was requested from the Brazilian authorities, for secrecy's sake not for espionage but for embezzlement, which meant that Hekailo could not be tried for spying but only for fraud. So Hekailo admitted everything he had sold, including the alarm system at Lemberg garrison for which he could have been shot if he were not protected from trial. What he stubbornly refused to confess and what Redl stubbornly tried to make him confess, was betrayal of the order of battle. Once he even answered his interrogator Redl that he could have no knowledge of such high staff plans; they could only have been sold to the Russians by an officer of the General Staff in Vienna, one of the small number who would have access to them. This line was understandably not followed up by Redl. But Hekailo did give away his accomplices, two officers serving on the Galician frontier. During the search of the quarters of one of these Redl shocked his colleagues by his methods. Nothing could be found, so Redl began talking to the suspect's little daughter, and by flattering the six-year-old on her cleverness and leading her on he induced the innocent child to tell him where daddy kept his papers. And there indeed was all the evidence they needed of daddy's guilt. Glad as the interrogators were to have been successful, they could not forget the use of methods hardly in conformity with the honour of a soldier.

That was not the only strange thing now recalled about the Hekailo case. Redl had asked for papers during the interrogation that were not needed for his duties, papers concerning Lemberg district stolen by members of the spy-ring which they did not have time to send to their Russian contact. When he insisted he received a humiliating refusal and at the time it was thought his eagerness was the same tendency to go too far in his keenness that he showed with the little girl. And that, too, now aroused memories. At first Redl was sure of this man's guilt – which was certain – and suddenly, after he himself had found the proofs, he swung right round and began to argue that the man was innocent and should be reinstated. He went so far with this argument that he was warned officially that he would be taken off the case, after which he was more careful. Then he offered to go to Warsaw, which was, of course Russian, to search for papers still missing; here too he was refused on the sound grounds that evidence enough for conviction had been found so that the missing papers were not important enough to risk an officer of the Austrian General Staff being arrested in Warsaw by the Russians.

Now, ten years later, it was clear that Hekailo was what would later have been called a fall guy. Having got himself into trouble with his frauds he was of no more use to his masters and could be sacrificed to cover others, including whoever had really given the Austrian order of battle away. The two officers implicated by Hekailo were still useful however and Redl was trying to save them as well as himself. He failed to do this and they were tried and sentenced to prison. This extension of the plot to get Hekailo blamed for the whole ring annoyed Redl's paymasters on whom his high income depended and to reassure them Redl betrayed a Russian staff officer who worked for the Austrians; he was hanged. From then on he constantly supplied the Russians with the names of Austrian and Hungarian Intelligence officers and their agents. Exactly who and how many was never discovered, for Alfred Redl was dead and could not be questioned. Nor was it ever known whether the Austro-Hungarian troop plans in case of war were given to the Russians; probably not in their entirety. An order of battle is not a sheet of paper but comprises a whole room full of files and would take time to photograph and copy; a spy who succeeded in such a coup would be more likely to an old and trusted filing clerk than an Intelligence officer. But by carefully reporting every remark heard and overheard among the closed circle of the General Staff in Vienna, as well as photographing what papers did come into his hands, Redl could build up a continuing picture which a skilled collator on the Russian staff would combine with his other information. The Russian planners would then make enough changes in their own dispositions to warn their opponents that they knew something; hence the need to saddle

Hekailo with betrayal of secrets he could not have known and remove suspicion from anyone else.

Those events took place in 1902 and 1903. By 1913 Redl knew so much that Conrad von Hötzendorf must assume that the Austrian General Staff had no secrets not known to Russia and Italy. That thought must have been a factor in his instant decision that a prolonged interrogation and trial could produce nothing to outweigh the damage to military and public morale it would cause.

He may even have been right in his calculation, but the secret could not be kept. It came out almost at once and by a farcical chance. A Prague football club was playing a match on the day after Redl's suicide, Sunday 20 May and one player did not turn up on the field. The chairman of the football club was the news editor of a local newspaper and when the player excused himself the club chairman was so incensed with him – the team lost the match – that the man was obliged to explain the whole story. He was a locksmith and had been sent for in the Sunday absence of military mechanics to open the apartment and then the desk drawers and cupboards of a Colonel at Prague head-quarters. In the course of his work he heard that the Colonel in question had committed suicide the previous night in Vienna. The locksmith retailed some of the things found in the desk, cameras, photographs, files, all sorts of things. He described too the effect of the discoveries on the officers conducting the search and the comments they made to each other. The news editor put two and two together and made four because Redl's suicide had been announced. If he printed the story his news-paper would at once be censored, if not confiscated. So he did what any other newspaperman would have done in similar circumstances; he sent the news to the correspondent of his paper in Berlin, who sent it back to be printed as a *denial* that the death of the much-praised Colonel Redl in Vienna was due to his career as a spy having been discovered.

So this is really a very modern story. Including the two questions left unanswered by it, unanswered questions being the only interesting ones. Why did nobody ever notice Redl's un-orthodox private life? And why did the enormous internal shock inside the Austro-Hungarian High Command not lead to wide reforms in the Army? The answer to the first question may be briefly, but not quite superficially, that Redl had no close friends; after all, the only man he could invite to dinner when he was in Vienna was a professional colleague. The answer to the second is that it is difficult to reorganize any old and complex institution, especially in times of continuous tension such as the first years of this century; and to get anything radical done in the Austro-Hungarian Army was like trying to draw a handful of cotton-wool through a tub of glue. When the heir to the throne, Archduke Franz Ferdinand, discussed the case with Conrad von Hötzendorf, both of them being convinced reformers, he did not say '*Now's* our chance!' He reproached Conrad with having condemned Redl to death unshriven. Just over a year later the Archduke died himself unshriven, the bullets that killed him being ordered on information supplied over years before with the unwitting co-operation of General Giesl and his brother through Belgrade by Alfred Redl.

6

The Sound of the Danube -
Gustav Mahler

ONCE upon a time there was a peddler woman who trudged
about the muddy country roads of Bohemia from hamlet to
hamlet. She carried a basket and a bundle on her back with
skirt and bodice lengths of stout cotton cloth and jacket and
cloak lengths of woollen frieze for the peasant womenfolk to
make their clothes, and ribbons and buttons to fasten the bodices
or decorate them. She sold tapes to make the drawstrings of
petticoats, calico to make the petticoats themselves, and when a
girl was to be married she would bring special material bought
in the nearest town and give advice as to how the few ladies
to be seen there were wearing their dresses this year. These
would be the wives and daughters of the prosperous citizens,
those who owned the local factory, the transport agency, a
shop-keeper or two. Sometimes they were the wives of imperial
officials, or army officers stationed at the garrison. With her
goods she carried what news of local interest there was and
what she picked up of the outer world. She gossiped from house
to house. She carried messages and acted as match-maker or
go-between in buying and selling; perhaps she sometimes made
small loans. She would buy the wool of a sheep and on her next
trudge bring the exchange for it; some pot or pan for the household. She had a licence as a peddler and every now and then
the weights and measures inspector who travelled about too
would check whether her metre lengths were correct or whether
she cheated. Sometimes the cheating was not that but the mis-
measurement of ignorance and the difficulty of stretching cloth

out in a crowded cottage on the only cluttered table in a bad light. But the weights and measures inspector accepted no excuses. If a two-metre length of linen tape was less than two metres and less than one centimetre wide, she was in trouble and if it happened more than once she could lose her licence. Much country clothing was still homespun and she would arrange exchanges: a piece of 'stuff' for a length of linen from a woman in the next village whose holding included a patch of flax. She talked in a sing-song mixture of the local vernacular and Yiddish and carried figures and orders in her head. If anything needed to be agreed with a stranger or if anything was worth more than a few Heller, a witness would be called in from next door so that buyer and seller could be clear about what was agreed.

She always knew if a boy was to be called up to the colours and which girl's eyes would fill with tears to hear the news. She knew what the rich old peasant's second wife did when her husband went to market and with whom; she knew how much money they had or did not have and how it came about that the corner field changed hands and who drank too much and who beat his wife. She slept in a barn or the outhouse of a tavern. To protect herself from gypsies or tramps or the occasional deserter on the run who might steal her lean purse she pretended to be able to curse people and cattle so that the ill-disposed kept clear of her.

When the snow began to fall heavily about the turn of the year she stayed in her dirty little hut on the outskirts of a village just like all the other villages; as soon as the roads were clear again she started off on her travels in all weathers. It was only deep snow so that the low houses were up to their eaves and the lanes impassable, that stopped her. The smallest hovels like hers were without window glass so that in bad weather it was dark inside when the shutters were closed. From year to year as she got older and more rheumatic, she put away the small coins one after another.

Her son took the coins after her funeral and bought a horse

and cart. He was a trader and a carrier and read books; he was ambitious and could even speak a few words of French. The people round about called him the waggon-scholar. As his horse plodded on its way he read his books in the German language and not in the local vernacular for the outside world was what he longed for. He tried to speak correctly, to lose the Yiddish; he would achieve something. He looked about for a wife but the available Jewish girls did not please him. He wanted a girl with some refinement, someone who would indicate his future higher status, perhaps with a bit of money. The match-maker found a girl, the daughter of a soap-maker in a nearby town who might not have accepted such a lowly suitor for his Marie if she had not been half lame. She did not want her suitor either, she wanted another man who never gave her a glance; but suitor and father between them overruled her wishes. A girl who limped and was not strong could not pick and choose.

No doubt the dowry was small, smaller than a healthy girl would get for an advantageous marriage, but a nice balance was drawn in such matters then. And now, more often than sentimental people suppose. The boorish carter wanted refinement and took the rest in the bargain, and the family wanted Marie off their hands. Bernard Mahler took her first to one of those low village houses, an improvement on his mother's hut. Later it was said by their son that the windows were unglazed, but the photographs show a one-storey peasant house of a kind that always does have glass in its double windows and without fixed outside shutters, the alternative for very poor hovels. Perhaps the son exaggerated his family poverty, or perhaps he remembered that when he was small windows were broken and stayed unrepaired. After a couple of years and with two children, the family moved to the town of Iglau, in what is now Czechoslovakia and is called Jihlava but was then an almost entirely German town. A first son died in infancy so that Gustav Mahler was the eldest child. In Iglau Bernard Mahler opened a little drinking shop and made his own spirits, from fruit or wheat. The still would be in the cellar and the taproom on the ground floor with bare boards and a table or so with rough chairs. It was near a barracks and probably most of the customers were soldiers off duty. They and the neighbours called Mahler's wife 'Duchess' so evidently the refinement was obvious to all.

Bernard Mahler was variously described by those who knew him as obstinate, a man of great vitality, uninhibited. A photograph shows him as short and sturdily built in a respectable tail coat and holding a silk hat. The head is carried as if thrown slightly back, aggressive and defensive, a look added to by the wide downward moustache. The eyes glance shrewdly, defiantly. Not a nice face as far as the rigidity produced by photography at that time can be trusted. His hand is expressive. Rested on the studio table, it is closed, almost a fist; it looks as if he had just slammed it down. His wife was taken at the same time and with the same requisites, a small machine-carved table and a curtain. She wears outdoor clothes, wide skirts touching the floor, a cape edged with fur at the collar, a tiny bonnet with ribbons tied under the chin, and she holds a large muff of fur resting on the table. Her face is completely expressionless. Another photograph in what must have been her best dress, which looks like silk and with a ruched panel down the front of the skirt, shows her face better. Far from ill-looking, the level eyes and the wide mouth express the containment of deep unhappiness and controlled dignity. Something in the carriage of head and shoulders, although she is carefully posed, gives a hint of unevenness that implies that her limp may have been caused by one leg being shorter than the other.

From earliest childhood the children were witnesses and auditors of appalling scenes. Since Marie Mahler is more than once said to have been of very gentle temperament and her husband the opposite, it seems likely that he abused and beat her as well as being a menace to every servant girl. She had twelve children; five died in infancy, one at thirteen, one committed suicide at twenty-three and a daughter died as a young married woman. Child mortality in the first years of life was then about fifty per cent except in the wealthy classes, and in rural areas was very high. There was a good deal of inter-marriage in remote districts, and this was especially so among Jewish families where they were scattered in villages and there-fore a small minority. Marie Mahler's mother was of the same surname before her marriage as her husband which may imply a family relationship before marriage. Before the year 1860, the year in which Gustav was born, when changing domicile was made much easier, country people did not move about. This was so for the whole rural population but was even more difficult for Jews who needed special permission as well as being restrained by all the pull of land and habit. As one goes east from the Danube anti-Semitism gets worse, now as then. Bohemians and Moravians were always anti-Semitic but at that time the popular explanation was that the Jews attached them-selves to the Germans rather than to the Czechs. This shows that explanations were by then felt to be needed, at any rate in public, and the one used shows the growing force of national-ism. Indeed it probably exaggerated it, since nationalism was largely confined to the educated classes. That the Jews aspired to belong to German culture and society is quite true, for-tunately for the arts and sciences of central Europe, and it is a strange fact that of all the many and mutually hostile minor-ities of the Habsburg realm, the Jewish intelligentsia were the only ones who did not produce any 'national' demands for autonomy.

The only hostilities normally mentioned when discussing the Austro-Hungarian Empire are anti-Semitism and – among Slavs – hatred against the Magyars. This is deeply misleading. All the different clans and groups distrusted each other and where they were mixed together, disliked each other; these feelings were increased to hatred as nationalisms were propagated. Since all these people are ethnically so mixed into each other that their national feelings are almost entirely artificial, nationalism was in fact language particularism. Dislike of the Germans in Bohemia and Moravia belongs in any serious sense to a con-

siderably later date than the 1860s and until about 1937 was
not only much smaller than anti-Semitism and anti- every other
group but much milder too. In theory, which means in the
newspapers and political clubs, the Czechs considered the
Austro-Germans to be oppressors; in practice the Czechs went
to Austrian cities to make their careers and rose to high ranks
in the Imperial civil service and the Army. All classes above
peasant level were inextricably intermarried and spoke and read
both German and the Czech language with equal facility.

It should therefore be taken with a pinch of salt that Czech
anti-Semitism at that time was really caused by growing anti-
German nationalism. It had existed since the Jews were there
at all and has been sadly proved many times since the massacre
at the end of the fourteenth century in Prague when over three
thousand people were said to have been killed, which can only
mean that the ghetto there was practically wiped out. If hatred
of the Jews did have serious connections with anti-Germanism
this was caused by the old special position of Bohemian Jews
in the Empire; they were the patricians of European Jewry
and the only Jews before 1848 who could own land and large
property, apart from money.

And the story of Gustav Mahler is the proof of that attachment to German culture, among other things. For this grandson of a Jewish peddler, son of a wife-beating schnapps distiller,
became the director of the Imperial Opera in Vienna and was
one of the greatest musicians of his time.

A sentimental story has it that when Gustav was still very
small the family took over the house next door to the dram
shop and in the attic was an old piano on which small Gustav
began to play. In fact his ambitious father bought him a piano,
then the sign of middle-class dignity for the poor as a colour
television set is today. The double-bass player in the town
orchestra took a turn and a professional teacher of the piano
was found. At ten years old Gustav played for the first time
in public and was quite a sensation. He quickly became a provincial *Wunderkind* and not only practised for hours every day

as he must have done to be later admired by people who were able to judge a pianist, but repeated on his instrument the bugle calls and march music he heard from the barracks, the tunes of the hurdy-gurdy man and the folk-songs of peasant girls who worked in the tap for his father. Gustav had good reason to want to retire from the actual world about him and like all children made his escape from sordid noise and adult passions into play and dreaming. He played and dreamed music.

When he was only eleven his father arranged for him to go to a musical family in Prague and attend the grammar school there. But instead of the two sons of the house helping the child he was ill-treated and underfed and made no progress at school. It is said that this foster-family even took his clothes and shoes away and gave him old and worn-out things in their place; he also watched the near-rape of a servant girl in the house by one of the sons and was much shocked by it. This was so much the general fate of girls in service in those days, by no means always unwillingly, and so much part of his own father's habits that it seems likely that in telling the story when he was grown up Gustav concentrated into this one episode everything else he remembered of sexual scenes in childhood, some of which were brutally and horribly concerned with his mother and therefore had to be forgotten. Until he married himself he had a marked nervous jerk in his walk, an uneven gait which he picked up from his mother. He also bit his nails and was in general a nervous and neurotic boy. Great talents are a burden to their possessor; any talented child has a difficult life from inside its own being and Gustav suffered from his family life as well, suffered for his mother whom he loved and from the noisy and coarse surroundings. His father was a strange mixture and may well have been a man of such strong sexual drives that even if he had felt it necessary he would not have been able to control them; and in those patriarchal days a man of strong passions did not consider the women he used, nor was Bernard Mahler controlled by religion for he had expressly abandoned his faith. Yet he had enough books for it to be said that he possessed 'almost a library' and the boy who showed little interest or aptitude for formal schooling must have read a great deal in his boyhood for his knowledge was wide and varied. He also became locally well-known for his playing and improvisations on the piano, known, that is, outside the town.

One of the people he got to know was a man called Schwarz, the land-agent and agronomist of a large estate, who loved music. This man found some manuscript scores by a recently dead piano virtuoso, Sigismund Thalberg, whose work was of great technical difficulty, and when he showed this find to a friend whose name was Steiner his friend commented that he knew a boy who could play such things at first glance. Impressed, Schwartz invited Gustav Mahler who proved to be no less gifted than Steiner had claimed. Schwarz asked him to stay with him and finally wrote to the boy's father that Gustav should go to Vienna to the Conservatory.

Bernard Mahler was at first undecided and Gustav appealed to his new friend for help and got it. The letter written by the fifteen-year-old boy is a model of tact and calculation; the boy already knew how to get what he wanted. Schwarz went to see Bernard Mahler and the outcome was decided. Two weeks later Schwarz took the boy to Vienna and presented him to Professor Epstein at the Conservatory of the Friends of Music in Vienna. He was at once enrolled. Later Epstein paid half his fees, backed his request for the fees to be reduced on account of the poverty of his family, sent his own son to Gustav as a pupil and put other piano lessons in his way.

The Music School in Vienna was then part of the musical association and not a public institution, and was therefore fee-paying. This conservatory was a true republic of artists; the great and rich were (and are still) proud to be its subscribers and musicians who formed the orchestra it supported ran their own affairs including their choice of conductors. It was, until the abysmal wickedness of the Nazis drove away many of its finest players, without any question the finest orchestra in the world; if the Nazis had never committed any other crime they deserved eternal commination for their near-destruction of the Vienna Philharmonic Orchestra. It took years after the Second World War was over to restore it to its former subtlety and strength. An irreplaceable body of knowledge, experience and devotion to music, and to music alone, was dispersed in 1938. In 1875 when Gustav Mahler became a pupil of the conservatory of music it was the supreme and unchallenged arbiter and teacher in the whole world.

The peddler's grandson was instantly accepted into this high companionship, the teaching institute for the loftiest of the arts. It taught him his profession as if it were a *Handwerk*, a word that needs no translation and could be adopted into the English language which lacks a comparable expression. The development of any talent needs disciplined training and constant hard work. Creativity and spontaneity come not before training but like a gift from heaven, through it. The gifts of heaven must be paid for and earned; one of the instalments that lasts for life is the pre-eminence of work. The service of the chosen art must come before everything. It must come before personal wishes, before comfort, before money and success, before other people, before oneself. Egotism must give way before it from the first; not 'I' but music, is its first and harshest law. This is so of all the arts but music demands not only total commitment as any profession worth doing does, it demands a technical competence and physical dexterity which need daily renewal. The talent of a Mozart is useless if Mozart neglects to play with precision and ease. That precision and ease, that discipline, Mahler now learned.

Professor Epstein taught Gustav Mahler piano-playing himself. A composer, Robert Fuchs taught harmony. Composition and counterpoint were sternly ruled by Franz Krenn whose strictness with his students was legendary. A fellow-student at the time, Hugo Wolf, could not stand his rigour and told the Director of the Conservatory so; he lost his place and left the school. Wolf was a friend of Mahler's and shared his lodgings at times. These lodgings were constantly changed; like all musicians they were noisy neighbours by the nature of their work and like

all musicians could not understand that the other people in the
house would rather sleep than hear unruly young men singing
the last Act of Wagner's 'Götterdämmerung'. On this occasion
Mahler and two friends of whom Wolf was one, were put out
in the street at an instant's notice in the middle of the night.

Mahler learned from Hugo Wolf's error; his devotion to his
work was strong enough to stand the strictest discipline and on
the one occasion when he rebelled he at once wrote a grovel-
ling apology to the Director before the worst could befall him.
It was not all success. A first attempt at writing a symphony,
the parts of which Mahler had to copy out himself at night for
lack of money to pay a copyist, aroused the rage of Director
Hellmesberger. Weariness and its attendant bad eyesight had
allowed Mahler to copy notes incorrectly and these mistakes
were retained in the performance of his work causing fearful
dissonances. But at the end of his first year at the yearly com-
petitive examination for piano-playing he won first prize with
the performance of a Schubert sonata.

As well as this intensive work and the outside drudgery of
teaching childen piano-playing, Mahler had to finish his statu-
tory schooling, and this he managed, but only just, as an extra-
mural pupil at the Iglau grammar school in the summer holidays
of 1878. He must have had special tuition from his school, since
all schools were closed at the same time that the Conservatory
in Vienna was, and the holidays were the only time Mahler
had for his books. In that year too he won first place in the
composition examination which was always a competition,
with a piano quintet.

There was then no separate schooling for conductors at the
music school. Only in 1909 when the conservatory was made
into an official institute was a separate course for conducting
begun. Those who intended or hoped to become conductors
learned the structure and forms of music, were tutored in their
chosen instruments, playing in and with orchestras; and in
composition. They deputised on instruments other than their
own at times and when Mahler was not used as solo pianist at

student concerts, he took care of the percussion. The least of a conductor's duties is to beat time at performances in public; just that activity which is seen and overestimated by the public. Almost everything the conductor has to do with his musicians is done beforehand at rehearsal and practice.

During his student time Gustav Mahler found the two dominant influences on his own music; Richard Wagner and Anton Bruckner. Wagner and his works – which he called music dramas to distinguish them from Italian opera – were already very famous. However his determination not to allow any performance of his operas to be given that did not conform to his own ideas was a hindrance to their triumph outside his own immediate sphere. A group of his admirers persuaded Wagner to go to Vienna in the spring of 1875 to conduct three concerts, following the success of parts of *Tristan* and *Walküre* in concert performances conducted by his disciple Hans Richter. After this Wagner was then persuaded by increased royalties and the permission of the Opera House Director for some of his singers to go to Bayreuth for the following summer, to allow *Tannhäuser* and *Lohengrin* to be staged in Vienna.

Wagner was a cult. The newspapers were full of detailed gossip about his every move, he was followed about by people who had no idea of music; he was treated like royalty, like somewhat scandalous royalty. But his ideas and his music were still revolutionary; nor was his political rebellion in his youth forgotten and the professors at the Conservatory were not convinced by his genius, nor did they approve of his showy and vulgar personal style as they thought it; moreover Wagner was always running off with other men's wives. Many students, Mahler included, restrained their enthusiasm for the new music and 'the whole work of art', when their professors were listening. But it overwhelmed them, it was a revelation; once it was there nobody was ever the same again and this flood of new understanding broke into other departments of life than music.

Nothing is more difficult or less likely of success than to try to express one form of art in the terms or forms of another. All art means itself and can only be grasped in its own terms, and more than any other human activity music is itself, for itself and contains nothing but itself. Nor can the music of Wagner or any other great composer be grasped at once. The hearer must wait patiently and listen attentively before light will dawn. But once the dawn breaks the light becomes ever more brilliant and varied, constantly increasing, deepening and changing but never failing.

However, the interior content of Wagner's music which is not discussable in words, was not the only revolutionary characteristic of it. Being operatic and therefore including human voices as well as visual drama, it cut across the Austrian or Danubian concept of orchestral music founded in the development of the symphony and the sonata form. Even before the great master Haydn and certainly since his time, the concept of order and harmony built up from the fundament of the bass instruments became universal and for symphonic music has remained so. The great nineteenth-century composers continued in this tradition, expanding in numbers of instruments as concert halls were built larger to accommodate the increase in public love of music and in turn the enlargement changed orchestration and treatment. Up to Brahms the line ran expanding but straight and was followed in differing degrees by all other musical societies. Essentially the Russian and French musicians of the time remained in the tradition of Haydn, Mozart and their predecessors. At the time of Wagner's first conquest of the music public it was feared that his work would destroy the traditions which had produced the world's greatest music; this of course was not so. But in Vienna it was feared to be so and at first hearing, the tremendous psychic force and near-chaotic complexity of Wagner's music seemed to threaten the whole body of the art itself. Even more than this, so to say, professional fear, the interior meaning of Wagner's work was threatening. It shook people to the innermost chambers of their souls and still does. Unlike those who protested wildly against the new painting and architecture, those who were afraid of

Wagner were not scholastic philistines but dedicated musicians. They need not have feared for the eternal glory of Mozart or Beethoven whose work will last as long as civilization; but their unspoken and almost unconscious fear was not quite unjustified; Wagner was and is Prometheus. And the first property of the fire stolen for men by Prometheus is to sear and destroy. Anyone who has ever risen stunned and uncertain of where he is or what is happening from his seat after the last chords of Tristan knows that.

So the world of musicians and the musical public were divided into Wagnerians and anti-Wagnerians. Gustav Mahler became and remained a Wagnerian, following another much admired composer who is only now, after the half-century division of European civilization, becoming widely known. This was Anton Bruckner, who was then teaching and lecturing on harmony and counterpoint at the Conservatory and who was a Wagnerian. Today Bruckner's music sounds clearly in the direct line of the Danube tradition, but it is also true that his music could not have been written as it was if Wagner had never been born. That is even more true of Mahler, both in respect to Wagner and to the ignorance about his music outside central Europe until very recent years.

It has been made easy not to know about Mahler's music because of the demands made by him on musicians, both in numbers and skills; in size of orchestra and length much of his symphonic work is very difficult to perform and to listen to. His harmonic and contrapuntal structure is intended to produce a dense interweave of sound and requires the extremes of attention and rehearsal from groups of players so large that they are not likely all to be familiar with each other. The length of some of his work is also exhausting to the audience, as I myself recall from a first hearing of *Lied von der Erde* years ago in Berlin when the reception was in the main a rejection and I found myself alone and inarticulate among a group of friends who more or less agreed that it was no wonder Mahler was unpopular. I have since understood that verdict while still not agreeing with it, for parts of Mahler's earlier symphonies have a curious quality of unreality. This is not the unfamiliarity of work so *avant garde* that one cannot 'hear' it, it is rather that by its structure and form one expects to grasp the music and then fails or partly fails to do so. It also contains a quality distinct from the actual sound, of being related to the world about us in some way that produces the impression of its being prophetic, but prophetic for today and not for Mahler's lifetime and this is uncanny. It may be that the music having lain fallow for so long, its sound echoes in the ear which has meanwhile traversed other sound-experience, as being of the past and yet fits itself at once into the present. It is the near-opposite of the effect of Wagner's music in which the hearing mind takes in the meaning with a deep shudder of recognition; to listen to Wagner is to 'know' what he 'meant' and to know because it has come true, and is still in the act of becoming true. The opaqueness of these remarks will perhaps serve to convince the reader at any rate of the difficulty of expressing anything at all about music in terms of words.

The student Mahler who loved and admired Anton Bruckner was present when Bruckner's Third Symphony was a complete failure in an almost empty auditorium. Not only at the time as a boy but all his life as a powerful conductor and director of orchestras, Mahler insisted on familiarizing the public with Bruckner's work, helped him with publishers and put his own royalties from music-publishing at the disposal of the publisher so that the uneconomic risk of printing Bruckner's work could be undertaken. It is entirely possible that most of this work would have been lost in the uproar of the twentieth century if this had not happened.

In 1878, the same year that he achieved his school-leaving certificate, Mahler began to write first text and then music for a never-performed fairy-tale oratorio, by changing the story of the 'singing bone' into a bone carved into a flute that plays by itself and exposes a murder. The King's wedding is disrupted by the flute recounting how the King killed his brother to gain bride and kingdom. As the guests flee, the lights flicker out and the castle crashes into ruins. This was a second start at turning an old tale into music. The first he shared with Hugo Wolf and started upon it but when he showed what he had written to his friend, Wolf was so upset that they quarrelled and the friendship never recovered. At about the same time, that is at the end of their teens, Wolf, who was in any case unstable, caught syphilis and from that time on was constantly ill and at last insane with the dreadful progressive paralysis of this disease.

Since underground drainage and the piping of drinking water in towns had eliminated the various epidemic plagues in Europe, increased movement and overcrowding filled the gap of fear with the two curses of the nineteenth century. Everyone was afraid of tuberculosis and this fear was openly expressed. The fear of the venereal diseases was even greater and secrecy because of their sexual origins made it a hovering dread over whole generations. The German doctors who isolated the viruses of gonorrhoea and syphilis were born about the 1860s and no doubt many doctors addressed themselves to this terrible problem just because of its considerable increase and its creeping presence in the prosperous and educated classes, for it had always been considered a disease of soldiers and itinerants and not of respectable people. Blake's menacing words express it exactly: 'How the youthful harlot's curse . . . blights with plagues the marriage hearse.' Warnings were given in such vague circumlocutions, as indeed they were to Mahler and thousands of other young men on leaving their homes, that they were hardly understood; the symptoms were not described to them out of a mistaken prudery, and they could not recognize the moment of danger. Even doctors would simply adjure young men to be continent and leave it at that. Each had to discover for himself from friends the signs that should warn them, and often they learned by irreversible experience. The whole history of the nineteenth century is full of the ruins of individual lives and entire families from this frightful scourge and its inherited weaknesses.

The most fortunate gift for any young man or woman was a steady love affair; without that good fortune they were condemned to the 'purity' enjoined on them by religion until they could marry. The alternative was a constant fear as debilitating and fruitful of neuroses as the effort of controlling the libido.

Vienna was no better and no worse than all European cities, but because of a long tradition of realism the problem was written of there, of course in vague terms, and diaries and memoirs mentioning this universal preoccupation were published uncut long before anything of the kind could appear in English. Almost all the contemporary journals and letters from one young man to another contain mentions of the temptation and the fear. Hugo Wolf was unfortunate. Gustav Mahler was both more cautious and more lucky. A frail child, he hardened himself in adolescence by much exercise and a careful diet which for a time included vegetarianism in imitation of Wagner. Although he was only just over five feet in height he was very strong and there are accounts of his bodily lifting up singers who persisted in standing in the wrong position – and singers were hefty in those days – and removing them to where he wished them to be. The self control he imposed on himself as far as casual girls were concerned has been adduced as evidence that he lacked normal desires but in fact he was fortunate enough to have several love affairs before he married while carefully avoiding the promiscuity that was always the greatest danger.

This prudence was a firm characteristic of Gustav Mahler's and was dictated more than anything by his devotion to his profession to which every other consideration gave way. His enemies said then and long after his death that he intrigued and calculated and was pathologically ambitious. His persistence and intransigence in rehearsal was paraded as a fault. But all these things were not for Mahler a matter of personal striving for place or fame and certainly not for money; he identified himself with music. He worked untiringly, driving himself to the limits of his vitality and drove others with himself. He was a perfectionist in the concert hall and the opera house and demanded perfectionism of all who worked with him.

In 1880 Mahler committed himself to conducting by engaging an agent to find him a summer job which was duly found at Bad Hall where there was a tiny summer theatre for the spa guests. No doubt this was not thought of at the time as more than a temporary means of earning money. He was not quite twenty. To compose Mahler must have money for leisure and privacy; to get it he was obliged to give up both for much of the year and for most of his life. The following summer he went to Laibach, which is now Lyublyana, a much bigger theatre. Here he was constantly required to conduct overtures, interval music and operetta, sometimes to compose interval and background music for plays, and of course, to conduct concerts and operas. At this theatre he is first mentioned for giving individual rehearsal time to players and singers – singers who would be mainly guests engaged for a particular part. This solo rehearsing was at once a most valued innovation and one of the things that his colleagues most complained of. According to their own devotion to their jobs they either hated it and resented the time it consumed or found it enlightening and inspiring.

Theatres and concert halls built in the last quarter of the nineteenth century were much larger than previously and required far more practice from the larger orchestras and choruses needed to fill the expanded spaces with sound. Rehearsal times therefore became longer and were more rigidly organized. Mahler was one of the first conductors to co-ordinate this trend into a much-needed firm organization. It made him at first unpopular, but was the chief reason for his supremcy when at last he took over the Opera in Vienna.

'At last' is exaggerated. Mahler's career was a steady and rapid climb upwards. His rise is attributable solely to talent and hard work for he was by no means popular. Small, with a shock of black hair and a hawkish nose, he wore in youth a full beard to increase his age in appearance at any rate. Aggressively determined, he would positively dance with energy and impatience when working. At twenty-three he went to Olmütz in Moravia where the conductor had departed in a hurry after a public scene in the middle of Meyerbeer's *African Girl* when he came to blows with the cast and the police were called in. Probably he was drunk, or perhaps they were all drunk, for the theatre was in a state of disintegration. The actors and singers were often unpaid, the scenery so decrepit that bits fell down on the actors' heads. Everyone was, unsurprisingly, quarrelling with everyone else; to cap everything the scandal over the conductor happened well after the beginning of the season when a replacement was hard to find. But Mahler needed a job and he took on this unappealing one. His agent warned the theatre Director before he went to Olmütz that the new conductor was not the man to put up with the disorder that reigned there; in his turn the Director made a speech to the assembled company asking them to have patience with the new young man.

Mahler was even worse than they expected. After the first chorus rehearsal the singers complained that they had all been drilled hoarse. It was the turn of the soloists next. Mahler did not even introduce himself, so angry was he at the fashion in which the deified music was being treated. He gave them curt, brusque orders in such a tone that the demoralized company had no time to protest and before they could recover their nerve the habit of work had been restored. In ten days the previously sparse and dissatisfied audience was vigorously applauding a performance of Verdi's *Masked Ball*.

The company made fun of Mahler's appearance and his horn-rimmed spectacles; it was a great joke that the new conductor drank neither wine nor beer after performances, but water. Mahler seemed not to and probably did not, notice their sulks or jokes. All he cared about was that they should work, and work they did with lessening ill temper as audiences increased and performances became less like pastiches of a still unheard-of Marx Brothers film.

Mahler hated it. He felt dishonoured by the low standards he fought with and kept Mozart and Wagner out of the programmes so as not to have to dishonour them with himself. At first his only comfort was that he suffered in the cause of Music and sometimes he felt lamed by the carelessness and sloppiness about him. But he forced his will on the company, jumping up on the stage during rehearsals and demonstrating what he wanted, bullying cast and musicians into taking him seriously. After a few months, when self-respect in the company had been restored and success was certain within their provincial standards, the town council reached one of those decisions that make high comedy. It decided that the theatre was bankrupt and could not be rescued without investments they were not prepared to make. In the middle of the season the theatre was closed and the company dispersed.

The news of the death of the master reached Mahler in Olmütz and he wandered alone and grieving for Wagner about the streets of the small cathedral town. But not for long. Negotiations were afoot through influential people who had seen Mahler at work and he received an offer to be second conductor at the Royal Theatre at Kassel from that autumn. In the meantime he got valuable experience as chorus trainer for an Italian company making guest appearances at the Carltheater in Vienna. This was the former Opera theatre, now the second since the huge and imposing new house on the Ring had been opened in 1869. But it was Vienna and his work there brought Mahler for the first time to the notice of the metropolis.

The Opera House at Vienna was designed by two architects. Eduard van der Null and August von Siccardsburg made their plans when the roadway where the Ring was then being laid out was much deeper than the finished boulevard. The consequence was that a massive building planned to rise above a sunken roadway appeared when finished as dumpy, too flat in proportion to its width and depth. It was one of the many miscalculations of proportion of the time. The Viennese complained as always and expressed themselves as always in malicious jokes. The Emperor was disappointed and said so. Van der Null, who was in any case a melancholic, committed suicide before the new house opened with 'Don Giovanni' on 25 May 1869. Siccardsburg was so much upset that he shortly afterwards died of a heart attack. It is said that the Emperor was so shocked at the deaths and the possibility that his own words may have been repeated to the two architects and have added to their distress, that from then on he never allowed himself a candid opinion but always stuck to the neutral courtesy of 'it was very nice, I was very pleased'. This phrase which became almost legendary provided one more reason for posterity to label Franz Joseph as stupid and unfeeling.

Nevertheless inside, the new Opera House was almost perfect for its purpose, handsome, impressive, with excellent accoustics and every conceivable device and convenience it needed. It was later copied many times in cities all over the world. But the fate of its architects mirrors that of a number of others who have held high appointments in the Vienna musical world and particularly in the Opera. The Viennese are said not entirely without justice to kill off those who serve them in the cause of music, and the list of those who accepted the risk and died untimely together with those up to the present day who have got away in time, would be a long one. The combination of standards so high that they begin where most other people leave off, and the eternal intriguing and quarrelling, is a lethal one. Today these hazards are greatly increased by an apparently insoluble problem of bureaucracy; in the old Empire that at least was not the case. The Opera was paid for like the Burgtheater out of the Emperor's pocket and both theatres were controlled by the Imperial Chamberlain, the equivalent in England of the Lord Chamberlain, who made the necessary appointments after taking authoritative advice and whose decisions were final. The Emperor himself never imposed his wishes; as he said when a hint had not been taken and someone suggested that he could issue an order, 'I may wish but I do not command'. The Emperor's wishes on that occasion were made known to Gustav Mahler and it was he who ignored them; but that was later.

From his appointment to Kassel the pattern of Mahler's advance was set. He moved from there to the reorganized German Theatre in Prague while waiting for a new appointment as second conductor under the famous Arthur Nikisch at Leipzig. Nikisch was toying with an offer to go to the three-year-old Royal Opera House in Budapest – in Hungary everything that elsewhere in the Empire was Imperial, was Royal – but he fell ill and was obliged to take a long holiday and this not only cleared the way for Mahler in Leipzig but opened the chance of a further rise to Budapest, after Vienna the second Habsburg city. He even expressed this calculation candidly to friends but this not very scrupulous shouldering out of a sick man should not be thought of as an individual characteristic of Gustav Mahler's. That is the way of ambition in the great world and those who will not use the way of the world can expect no success in it; there are such intrigues in all success everywhere and the reason they are supposed to belong to the theatre and politics is simply that these professions contain an essential element of publicity. All Mahler's moves were accompanied by such manoeuvrings and they were all the result of careful preparation and calculation. Where his plans were opposed as they frequently were, this opposition was ascribed by his wife in his lifetime and by music historians later, to anti-Semitism. His enemies, naturally, used the reversed argument and said that Mahler was a ruthless intriguer because he was a Jew. That was a case of using any stick to beat a dog with. Mahler's steep rise in the world caused a good deal of envy in those he overtook in his climb who preferred as always to cover their own less blazing gifts with the blanket of moral indignation. It is a comical facet of the controversy that many of his colleagues and those who wrote about these events were themselves Jewish, which reduces the entire argument to childish squabbling and there it would have remained if later events had not quite independently given it sinister seriousness. In themselves the quarrels were not sinister and this is proved by Mahler's career. For if anti-Semitism was in the Empire endemic and savage how did Gustav Mahler rise to the greatest height of his world and why do so many of his colleagues and his opponents have Jewish names?

In Leipzig Mahler worked to the limits of endurance. In one season he conducted 214 performances with 54 different works including two new Wagner productions, *Walküre* and *Siegfried*. He also discovered at the house of Carl Maria von Weber's grandson an unfinished opera. He finished and rearranged this work and Weber's *Three Pintos* was produced in Leipzig and was taken up by several other opera houses. Mahler's score is not admired today because he introduced a Wagnerian strain into Weber's music which does not combine well with it, but it was admired at the time and introduced its arranger to Richard Strauss among others.

Forgotten opera scores were not the only thing Mahler found in Weber's home; he fell in love with the lady of the house and even urged her to run away with him. They did not run away but the suppressed passion produced vitality that became an even greater passion; Mahler fell in love for life with the symphonic form and his desire for Frau von Weber was the inspiration of his First Symphony based partly on themes already used by him in a song-cycle. From this time on the symphony was Mahler's form of musical expression.

He often used voices in his orchestral works, and indeed his earliest music was for voices with instruments. But he never wrote an opera, which seems strange because he spent much of his career as an opera conductor. He was fascinated by vocal and choral music, however, and it is significant that Mahler's *Lied von der Erde* is, in fact, his Ninth Symphony. He did not number it because he was superstitiously conscious that neither Schubert nor Beethoven lived beyond their ninth symphonies. And, like Beethoven's masterwork, *The Song of the Earth* is a choral symphony. Mahler wrote his Ninth Symphony, but his Tenth remained unfinished.

In that autumn of 1888 Mahler was offered the directorship at the Royal Opera House in Budapest for ten years at a high salary. He needed it; his father was mortally ill, his mother an invalid and the four Mahler children who were still at home looked to their eldest brother for help. In the next year both parents died and his married sister was ill. Another brother was a good-for-nothing who in the end emigrated to America, it is said for urgent reasons. Mahler sent his youngest brother and sister to friends in Vienna and took his eldest sister, Justine, to keep house for him. With Justine family affection intensified into one of those near-incestuous loves that cause such trouble for the sufferers. Gustav was so jealous of his sister that a little later when she fell in love with a first violinist of the Vienna Philharmonic Orchestra she was reduced to deceiving her brother. The lovers met in secret and did not marry until Gustav himself did so. And in spite of her own love-affair Justine was equally jealous of Gustav. Intensely possessive and passionate, working to the limits of his strength, struggling with the development of his own creative forces, Mahler's life was a tempest both inwardly and outwardly.

But not all was drama. In Budapest Mahler took a hand at comedy. The singing at the Budapest Opera was polyglot and the rhythmic havoc created by the various phrasing of what was sometimes several different languages at a performance shocked Mahler profoundly. But Magyar chauvinism made the question of language a delicate one. The chorus and local singers were trained in Hungarian; it was unpopular, nearly impossible, to suggest that this might not be a good thing in an art-form that depends as much on language as on music. Soloists would sing their parts in which ever language the opera was written, and sometimes whatever suited themselves. It happened that a Rigoletto, for instance, would sing in German and the other chief roles Italian while the chorus used Hungarian. It was bedlam, and it illustrates very well the sad idiocy of language exclusiveness, for however beautiful, Hungarian was unknown to the vast majority of singers. To solve the problem, Mahler neatly used its cause. He insisted that either everyone should sing in Hungarian, which of course was impossible, or should sing in the language the opera was written in. Apparently nobody noticed the contradiction in this ruse and it worked. The mixing of languages ceased.

The reader will by now know enough to be sure that Mahler did not fulfil his contract in Budapest but made another change, this time to Hamburg. As with all his steps upwards, this one was carefully planned and carried out. For many years it was disputed that Mahler's movements were carefully calculated; above all his wife, who quite possibly believed it, described his progress as not voluntary but dictated by the enmity and jealousy of rivals and anti-Semites which drove Mahler from opera house to opera house and interfered with his composing. Quite the contrary: Mahler knew perfectly well what he was doing and that includes his much later departure from the goal of his ambitions.

In Hamburg and on holidays from his work there, at every moment he could wring out of his official duties, he was composing. Every penny he could raise, from his own funds and by borrowing from patrons, went into the presentation of his Second Symphony and other work in Berlin where his music achieved its first major public success. In Hamburg too he met the first woman he could treat as an equal; that is, whom he felt to be a real human being and not the object of desire alone. Mahler and the singer Anna von Mildenburg as she called herself were for a time engaged and much of the knowledge of this period comes from his letters to her. He trained her by personal rehearsing into a magnificent Wagnerian soprano and they were devoted colleagues in Vienna long after the love-affair was over.

It was 1896 and Mahler was thirty-six. The Director of the Imperial Opera in Vienna was ill and ageing and it was known that a conductor was to be appointed to assist him. What was not known was that the general manager of the Court Theatres intended to replace the old Director with this conductor when he had worked himself into the post. The Opera administrator was instructed to find such a conductor and see that the transfer then went smoothly and discreetly. The administrator was called Wlassack and as with all really interesting intrigues it was doubtful whether Wlassack was using others or being used by them, and that is equally so of other players in the ensuing chess game. Several talented and well-known conductors at the larger German music centres were possible candidates. Not all of them would want to go to Vienna if it came to the point, but no ambitious conductor wished to be unable to say that the chance had been his to refuse.

The circles of intrigue began from the outside, converging towards their centre. Although he wrote privately to a friend in Budapest that Vienna was his target, Mahler said in public, including to Count Apponyi who had the Budapest appointment in his hand, that he felt nostalgia for the Hungarian capital. From his summer home in the Salzburg lake district he cycled – Mahler was a great bicyclist – to Bad Ischl which was fashionable because the Court was there in the summer. Among the acquaintances he called on there was Brahms whose horror at Mahler's Second Symphony did not dim his admiration for the conductor Mahler; and Brahms, of course, had great if quiet influence. So had the terrifying critic and anti-Wagnerian Hanslick, whose cruel caricature Wagner wrote into *Meistersinger* as Beckmesser. Although he was passionately loyal to Wagner, Mahler consulted Hanslick and that shows how determined he was for when Nietzsche, a much greater man than Hanslick, fell out with Wagner Mahler's enthusiasm for the philosopher had turned to enmity. It was not disloyalty to the master but a sacrifice made to him; Mahler had not the least intention of neglecting Wagner's music once he gained his eminence. Every influential musician, courtier and patron gained the firm impression that upon his advocacy of Mahler's cause hung not only Mahler's ambition, but the fate of music in Vienna. There is no doubt that Mahler was sincere in this and in fact it turned out to be true.

A major move was made by Anna von Mildenburg. Her teacher was Rosa Papier, a great alto who broke her voice singing mezzo-soprano parts for Wagner, parts far too high for her, and then became a well-known teacher. Rosa Papier was an old friend of the Opera administrator Wlassack. All summer and autumn the campaign continued. In December came the crucial moment. Mahler officially applied to be considered for the appointment and asked Wlassack to use his powerful influence for him. Count Apponyi wrote an urgent recommendation. His enemies accused Mahler of being harsh, short-tempered and inconsiderate. Moreover he was a Jew and high Court appointments could not go to non-Catholics. Mahler had already informed Wlassack that he had carried out a long-considered conversion to Catholicism some time before. By February matters were arranged, and the press, which had been discussing for months who would become the new conductor, still knew nothing.

As soon as he was certain of success, Mahler forced through the agreement of the Hamburg Opera to his release at the end of that season in June so that he would be free to begin work in Vienna well before the new season began in September.

The incumbent Director of the Imperial Opera countersigned the appointment of his new conductor without knowing that it was already agreed that Mahler should shortly be advanced to his own position. The contract as conductor was for one year, apparently as a probationary period; in fact so that Mahler could then become Director. The agreement to this contract by the Court was rushed through in one day although the process normally took some time.

Why the urgency and why the secrecy? Mahler was a controversial figure both as composer and as conductor. Singers, chorus and orchestra dreaded his stringent demands on them; and many of the most famous singers disliked the loss of their personal dominance on the stage. They must be presented with an accomplished fact and they were. The public was astounded by the announcement and the great argument that would certainly have bedevilled and perhaps even prevented the appointment was only a rattle of fireworks instead of a bombardment of heavy artillery.

It was the perfect intrigue, neat, discreet and successful. Vienna for once changed opera conductors without a scandal and everyone immediately claimed to have known all the time. How was such a secret kept for six months in a city where there are notoriously no secrets? There can only be one answer: it was in the interest of all the participators to keep the secret. Court officials, administration and the old Director all wanted the man who would bring new glory to the Opera. He himself swayed between elated pride, messianic intention and fear at the immensity of the job before him.

The anti-Semites raged; it was an outrage that this son of a tavern-keeper, the grandson of a peddler, should rule in the Imperial Opera.

His serious critics, those who didn't care if the Director of the Opera were a Hottentot or Chinese or the Emperor himself so long as he made great music, made other complaints. Mahler was never satisfied, never at rest. He drilled chorus and orchestra like an army. The star system gave way to the Company and the greatest voices took the parts they were suited to and not the most exciting ones. He was not content with one Wotan, but in one week one singer took the part in the Ring and at the next presentation there was a different voice, a different concept of the role, an altered production. Any one of four bass-baritones, wrote one critic, might be singing Wotan; one never knew where one was. Apparently it did not occur to him to marvel at an Opera company that contained four possible Wotans, and all members of the company: not guests. The old system of a great singer to whom the whole company played up and who expected applause for his arias and even sometimes for his entrances was absolutely forbidden in Mahler's time. The composer was the dominant arbiter and the composer alone. The company must try without ceasing to understand what the music demanded, and neither vanity nor great talent must be allowed to unbalance the whole work of art. Even in Mozart operas the traditional applause in the midst of a scene was furiously forbidden and the orchestra played on without the customary pause. Cuts in operas were unheard of. The public was tyranically forbidden to move about in the boxes. The doors were closed before the conductor raised his baton and late-comers must wait until the curtain came down. This last rule has now become an iron law in any opera house worthy of the name, but it was not so before Mahler's time and people went to the opera as to a party, to see and be seen. Mahler's view was that if people wanted to have a chat they could go to a coffee-house.

The lighting in the auditorium was reduced almost to dark-ness to increase the effect of the stage lighting and much ex-periment went on to make the lighting serve the music and the action of the performance. The balance of an act or of a whole work was changed so that the drama of the 'story' itself dictated high-points and not the entrances and exits of the chief pro-tagonists, who were of course the chief singers.

The stage and scenery were subordinated to the music too; unnecessary and superficial decoration, costume or 'business' un-related to the theme disappeared. Presently Mahler found an artist who understood his purpose and who revolutionized stage design. Alfred Roller was an important painter of the Secession movement, a friend of Klimt's and of Max Klinger the sculptor whose statue of Beethoven was installed in the centre of the Secession building to the music of Beethoven's Ninth Symphony conducted by Mahler. After Roller began to work with Mahler in the Opera sets were drastically redesigned to expose and further the dynamics of the music. The orchestra pit was sunk deeper so that the music swelled up to a confluence with the voices and not in rivalry against them. This was an idea taken from Wagner's own theatre at Bayreuth where the pit is covered over entirely, and was one much condemned by the critics who were used to hearing the individual parts of the orchestra rather than a blended body of sound.

Another important member of the Secession circle was Carl Moll and he had a beautiful and fascinating step-daughter, Alma Maria. Klimt was in love with Alma Schindler when she was sixteen, but her stepfather intervened with the undoubtedly true fear that Klimt could make a young wife nothing but un-happy. She was twenty when Mahler first met her and he fell in love at first sight. Within a week or so their marriage was irrevocably decided upon.

The word irrevocably is used with intent. When Gustav Mahler attained his dream of the directorship of the Imperial Opera, Anna Papier who had helped materially to achieve his aim wanted Mahler to send for Anna von Mildenburg to join the company. Mahler's housekeeper and sister Justine used every weapon at her disposal to prevent this but did not succeed although for other reasons the personal relationship between Mahler and Anna was at an end. Justine was as jealous of her brother as he was of her; a case for Sigmund Freud one may well think, some years before Mahler did actually consult the soul-healer as the German phrase rather precisely expresses Freud's function. When it came to Alma, however, Justine recognized that the girl's beauty and personality, not to mention her erotic vitality, was outside the range of any opposition. Justine tried and the two women were always at least wary of each other afterwards, but the sister must have known she was beaten and she and her violinist lover were married on the day after Gustav Mahler was wedded to Alma Maria Schindler in the Karlskirche in Vienna.

Alma Mahler can be as well known as it is possible to know a human being one has never met. She wrote an account of her life with Mahler soon after his death which for the time, and indeed for any time, is astonishing in its candour. Much later she incorporated the material into a complete story of her life. That story, published in Vienna in 1949, is a valuable historical source if memory of factual events is checked against other evidence. As a psychological document it is even more valuable and by itself it provides an answer to the unrealistic concepts of the present-day Women's Liberation Movement.

Alma Schindler was brought up in a community of artists including some, and not only Gustav Klimt, whose personal lives were immoderately and openly profligate. She was not only commandingly beautiful, intelligent, educated, full of character and charm; she also had musical and literary talent. Though not rich she was certainly never poor; the struggle for bread was spared her and she was surrounded by many influential friends. Moreover she was young when the freedom of women was believed in as it could only be believed in at a time of expansive liberalism not yet touched by the reality of experience. Alma Schindler was in her own person the New Woman who was so much talked of then and later all over Europe and America by a million men who sincerely thought of women as their equals, that is as human beings, and continued to use them as females. Her entire life into old age was spent in the service of men and during her youth, of children; above all it was ruled by her own sexuality and the passions of sexual feeling she inspired in men. Anyone who still believes that a woman can free herself from the psychic makeup of femaleness and from her own body and relegate her personal life to one part of her being as men naturally do, should read Alma Mahler-Werfel's account of her own life. The importance of her testimony lies in its unwittingness for in spite of her very feminine candour and a lively self-concern she never drew the conclusions her experience so clearly proved. Or, at any rate, she never formulated and published them and there is no sign in her writing of her having understood them as distinct from sometimes protesting about them. Alma was the living demonstration that all civilized and cultured societies are built on the acceptance of women that they are women and cannot be imitation men.

Almost the first thing Gustav Mahler demanded of his future

wife was that she should give up entirely the use of her own talent; and to this demand she at once agreed. To point the story with classic finality, the pair were lovers before the wedding and Alma already knew that she was pregnant at their marriage. The gate was closed; even if she wanted to she could not go back. Until Gustav died in May 1911 Alma carried about with her on all their travels the manuscript scores of her first compositions.

The peddler's grandson was king of music in Vienna and had married a golden girl. His achievement was so far from anything that his parents could have conceived that it must have seemed sometimes like a dream. For his mother at the time of her death Gustav seemed to have scaled the heights of success, but if she had lived to see him a few years later she would hardly have believed her own eyes. As for his grandmother, she would certainly have concluded that the boy was spinning fantasies. His father and his grandparents depended for their livelihood on the goodwill of a rural weights and measures inspector, who as likely as not would be a pensioned sergeant of the Imperial Army. Gustav was in a position to ignore without even a reply the wishes of the Emperor himself in the Emperor's own Opera House.

7

The Successful Artist - Gustav Klimt

GUSTAV Klimt was no haggard young genius starving in a garret rather than use his talent for pelf. He was attractive enough to have played that part and liked women enough, not to mention wine. But he was too simple for such inverted or invented notions as hatred of money just because it was money. That attitude is for artists before recognition. Or those who miss it; quite often, although it is impermissible to mention it, because they have no talent. In fact Gustav Klimt took up no position at all about his achievement and probably never thought about it; he took it for granted and devoted his energies to doing the things he meant to do and doing them as well as he could. Those two things were painting and loving women. From his childhood he never knew failure; poverty he knew as a child in a working-class home and that was the spur to work at his gift. Furious battles raged about him in his prime, but for him they were alarums and excursions in the wings, sometimes loud enough to cause annoyance but never taken so seriously as to interfere with what he wanted to do.

There is nothing like the memory of grinding want to spur talent and the memory that stabs sharpest paradoxically is the near-forgotten one that lives well down in the pysche, blurred and formalized into a presence that can be accommodated but never quite fades even when the artist has been leaning for years on the cushions of recognition and well-paid commissions. That memory was the impetus to work; the interesting question is where the talent came from. In Klimt's case in the eighteen-sixties, a gold and silver engraver and a girl who once dreamed of being a singer put the genes together in just the mysteriously right mixture. Of their seven children, two were talented painters. Gold engraving suffered with other luxury trades during the serious slump of the 1870s; with so many children the family was desperately poor. But the house where they lived and where the father worked, one of those typically low one-storey houses of eastern Austria, was almost in the Wienerwald well outside the western edge of Vienna. The killing formalism of tenements was spared them all, the pressing nearness of hundreds of other poor families whose common and apparently inescapable fate breeds desperation. They could always get *out*. On Sundays they walked across the lush meadows and through the woods where the groves of tall beech trees breathed their enigmatic comfort and in the spring small flowers, celandines, wild violets, cyclamen, seeded their precise images for ever in Gustav's seeing mind. Their mother always sang and the children sang with her; she sang not for large audiences as she had wanted to when she was a girl, but just for herself and her family, a private joy. They were often hungry for some years, but neither frightened nor hemmed in.

Gustav, a year older than his brother Ernst, was to be apprenticed to the engraving trade like his father but the teacher at the local school told his parents that such a talent for drawing should be trained. He was just fourteen when he passed the tests for entry into the School of Applied Arts, an Imperial Institute; the State would pay for his education and to earn a living the two boys painted little portraits, mostly from photographs, for the neighbours. They got six Gulden for one of these, neatly set in a mount. They had the good fortune to have a first-class teacher called Ferdinand Laufberger who saw that they learned thoroughly all the techniques from wood-cutting to oil-painting. Like their teacher, they made their own colours and tools. In the old-fashioned phrase they got a thorough grounding. It may well be the greatest possible luck for an artist to have a teacher in youth who is competent and enthusiastic and who takes an interest in his pupils. At school the two brothers made a friend as well and when their apprenticeships were finished they took a studio together with Franz Matsch and the three worked together. Matsch showed business as well as painting talent and got their first commissions for them, for which each submitted a sketch for the client to choose from. Large paintings were carried out by all three, each taking a section in the traditional way.

In their student days they all three admired Makart, the 'great' painter of the day and bribed his servant to allow them into his studio to study the work-in-progress of the great man. Technically Makart really was a good painter; what was wrong with him as an artist was that he was too involved with the fashion of the time, so clearly to be seen in the buildings of that period on the Ring. Makart imitated the past, going back as far as the fifteenth century, and allied the mimicry to the style of his own time, producing an extraordinary mixture of history romanticized with the almost insane complication and adornment of contemporary taste. Naturally one man cannot have caused the fixation on a never-never land of imaginary former times, but Makart was its most noticeable exponent and stamped his pathological inability to leave anything alone on his time in Vienna. Not a line could be left clean, not an inch of surface without its meaningless rose stitched to the curve of a skirt, its curlicue stuck to the hand-grip of a chair, the smothering of every centimetre of canvas with busy detail unrelated to the subject, added, piled on, fidgeted with. There was some reality that must be crowded out of the eye, the mind. Something looms behind Makart's pictures, something large and simple, something that must not be allowed to exist. They have nothing to do with the exuberant self-confidence of the late eighteenth century, for instance with Maulpertsch, or with the loving fidelity to landscape of the early nineteenth century; one looks in vain for the dreaming calm of Waldmüller. There is a craziness about Makart that sharply focuses the period in all Europe, the time when proportion was lost.

It may partly have been the considerable expansion of wealth among large classes once the depression of the 1870s was over; the railways increased travel for pleasure and when the new-rich went to Rome and Florence they came back full of the idea of having a palazzo like one seen in the south and pictures in it to match. Just as the photograph ended the great art of portrait painting, the unassimilated shock of the Italian renaissance in groups of people with no settled taste killed their inborn inherited sense of how things should look, their own natural aesthetic. Where their own past was clutched at it was the sentimentalized middle ages; that is, a period even in its reality a long way off and meaningless in everyday life. The valid native tradition of the previous two centuries was simply ignored and so was the authentic transplant of the renaissance to middle Europe; in 1885 Fischer von Erlach might never have lived. Neither Makart nor his customers wanted to imitate the aristocracy of their own past and that is one of the strangest things about the huge wave of false fashion that swept Europe. There was certainly no lack of snobbish admiration for the great old families in social manners, but everything that had been real about those entrenched and ancient clans was rejected: their power, their patronage, their sense of proportion, above all their realism. Was this perhaps an unread sign that the old aristocracy had so lost its vitality that the new rich felt no genuine pull towards it and envied only its titles and its access to Court?

Nor can it have been the vastly increased use of power-driven machinery that of itself destroyed the sense of what is proper and seemly. There is no intrinsic reason why objects made with the help of machines should be ugly; like money, machines are invented by men as a means of getting things done and are in themselves neutral. Driven by water or animal power they had existed for generations; it was the number and the means of driving them that changed, in the arts and applied arts as in industry. In the theatre, for instance, the late seventeenth and the eighteenth centuries were a time of fantastic ingenuity in machinery for lifting and changing scenery, simulating flying figures, sailing boats, revolving whole scenes, producing effects of storm or fire. (In this they rediscovered classic Greek techniques.) Yet the buildings in which these devices were used were some of the most beautiful in Europe and many later theatres were copied from them, so practical was their basic design.

But there is no doubt that somewhere in the course of the great and rapid changes of methods and in the huge increases of population together with the mass movements of people into large urban complexes which were no longer cities, the interrelation between hand and eye, eye and mind, a man to an object made by him, was lost. People were alienated from their own products in individual cases and socially deep divisions of feeling and meaning were opened up between those who lived with land, weather, animals and those who could live their entire lives cut off literally from real life; it was possible for the first time in history for thousands of human beings to live without ever seeing or touching anything or any physical being in its natural state.

Against this state of affairs Klimt began gradually to revolt; and the progress of his rebellion can be seen in his work even though a considerable amount of his major work was burned or otherwise destroyed, is in private houses or, as in the case of the Burgtheater, was heavily restored after the rebuilding of the theatre in the 1950s.

Some of the earliest commissions the two Klimt brothers and Franz Matsch carried out were theatre decorations. They painted together curtains and ceilings for several provincial theatres before some of the ceiling painting in the new Burgtheater was given to them. The director of the Academy of Applied Arts showed their work to the architect Baron Hasenauer who at once determined to employ them. This was on the strength of their copying Makart's work; in fact Makart himself died before he could carry out his design for the ceiling of the Empress Elisabeth's bedroom in the new Villa Hermes out at Lainz to the west of Vienna. The actual painting was done by the Klimts to Makart's sketches. In the Burgtheater they painted some of the staircase ceilings, working directly on to the masonry which they covered with powdered marble bound by glues as ground-work. These decorations depicted stages in the history of the theatre and their families and friends appear in them among the public. There is one group of an audience watching a Shakespeare play in contemporary dress which shows Gustav and Ernst Klimt and Franz Matsch all together. These early works are, of course, formal decorations and not products of the imagination of the painters; they are also still clearly derived from the example of Makart but already they show far greater clarity and simplicity. They already demonstrate too a continuing characteristic of Gustav Klimt's and that is his extra-ordinary facility in changing his style. Throughout his life he painted in many quite different ways with equal effectiveness. He moved to and fro from naturalist portraits to impressionism, to exact anatomical studies, brilliantly expressed nude drawings of great economy, fantastically idealized and decorated por-traits, landscapes in half a dozen idioms; a bewildering array of masterly techniques. In some of his landcapes a familiar view becomes more real than one's own sight, while others are in-formed by his own inward vision so that they are metamor-phosed into quite different insights for the viewer.

Before the old Burgtheater was closed and pulled down, it was fixed in paint by the two Klimts, Gustav showing in watercolours the auditorium from the stage and filling it with instantly recognizable portraits of the great and beloved of the time: Brahms, the great surgeon Billroth, Mayor Lueger, and one of the most popular actors of the age, the comedian and singer Girardi. And everywhere amongst them the figures of lovely women. For this aquarelle Klimt won the Emperor's Prize of 1890.

In the next year or so the trio painted some of the art-historical staircase illustrations for the Museum of the History of Art (Kunsthistorisches Museum) and these can still be seen today just as they were. They are in the academic style of the time but again with that clarity of line dominating more and more over the bad example of Makart. It must have been during this period that Klimt learned much about the antique and exotic he later adopted as backgrounds and allegories in some of his most famous work. Nor did he ever lose the intimate tracery of the small scattered blossoms of his childhood wandering in the fields and woods and just as he kept in his mind's eye the cells, threads and tissues seen under microscopes in the medico-artistic lectures he attended in his student days. These intimate forms, the inner being and stuff of life, recur constantly later in what at first glance appear to be completely artificial compositions of mosaic-like coverings of startlingly real human features and limbs.

Although Gustav Klimt did travel about during the 1880s and 1890s he was never happy for more than a few weeks away from his own city, where without sentimental phrase-making, his heart always was. He was a child of Vienna from birth to death and the longing for new scenes, for change, was alien to him just as the easy-going tolerance of differentness which is so very Viennese was native to him. He never wanted others to be the same as himself, but to be themselves and neither cared nor could understand why he or they should be expected to conform to prescribed patterns.

In 1892 his home and the world was darkened; his father and his brother Ernst both died. That was the watershed, the point of no return. Klimt was then forty years old so his character cannot have changed. But he began to show outwardly an increasingly stubborn refusal to compromise. A certain bluntness in the way he met others, which belongs to any artist but which is not always openly expressed, was from that time on a dominant and visible part of his temperament. He ceased to be amenable to social or fashionable conventions in his life, his work and in the way he went about his work with clients. This intransigence must always have been in him for it is a fundamental characteristic without which no one can really be an artist but the suddenness of the change of manner suggests something more than the fact that his brother and his friend

Matsch had been in charge of the business side of their careers. This was certainly the case and although Klimt and Matsch remained friends they gradually separated their working lives so that as Klimt began to do his own business he lost the adroit diplomacy of Matsch. Either Klimt could not be diplomatic or he could no longer be bothered. Probably the overriding need to be himself in his life as in his work would have resulted in the series of ferocious and absurd scandals that followed each other a few years later. But it remains strange that a painter who had been so favoured, and continued to be so, by the official world that held the power of patronage should in a few years have become the object of such public enmity. The academically artistic world turned against Klimt before his work became so estranged from the accepted modes as to account for the breach. It seems likely that with his brother and Matsch Klimt lost an easy liaison to the outside world at the same moment that shock and grief showed him that time was not endless and he must cease wasting it on inessentials if he was to fulfil his own vision.

The now open intransigence must have been quite startlingly visible for there is no other reason for the rejection by the Künstlerhaus – the equivalent of the Royal Academy of Arts in London – of a wonderfully well-painted but perfectly conventional portrait of an elderly tea-merchant. The accompanying portrait of this man's wife was hung, but so badly that Klimt said with open contempt 'the honourable hanging-clique has posted my last work in the lavatory', using a word that can mean either that or exit, to point the angry joke. It cannot have been these portraits that the Academy and Klimt were quarrelling about; the mutual dislike was already there.

No doubt it was partly due to the way Klimt now lived. A visitor to his studio has left his impression that it was filled with a crowd of unclothed models, lying about, chattering and moving to and fro while Klimt stood at his easel in the centre of the room and sketched first one and then another of the slender, rangy red-heads and dark-haired women. There were thousands of these sketches, almost all women and almost all nervous, thin, passionate women; the smooth, rounded and creamy blondes so beloved of his fellow-citizens clearly did not interest Klimt. He drank a good deal of the local wine and had a mistress – apart from the models – who was a dress designer and helped to introduce the new feminine fashions into Vienna which revolutionized women's clothing. But he never married and never allowed himself to be restrained from his physical and artistic adoration of women. It can easily be imagined how this open lustfulness enraged other painters who conformed to the conventions of the time; envy alone must have made them hate Klimt even if he had not been their superior as a painter. And what is more his sketches and paintings of women have the splendid erotic force of their own sexuality and are not idealized as was usual at that time. There they are, living women with muscles and pubic hair and breasts like breasts and not like the symbolic nudes on marble fountains.

This sensuality is equally visible in the portraits of well-known ladies of society during those years by Klimt. Perfectly correct, fully dressed, outwardly conventional, but eyes and lips convey disturbingly the woman inside the exquisitely coloured and floating dress. Some of them are fantastically decorated and some very simple. In some there is intricate patterning of drapery and background, some have gold surrounding the figure. In some, oriental figures posture and plant shapes, or what are usually taken to be plant shapes, are scattered across the canvases. Many of these strewn forms are in fact flowers but some are the cells and tissues remembered from the microscope. They are biological and physiological hints of inwardness or mortality, just as the gold is encrusted wealth and the frequent eastern background figures convey strangeness, what is unknowable in the sitter. Or in the painter, or both.

Klimt and his friends met in the afternoons – where else? – in a coffee house near the city open market for fresh food and vegetables. In the last years of the century they became an informal group inside the Academy of Arts and when this group was attacked by those artists who did not share an enthusiasm for new styles and ideas, Klimt and others resigned from the official association and the group became a 'movement'.

Such changes from accepted styles to new ones are almost a stereotype of 'The Artist's Life'; not that they do not occur in many other walks of life, but that the portrayal of the world and life in any form must address itself to a public if not the public, and is therefore attended by publicity. The controversies that shake the medical world regularly are carried on in near-privacy and the reason for this is only partly that the layman does not understand them. The layman also does not want to know that there is constant change and doubt in the medical world for such argument threatens his quite false confidence in medicine. But the portrayal of the cosmos is felt to be within the competence of everyone, and quite rightly too. As always, in the case of Klimt and his friends, opposition to change was fired as much by practical considerations as by dislike of anything new. Klimt was not only a successful portraitist and continually favoured with big official commissions, but he was proposed for the title of Professor of the Academy of Graphic Arts, a much envied distinction which his enemies prevented his attaining. The grandees of the Academy did not want this rake, this working-class nobody, to be of their number. He and his friends knew what to do about that; they founded their own anti-Academy and called it Secession. And since they were not poor the first exhibition in 1898 in the hall of the Gardening Design Society was followed by the building of their own exhibition hall near the Market and surmounted by a dome of gilded metal bay-leaves called by the Viennese the golden cabbage. It was one of the first major buildings of the new architecture. The academicians were furious. They were even more impotently enraged when in 1902 the Secession show was visited formally by the Emperor Franz Joseph.

The occasion was painted, naturally, and hangs now in the Historical Museum of the city. Franz Joseph is being greeted by the aged Honorary President, the distinguished water-colourist

Rudolf von Alt, and by the first active President, Gustav Klimt. Round about them stand their associates, solemnly attired in white ties and tails for the illustrious guest who almost literally crowns their rebellion. The naturalist, completely straight-faced painting is one of the delightful jokes of the time and one cannot even look at its demure respectfulness without beginning to laugh. The deference to the Emperor is real enough; the joke is against those who ground their teeth but were not present. The womaniser, the winebibber and the untouchable Emperor in the same room! He cannot have known what sort of people these so-called artists were! Of course, they said under their breath, the Emperor knows nothing about painting; that went without saying. It was quite untrue but was said none the less. But no amount of oblique scorn could disguise the fact that the rebels had in fact not been excluded but had shut out the formalism of the Academy and the All-Highest Ruler himself had set his seal on the insult.

For the great scandal was already there. The Minister of Education ordered three large ceiling decorations for the main hall of the new University. They were to show *Philosophy*, *Medicine* and *Law*. The first sketch for philosophy was judged by an artistic commission on which members of the University were represented. This committee suggested small alterations and these were agreed by Klimt; the design was then unanimously approved. The Minister later tried to protect himself behind this committe, so evidently some opposition, either to Klimt himself or to his work, was expected. The finished painting, not this time executed straight on to the ceiling but painted separately, was shown for two months at the Secession before being mounted. Thirty-four thousand visitors were counted, many of whom had come to see what the fuss was all about rather than to assess a work of art.

Naked figures sweep upwards through space, scattered with stars over an amorphous dark swirl from out of which an allegorical head is suggested, posing the riddle of life. At the lower verge the calm, wise eyes of a female head wrapped in sombre draperies symbolizes Philosophy itself. The composition in itself might well have caused some genuine argument for the human figures, old and young, a child, an embracing couple, are all crowded to the left while the rest of the canvas appears almost empty; the universe with its eternal question. The draughtsmanship is masterly and the helplessness of the humans swept through life by the indifferent force of nature arouses intense sympathy.

But not in the scholars. One splendid Professor committed himself to a classic statement of prejudice : 'I don't know Klimt or his picture. But I hate modern art so much that I oppose it wherever I can.' A protest was signed by seventy professors and sent to the Minister claiming that the work did not harmonize with the neo-renaissance University Aula (main hall) and its mounting should be forbidden. A counter-motion advising the mounting of the painting in its destined place and its comparison with the other two panels before any judgement was made, gained only ten signatures. Among other objections, it hardly needs to be said, the painting was said to be obscene, an accusation to be even more violently repeated when *Medicine* was shown. In the meantime *Philosophy* was sent to the World Exposition in Paris and won the Grand Prix, an honour that produced no second thoughts among its enemies in Vienna.

Medicine was even worse, or better according to the viewpoint. Here the stream of human figures is on the right of the canvas. To the left a single female form, the source of life, attached to the swirling crowd by the outstretched arm of a man amongst it. A skeleton, a very old man, a pregnant woman, a pair of lovers, a mother and child and others are fronted by the dominant form of Hygeia about whose outstretched arm the snake of Aesculapius winds, its head in the flat chalice held by her other hand. This stern, inscrutable form is exotically draped. Across the naked human figures are scattered sharply focused cells.

Doctors objected that Klimt's picture was nothing like the graphic presentations they were used to and failed to show the two functions of medicine, healing and the prevention of disease. Both these things were true as far as they went; but the real objection was the brilliantly suggested impotence of the human condition that reduces medicine by implication, making doctors appear unavailing. When a reproduction was printed in the Secession magazine 'Ver Sacrum' (sacred spring) the public prosecutor seized it as obscene and a public affront. The Court did not uphold his prosecution. Asked for his opinion, Klimt said 'I haven't the time to interfere in these squabbles . . . for me the decisive thing is not how many people like a painting, but *whom* it pleases.' His real answer to the scholarly philistines he painted. A charming girl sits with her back to the viewer, her bottom towards them, looking over her shoulder with a smile. He called it *To my Critics* and then changed its title to *Goldfish* in reference to such a fish swimming towards the girl. This was not belated tact; everyone knew the real title. Klimt simply wanted to emphasize his indifference and scorn by making a meaningless concession with a pointless change.

Anything Klimt did at that moment would have aroused further fury. Since he was working intensively, he did not fail to provide fuel for the fire. Max Klinger's wonderful statue of Beethoven, who in his day had faced the same insensate rage, was to be enthroned in the centre of the Secession and Klimt made a frieze on the walls round it. The public giggled at the nude figures; the critics labelled them an orgy of nakedness, painted pornography, pathological fantasies. Others rushed quite unneeded to Klimt's defence. People seemed to have taken leave of their senses and every publicity seeker in Vienna added his meaningless comment.

With the showing of the third university ceiling the uproar became not only louder and more scurrilous, but lost its tenuous contact with common sense altogether; because to this representation of *Law* there was a valid objection to be made which was not made, although it must be underlined that this had nothing to do with the quality of the painting. Klimt's *Law* was even less reassuring than his view of medicine. A tormented and old male figure and three female nudes are encoiled by huge octopus-like tentacles. Over them stand, in embroidered draperies, three aspects of the subject. To the right a dark woman with her head askew holds the tablets of the Law. In the centre a female with closed eyes, in ceremonial robes, uplifts her left hand with two fingers extended – in blessing or commination? In her other hand she holds the huge sword, its point downwards. The third figure is even more enigmatic; fair-haired, conventionally pretty, with an almost coquettish tilt of head and posing of hands, half-draped. This figure has no waist-line and her stomach appears to be convex; is she pregnant and if she is, with what? Can it be possible she represents the un-reality of accepted concepts, inhuman in their neat formality? There are masculine heads grouped at the feet of the central figure with the sword but they are subordinate to the symbols. The background shows rough stone masonry like that of a fortress or a prison. No, not a comforting view of jurisprudence. And at that time of belief in Law, intimidatingly subversive.

In the finish Klimt repaid his fees and requested that his works should be returned to him. There was another lawsuit before he got them back. In spite of the verdict of the protecting committee, the Minister of Education was forced to resign; the arts are taken seriously in that part of the world.

Why did the uproar happen? Other people were producing work in painting and architecture just as revolutionary; many of Otto Wagner's designs aroused considerable argument but it was comparatively reasonable discussion. There is a mob in every major city which will snigger at anything real and fresh; this canaille is by no means always or exclusively formed by the simple and the untaught. As everyone knows who has ever had something to say that goes against preconceived notions, the scurrility often comes with the coarsest vulgarity from those who might be expected to know better. This is sometimes the case where a group of professionals see the threat of material loss to themselves if a new vision establishes itself, and this accounts for the general hostility of 'critics' to the noncomformist.

It remains strange that the press in general joined the absurd outcry against Klimt, for the press then in Vienna was not only of high aesthetic standards but was itself largely edited and written by noncomformist 'outsiders'. The animosity of the University professors was motivated by their own interested view of their subjects and an understanding of philosophy, medicine or law does not presuppose aesthetic judgement or taste. The scholars condemned Klimt's 'philosophy' because they saw it through eyes heavily squinting towards a picture of Socrates seated in an olive grove and lecturing to a respectful group of handsome young boys. Doctors are bound to be suspicious of a view of their calling that implicitly suggests their powerlessness to change nature.

From the compositions of the three finished paintings it is clear that *Law* or *Jurisprudence* was intended as the centrepiece with *Philosophy* to its left and *Medicine* to its right. Probably the Minister of Education and his committee were unable to discern from the sketches submitted to them just how different the finished work was to be from the current fashion. They may too have failed to see in advance how disturbing the overall 'message' of the decorations would be, for they envisaged them simply as the formal completion of the new central hall of an existing and old institution. A university must in the first place be dedicated to the storing and handing on of the accumulated knowledge of the past to the future. Klimt's paintings formed not only a break in method. The concepts they express challenged a whole mental and moral system of accepted values. They were in themselves a revolutionary statement, a moral question that demanded an answer. To simplify, which is to oversimplify, the pictures express more clearly than any words could do an assertion and a question: that human beings are helpless, naked and ignorantly in bondage to the indifferent force of nature; that being so, what are philosophy, medicine and law *for*? Have philosophy, medicine or law any answer to the torment of reality? And the very posing of such questions contains in graphic form the proposition that the answers are

'Nothing, None'. This is a very serious proposal when it is placed in the centre of the organizational and official collecting place of scholarship in a society.

In this sense the academics and their allies among the scholars had a valid argument in their opposition to Klimt's paintings. This must be conceded especially if the problematic view of law is the centre as it is in real life, the fundament of civilization. To challenge law as a concept is to direct a question to the foundation of society, to civilization itself, and such a question at that time and in that place – one of the oldest universities of Europe – was unbearable and almost inconceivable. It is a dangerous thing to do anywhere and at any time and responsible people should consider deeply just what they are doing when they say as Klimt was saying, that law as such is an octopus that tortures human beings. All law needs constant reform and adaptation but that is not what Klimt was saying; he questioned law itself and that must be judged perilous and superficial. The codex held in the hand of Klimt's symbolic figure was not entitled 'the code of law'; it says simply '*Lex*'. To call the picture *Jurisprudence* was a casuistry.

And this great question was not veiled, removed into the theoretical. The naked human figures are terribly actual, real. The idealization of Makart's painting technique is gone as if it never existed; so is the transfer of time to a past that never was. Klimt's intimate feeling for physical life and the detailed realism of his figures offended not morality, but the falsely sentimental unrealism of popular taste. The decadence of which the artist was accused existed, but it was in the public and not in Klimt. It would not be correct to claim, no matter how often it is in fact said, that Klimt was a prophet of the future. Klimt's eye was turned to his present society which fed itself on the past and a past at that which never existed. What people hated in Klimt was that his human figures, unprettified and undecorated – the surrounding elaborations only emphasized the realness of the bodies – made them see clearly. That they did not want to do and they cursed as decadence what exposed their own decadence. It is by no means so, as the popular view of the artist has it, that great artists always expose shams; quite the contrary, the arts usually reflect the shams of the societies they belong to, as the pre-Raphaelites did then in contemporary England. They retreated into the very historicism and prettiness that never existed in creative (as distinct from formal) portraiture painting in France at that time, and was overthrown by Klimt and his friends in central Europe. Pointedly enough in present-day Vienna a whole generation of painters has largely rejected the modern ignoring of realism in western Europe, which has retreated into subjective 'abstract' inhumanity.

Klimt himself was a painter for his own time. But the story of the great scandal of the university ceilings has an afterword. The three paintings were immediately bought for large sums – Klimt was always successful – when they once more became his property. They were all destroyed by fire at the end of the Second World War in the holocaust of chaos. It is said, as it inevitably would be, that they were deliberately burned by a German officer but that is not in fact known. It is uncharacteristic if it was so, unless the officer had been ordered to burn them, which is highly unlikely at that moment of European disaster. But if a few of the combatants did see Klimt's view of philosophy, medicine and law in the landscape of horror that was 1945, it is almost understandable that they might have felt an overpowering impulse to destroy it. What indeed was left of the rule of knowledge in that moment except the power of the artist impotently to warn?

8

Herzl in Vienna

THEODOR Herzl, the founder of modern Zionism and ideological father of the State of Israel, is famous. Herzl as a citizen of Vienna is not only much less well-known but has been understandably distorted by the importance of his political achievement, by subsequent events in central Europe and more than by either, by having been made a latter-day Moses. That he was, quite literally. The human being, however, was when alive, far from monumental. Inside the marble statue of the prophet was a deeply divided, lonely and unhappy man who never once succeeded in establishing a close and lasting relationship of his own choice. The two continuing ties of his life were dictated; with his parents by nature and with his employers by a necessity characterized on Herzl's side by impatience and resentment and on the other by an increasingly weary and wary toleration.

Theodor Herzl was thirty-one years old, two years married and father of two children when he took up his first and only full-time job. He was delighted by the offer to be the correspondent in Paris of the *Neue Freie Presse* because he felt the need of a steady salary; but he thought of himself as a playwright. As a student he had set himself a goal, to have a play produced at the Burgtheater in Vienna. In doing so he classed himself with the greatest writers in the German language past and contemporary, but this was an enormous overestimation of his histrionic talent. In all, sixteen texts were staged including collaborations and operetta. When a play was at last accepted by the Burg it was the product of a collaboration and formed part of that body of light alternatives to the great classical plays which is needed in all the European repertory theatres. Herzl's plays were quite simply not very good. With one exception he copied popular successes derived from contemporary models and contrived in every other sense, of plot, dialogue and characterization. The exception, *The New Ghetto*, a serious psychological study of emancipated Jewishness, was unhappily as wooden and unreal as those plays written solely to make money. There is little doubt that if Herzl had not been known as a writer of light commentaries and short stories for the most powerful newspaper of the Dual Monarchy, and if he had not been acquainted through the newspaper with a number of theatrical personalities, he would never have achieved his ambition to appear on the stage of the Burgtheater. But he felt himself, at least for a time, to be a rival of Arthur Schnitzler, which can be taken as a measure of his own opinion of himself. It is not easy to discuss German writers in terms understandable to English-speakers, but Schnitzler was almost a genius whose fame only did not reach London, Paris and New York because the spiritual chasm of the 1914–18 war cut the culture of Europe in half. It is rather as if a journalist on *The Times* who has had short stories published just because he is known to work for that august journal were to compare himself in his own mind with Henry James. In view of his actual achievement the comparison may appear absurd, but Herzl does not need the hagiography of those who benefited from his sacrifice of himself; there is always something humiliating, even insulting, in the adoration of the heirs of a great man. If he had not misjudged his talents and the direction in which they lay, Herzl would probably never have reacted with such inner force to the goad of anti-Semitism, could not have achieved what he did. It was as much his disappointment with the theatre, just near enough to success for some years for that disillusion to be decisive, that turned his restless vitality into other channels as it was the plight of the Jews that drove him. Indeed he knew little of the desperate conditions of Russian Jewry until the last years of his short life. It was disappointed ambition that fired him; that and his unhappy marriage.

The hard fact of lack of success taught Herzl that he would never be a major name in the theatre. He reacted outwardly by cursing the theatre directors who failed to appreciate him but he knew the real reason and it comes through in his letters. The complete and immediate failure of his marriage cured him for ever of any hope or desire for personal happiness. This was blamed on his wife and Herzl discussed it with intimates solely in terms of his own anger, his misery. Nothing is less likely to be correct than the judgments of outsiders on a marriage but neither success nor disaster in marriage is ever one sided; nor is it a matter as a rule of praise and blame but one of temperament. What is known of the Herzl partnership is entirely one sided. If Julie Herzl did tell her story it has not survived, nor is she with one startling exception, ever quoted. The comment she made in the early days of her acquaintanceship with her future husband, was in answer to a question as to the point of pursuing an affair for which there could be no future; she replied simply 'the present'. There seemed to be no prospect for a rich girl in a would-be suitor with no profession and in fact Theodor abruptly broke off the friendship without explanation to Julie but for that reason, as he told friends. Julie's answer on that occasion shows a directness of perception that implies intelligence and realism; moreover if she did not intend to lose the present for other chances, she clearly felt something for Herzl from the start. Within weeks of the wedding there was trouble. Two years later, not for the first time, the possibility of divorce was formally explored. Herzl's wife was pretty, rich and pampered. The husband was intimately and passionately attached to his parents who constantly interfered. Julie is said to have been hysterical, to have staged suicide attempts and is described at least once as psychotic without objective evidence of this being produced. During her first pregnancy her husband left home for a longish journey and again at once after the birth of a longed-for son. Just after the first child was born he wrote a play lampooning women and marriage. He addressed Julie in letters as 'my dear child' and signed himself as her father from the start. To another correspondent he referred to his return home after a separation as giving Julie one last chance. The cause of that departure, a year after the wedding and just after the birth of his first daughter, was Julie's refusal to apologize to her mother-in-law. Most of Herzl's letters to his wife have disappeared although the empty envelopes were kept. In all the published accounts it is taken for granted that Julie was culpable in spending her large dowry on the household and her own expenses.

According to the assumptions of the time and place these are circumstances which indicate an unusual attitude on the part of a husband towards his wife and of outsiders towards both of them. Nor was the marriage a sudden decision for they knew each other for three years before the wedding. It seems unlikely in the sociable little world of rich bourgeois Jewry that a history of Julie's mental instability would have been neither noticed nor mentioned in that time. Still, all three of the Herzl children were definitely unstable if not insane. Two of them committed suicide and the third died in Theresienstadt when it was a concentration camp during the Second World War, after spending years in mental hospitals. Herzl's only grandson also died by his own hand. It cannot be said now from which side of the family this strain was introduced for Herzl contracted a venereal disease during his student days, an affliction often leading to hereditary physical and mental weaknesses.

Herzl adopted in his student years a pose of arrogant unconcern, a worldly supercilious air by no means uncommon in very young men. Even much later his fellow-Zionists have left complaints of his egotistic and autocratic ways. If Herzl retained this defensive affectation into his adult life with other men, it seems possible that he failed to abandon it too with his wife. Most men begin to lose such barriers as unneeded in their intimate lives and if Herzl kept it up an inexperienced girl would accept the pose as real and rely on guidance from what would appear to her as an experienced partner so that if not modified it would lead to deep disappointments and misunderstandings. Girls then even more than now, live in a fantasy construction before their initiation into the dense and tense mesh of real life and the transfer cannot easily be made without a period of desire and psychic surrender on both sides which fixes for some years and sometimes for life the 'realness' of the other person. Where rigid barriers are maintained on either side – and these are strongly implied in the continued attempt to treat a wife as a child while her husband sees himself as her father – there is bound to be trouble unless the wife accepts the falsehood. In Herzl's case the girl was rich and the possession of money always strengthens a wife's position vis-a-vis her husband; she was pretty, an acknowledged attraction to men and aware of it, and probably of strong erotic drives. Violent quarrels between young married people are sometimes a sign of too much sex rather than too little but where the over-excited nerves are on one side only this is normally a sign of sexual frustration and very likely Julie's 'hysteria' was no exception. However, it is not known for certain whether it was Julie who always provoked the devastating scenes that continually disrupted their life together because the accounts and hints we have are without exception from Herzl's point of view.

What can be said with certainty is that the marriage was a disaster from the beginning and that both partners were very unhappy.

It was during the journey in which Herzl escaped from his wife after the birth of his son that he was offered the post as Paris correspondent for the *Neue Freie Presse*. The offer was made on the strength of the essays, travel sketches and commentaries by Herzl published in the paper for several years past; this was the kind of writing at which he excelled.

The *Neue Freie Presse* was founded in Vienna after the revolutions of 1848. It was of Manchester-liberal politics but very far from radical in the modern sense of 'liberal', being very conservative in style as in opinions. Its fame was such that respectable and prosperous provincials often caused 'subscriber to the *Neue Freie Presse*' to be engraved on their visiting cards as Englishmen of the same time announced the names of their clubs. It was published and edited by Jews, like most of the major newspapers of the Empire, but did not emphasize its Jewishness while steadily opposing all discrimination including anti-Semitism. Its undeviating editorial 'line' was complete loyalty to the Dual Monarchy – a term which strictly speaking should only be used after the first Austro-Hungarian customs and trade agreement of 1867 – and to the person of the Emperor Franz Joseph.

Like many an excellent newspaper then and since its only serious fault was that its editors sometimes conceived their duty to lie in politics or diplomacy rather than in reporting what was going on. For this reason, to take examples of future importance, the *Neue Freie Presse* consistently failed for twenty years to mention the existence of the working-class movement or to discuss the wisdom of the German-Austrian defence pact of 1879. Nor was the Zionist movement ever discussed in spite of its being led by one of its senior editors. The exclusion from open discussion of a mass political party is so extraordinary as to seem impossible. Nevertheless it is a fact, and a fact repeated often in other papers, other countries in different contexts; not least in our own time. Nobody who has ever worked with news can have failed to notice the tremendous strength of habit and imitation in its publication, so that accepted views and trends are continually emphasized for years after their hold has been lost on real public opinion. Of course there were other, including specifically socialist organs which reported the activities of the working-class movement; but the newspaper which reflected Austria-Hungary in the rest of the world never even admitted its existence. It was the same with the forming of what came to be known as the central powers, or the Triple Alliance of 1882. There *may* never have been a sensible alternative to the German alliance for the Dual Monarchy, but there is no doubt that the lack of any discussion in the dominant organ of public opinion in Vienna made any such possibility distinctly less likely than it might have been. In these two large areas of news the want of public information had serious, indeed fateful, and long-lasting consequences.

In the matter of Zionism the results were not so massive, for the movement gathered strength somewhere else. The publishers and with one exception the editors of the paper believed in the assimilation of the Jews into Gentile if not into Christian society and this made them implicitly anti-Zionist. But modern Zionism, although its progenitor was Viennese, was not centred in Austria but in Russia which then included much of Poland. In ignoring this development the publishers of the *Presse* felt that they were declining to be used for propaganda in a cause they thought misconceived and mischievous to the welfare of both Jews and Christians in the Empire. They rested their conviction in the long course of amelioration of life in real terms for Jewish citizens which dated from the reforms of Maria Theresia in the eighteenth century and which had advanced rapidly since 1848 and the accession of the Emperor Franz Joseph. It was a process of assimilation, including that of much intermarriage, which was actually taking place and visibly succeeding. Most educated Jews believed it would overcome the large influx of 'eastern' Jews from Galicia, Transylvania, and by infiltration from Russia. They looked upon publicity for Zionism and even its existence as a hindrance in a beneficent process. The considerable immigration of poor Jews was caused by the official and violent anti-Semitism in Russia and in turn it caused a widespread but still inert and officially disapproved anti-Semitism in the big towns of central Europe. Figures are largely unreliable for many of the Jewish immigrants were illicit but for a time at any rate newcomers reached a noticeable proportion of the indigenous populace of Vienna; Jews were, of course, not the only group of fresh arrivals, and the Czechs were just as unpopular as the Jews. Between 1859 and 1890 the whole population rose from just under half a million to 1.34 million.

The discussion of this new atmosphere in the capital is not

made easier or more objective by the use of terms such as 'brutal violence' by recent commentators influenced by the much later twelve years of the Nazi time and its dreadful events. The demonstrations and riots in Vienna about the turn of the century, as in Paris and London, were not in fact inspired by anti-Semitism. They were hunger riots, industrial disputes and populist demonstrations caused by the hesitation of the Imperial authorities to recognize an enormously popular local politician as Mayor of the city. This repeated refusal to recognize an elected Mayor was loudly backed by the press which was largely Jewish and this increased anti-Semitism both in Karl Lueger himself and among his followers. But to write of brutal violence in the streets of Vienna at a time when officially encouraged pogroms in which dozens and not seldom hundreds of people were robbed and killed in Russia is quite simply untrue. Sometimes Jews were beaten up, sometimes Jewish as well as Gentile factories got their windows broken, there were diatribes against Jewish and Gentile financiers. There were several rural cases of Jews being accused of the ritual murder of Christian children in which the defendants were acquitted by the Courts. But nothing remotely like the hundreds of thousands of the Paris mob screaming 'down with the Jews' and 'hang the Jews' that surrounded the military academy when Captain Dreyfus was stripped of his officer's insignia and his sword broken, was ever seen in Vienna. The real reason the disorders, which included anti-Semitic outbreaks, caused such outrage in Vienna was precisely because they were so extraordinary in a populace noted for slowness and even indolence as well as for urbanity. The reasons for the unrest of the times all over Europe were the rapid and great changes in economic and social life which made large masses of the people emotionally unstable. Irresponsible propaganda made the anti-Semitism worse but the reasons for it are not so mysterious as it is often supposed. Theodor Herzl recognized them clearly as being rooted in economic strains, which they were. The cause of a large immigration of noticeably 'different' Jews to Vienna as to the large cities of Germany, lay in the extensive pogroms in Russia and to a lesser extent in Rumania. These poor people of lower social and hygienic standards than the Viennese, worked harder for smaller wages than the native working class and were naturally more frugal and vigorous as small traders than the old lower middle class. They were consequently disliked and their undoubted virtues as citizens looked upon as faults.

But they were as much disliked as immigrants as Jews and the difference in the reputation of Viennese Jews compared with the 'easterners' was enormous. In other words, the anti-Semitism in Vienna up to the First World War was largely a class feeling and was widely shared by Jewish Viennese, including Herzl whose strictures on Jews and Jewishness would have been considered sharply anti-Semitic had he not been a Jew himself. Herzl's attitude to Jewishness until his middle thirties was that it ought to disappear, and his views on 'money Jews' remained virulently hostile.

It is always difficult and perhaps particularly so in this case, to imagine what an atmosphere was in the past. There is a certain latent xenophobia in all big cities, strongly to be felt for instance by any stranger living today in Paris or London. As a matter of personal experience this rejection of strangers is rather less in Vienna than in many cities, probably because it was for centuries a focal point of many races and languages and the Viennese themselves are very mixed. Vienna to this day is full of people who are only partly of German stock and yet are not quite foreigners, but as it were, adopted. Until 1918 there were many families in government and military service whose origins were foreign, including for years a Prime Minister whose family came from Ireland and went back there. Later events make it hard to judge how different from such people educated and prosperous Jewish citizens were made to feel and how much of their feeling of being different was subjective, cases of what Herzl called the New Ghetto. It is certainly a fact of ordinary observation that Jews often insist on their different-ness before others even notice that they are Jewish. At that time

Arthur Schnitzler complained of being made to feel his Jewishness, but until he became famous he and his family mixed almost exclusively in Jewish circles so that his great success as a writer took him into a much larger society in which he may — as anyone else of non-Jewish background might — have felt provincial and defensive. In a society where careers but not social standing were open to the talents long before Napoleon invented the phrase, feelings of being treated as socially inferior can by no means have been confined to Jews. All mixed societies strongly impose their own customs on newcomers and do it explicitly; this is a major difference between London and New York and between Paris and Vienna. In neither Paris nor London will anyone tell a stranger how he should do things because the native way of doing them is taken for granted as the only possible way. In New York and Vienna one may be told and if the skin is thin one may resent it, gratitude only seeping in with experience.

Theodor Herzl's childhood was spent in the city of his birth, Budapest. The Herzls did not move to Vienna until he was eighteen. They had intended the move so that Theodor could attend Vienna University but it was hastened by their grief at the death of the only other child, Pauline, at nineteen from typhoid fever. Psychologically this was a complex change for the boy.

All Jews were of German language and culture no matter what language or vernacular was spoken around them and from far to the east looked towards German society as being of higher standards. The transfer from Yiddish to correct German was a watershed of achievement for thousands of Polish, Ukrainian and Rumanian Jews. This was of course not so for the Herzls. They were educated and wealthy and had lived consciously as Germans in Budapest, speaking and writing the pure German of cultivated people without local dialect or accent. In 1878, the same year as the loss of his sister and the move, Theodor entered Vienna University to study law; three major changes which were much intensified by the now complete concentration of his parents on their remaining child.

Jeannette Herzl was undoubtedly a text-book example of what in German is called 'the man-killing mother', a type by no means confined to Jewish families. An only son, he was brought up to feel himself intellectually superior and of superior culture to his neighbours who spoke Magyar; he was constantly flattered by the high hopes confidently expressed of his future. Yet he was a new arrival in the acknowledged centre of the German culture he belonged to as well as to the University. There was only the vacation gap between tightly disciplined school and University in his case and he had been encouraged to believe in his own genius without any competition from his equals; almost by definition he was going to have a bad time and he did. To cap everything Theodor was noticeably good-looking which is by no means an unmixed blessing in a juvenile male context; its advantages appear elsewhere and usually later.

He enjoyed Vienna, living on the spacious, leafy edge of the huge Prater and within a few minutes of a powerful and beautiful centre of every kind of aesthetic, intellectual and sensuous experience. The law did not much interest him – it was never intended that he should practise – and he showed only a mediocre success in its study. After settling down to the customs of student life he began to take part in both organized and free activity with his fellow students.

During Herzl's University years the reaction to the defeat of Austria by Prussia in 1866 and the consequent intransigence of the Hungarian half of the Empire had crystallized as a new and conscious nationalism. The Czechs too at this time wanted and got the use of their own language in local courts and administrative offices together with German. In itself an enlightened reform, this caused unease among the lower ranks of civil servants in Bohemia and Austria by adding another language to the skills needed for promotion. It also had the effect of restricting the easy transfer of officials of all language-groups throughout the Empire and thus provincialized and localized large territories.

This new feeling was internally divided into two trends; one showed attachment and loyalty to Habsburg Austria and therefore to the past and the other, composed of instinctive power-lovers for whom we lack a word in English, turned on Austria as power-lovers always do at any loss of power, with anger and contempt. They wanted to belong to the vigorous north-German dominance and in their extreme forms demanded the break-up of the Dual Monarchy, the assimilation of Austria into Germany, the end of Habsburg rule and eventually the end of the established Catholic faith enshrined in that rule. Austrian patriotism arose as a reaction against Magyar separatism and was a healthy and natural self-preservation, the attachment to an organization which had held the Danube against barbarism since the tenth century. The Hungarians then and the two Slav nationalisms later failed to understand this necessity until it was much too late and they had to learn the nature of power by irrecoverably losing it. This was a deep change of feeling in Austria which was naturally little understood by ordinary people and was a major cause of growing psychic instability.

The young Theodor, being passionately German, became a German nationalist, joining a duelling fraternity at the University called 'Albia', admiring the anti-Semitic Georg von Schoenerer and almost worshipping Richard Wagner. On Wagner's death in February 1883 a commemoration was held by the students at which among a good deal of other enthusiastic nonsense an anti-Semitic speech was delivered by Hermann Bahr. Herzl resigned from his fraternity with ill-feeling on all sides. This showed two of his strongest characteristics, courage and pride, for other Jewish students tried to stay with the nationalist movement until it openly rejected them. Herzl rejected those who would have turned on him before they could do so.

He had wanted to be a German knight as well as a German writer. Robbed of this ideal, he felt himself a stranger in the world. But he left University with a pass degree and with several unsuccessful attempts at getting short stories published already causing him depression. His mother had instilled into him an altogether too high expectation of his literary talent, with the result that when he found a kind of writing at which he excelled he felt disdain for it. He went for a short time to Salzburg as law clerk and enjoyed it but resigned from the law, giving as his reason that a Jew could never become a judge. Most writers about Herzl have taken his resignation and its reason seriously. In fact Herzl did not intend to be a lawyer and left the profession immediately when his training was finished; the appointment as law clerk being in Austria a required period of practical work. In this incident we see two constantly repeated misunderstandings at the same time: that Herzl resigned from his profession because of anti-Semitism in government service and that a Jew could never be a judge. Theodor did not resign after a short experience of anti-Semitism or anything else; should he have wished to return to the law later he could not have done so unless he had carried out his 'Praktikum' and he therefore went through it before leaving the law for good. The second common misapprehension was a logical and respectable consequence of the Catholic foundation of the Habsburg Empire and its derivation from the Holy Roman Empire of the German Nation founded by Charlemagne. It was not Jews who could not become Judges; it was any non-Catholic.

The shock of his quarrel with 'Albia' was a milestone in Herzl's life, there can be no doubt. A more general event at the same time which was one of the causes of the student anti-Semitism and therefore of Theodor's break with his fraternity, is usually considered to be a separate issue in his life but it was really the 'intellectual' background to his personal discovery of insuperable differentness. This was Eugen Duehring's book on the *racial* nature of the 'Jewish problem' which is now only remembered because Karl Marx wrote an answer to it. At the time it was famous and Duehring's reputation as a German scholar gave it a weight its contents did not deserve so that it was a dangerous incitement to hatred. Educated Jews read it and it was half-covertly much discussed in Jewish circles for some time. That it was accepted as serious argument when it was in fact scurrilous rubbish was indeed frightening and it was much more important than Wagner's well-advertised and childish attacks of anti-Semitism; great artists always have a certain licence for eccentricity. Duehring's treatise took on a spurious academic respectability in an era of belief in science and as Theodor noted, it was well-written and persuasive in its scholarly tone. It certainly had an effect on Gentiles and Jews alike for some years. For Herzl, with the sharp sting of the 'Albia' humiliation paining him, it opened up the black prospect of a world in which Jews could not be assimilated.

But he travelled at his father's expense, he wrote all the time and began to have things published, plays were at last performed, he married.

When Herzl first went to Paris he lived in an hotel, later his family joined him and with a certain inevitability his parents too for a time. But in Paris the stranger in the world became simply a foreigner in a foreign city. The correspondents of major newspapers in those days were persons of prestige. The representative of the London *Times* in Paris lived like an ambassador and was treated like one. From this vantage point Herzl, with the new feeling of being a neutral onlooker without a fixed identity, saw the operations of politics from close at hand; he saw how the world is run. And he hoped he saw too that anti-Semitism was something that belonged to central and eastern Europe.

To suppose that the Dreyfus scandal was what changed Herzl's view of the world is simplistic. His play *The New Ghetto* was already written and its author involved in complicated attempts to get it performed by the time Alfred Dreyfus was arrested. This play was a serious effort to argue that European Jews had carried the ghetto with them into the outside society they now lived in. Its writing was the last stage in Herzl's development before he consciously adopted the idea of a Jewish State. What the trial of Dreyfus for treason must have done to Herzl was to drive him beyond the point where he could deceive himself any longer that Jewish assimilation into European society was possible.

Because it did not happen in Russia or in Germany, or Austria or Hungary. It happened in France, in Paris. The persisting hope that for some reason anti-Semitism was an exclusively central and eastern European phenomenon was destroyed. Accounts of anti-Semitism then and since have often shown a curious dichotomy about France which at times amount to deliberate deception. The proposition was and is that anti-Semitism does not exist in France. The mob howling outside the court and again outside the barrack square on the dreadful occasion of Dreyfus's degradation at which all the foreign newspaper reporters were present, removed all hope that this pious fraud could ever become true. That dark and cold morning must have been a terrible experience of humiliation and despair for Herzl as well as for its central figure. It brought to a bitter focus the sheer unavoidable impossibility of Jews living with dignity in a Gentile world. That hour of theatrical drama brought down a curtain on more than the tragedy of Alfred Dreyfus, more even than the exposure of the concept of military intrigue using a base emotion to protect its weaknesses, and that it could happen *in France* ended a noble illusion of European civilization: the high concept that different faiths and clans could live together in mutual tolerance and respect.

Personal failure as a 'great writer', personal defeat in the crucial relationship of marriage, left Herzl's psychic vitality without direction or outlet. The moment of destiny was there at which the whole drive of his nature turned towards a purpose of hard and real idealism. It is a rare nobility of human nature to change the meanness of personal defeat into a cause that carries the individual out of his small ego and into humanity. From that time to the end of his short life, in the ten years that remained to him, Herzl evolved not Zionism, which had existed for nearly two thousand years, but the means of harnessing the longing for Zion into effective action.

Like all great ideas Herzl's was in essence simple. It was to provide funds to buy land for a Jewish State under the protection of one of the great powers and thus to turn the Jews of the diaspora into a nation. He expressed this idea in 'The Jewish State' published in 1896. He had no funds and no great power. The rest of his life was a confidence trick of staggering virtuosity.

The first Dreyfus trial was in December 1895 and in the following September Herzl returned to Vienna as literary editor of his paper. He returned to a city in which the atmosphere had radically changed. Not only Jews were now dismayed by the submerged fears channelled into anti-Semitism by the irresponsible electioneering, the arousing of base emotions, of Karl Lueger. Among them was Hermann Bahr, by that time a well-known writer who had made a complete turn, or perhaps truer to say had grown up, from his student days when he introduced anti-Semitic comments into his panegyric for Richard Wagner and thus caused Herzl's resignation from his student fraternity. Bahr had recently published a survey of anti-Semitism and come to the wise conclusion that it was an opiate as well as a kind of fashion. The need of this mental drug was not caused by widespread want because it was a time of considerable prosperity. The spreading of any irrational emotion, including hatred, among large groups of people is caused by great and continuing changes in economic and social customs, including benign changes. If the customs and habits of masses of people are in movement for too long and without reasons understood by everybody, which they rarely are, atavistic fears come to the surface. Nothing is more infectious than fear and it can spread like wildfire even without encouragement. Modern communications which belong to the late nineteenth century (they have only been intensified and accelerated in the twentieth) both constituted change in themselves, and speeded the spread of unease. It is not easy for the Americans or the British to understand the fear of encroachment which is a condition of life for peoples who are bordered entirely or mainly by land frontiers. At the same time internally an old and conservative large group of the population in several countries, including Austria, was menaced by economic changes.

Any impoverishment or threat, whether explicit or not, to the stolid lower middle classes which in all societies are at once the anchor and the cushion – no apology for the mixed metaphor which is intended to startle – of the mass psyche, is dangerous. A society that *allows* the stability of this group to be undermined is allowing a crime against itself to be committed which will inevitably revenge itself on the whole polity. A society that *encourages* the undermining of the stability of its lower middle classes is in a state of degeneracy that amounts to a death-wish. The actual removal of a widely based populace of small property-owners must and always does result in the imposition of a lost real stability by police rule. But any serious threat to that block of ponderous humanity is enough to produce irrational as well as rational fears which will show in growth of superstition, belief in universal nostrums, perverse longings for strong leadership, which is the last thing the middle classes need. Clownish fads and fashions of all kinds; envy, febrile angers, adoration of public figures, hatred of non-conforming groups, and many other unpleasant symptoms all issue in mass forms as a kind of psychic hypochondria.

These states of mind, repeated thousandfold in individuals, will fix themselves upon any noticeable group of strangers as hatred unless the causes of fear are understood and removed. A well-established middle class may take generations to undermine but the injection of more than a certain, as yet undetermined, proportion of identifiable strangers will hasten the process.

In Austria the lower middle class was deeply and widely

established. Its fundament was the dispersed ownership of land in small units, so that many thousands of families knew from birth that they were safe. To this establishment belonged the custom, codified by the great Maria Theresia in the eighteenth century, of artisan apprenticeship that ensured a sound training in useful trades to all non-landowning persons such as younger sons. The word 'Bauer' has a meaning of social rank in rural Austria to this day and is only used of the head of the family and his wife, the Bäuerin; they are called in their own parish not by their surname but by the name of their holding. Smith who owns Greenacres is not Schmidt, he is Grünacker Bauer. The customary and real standing of a farming woman, bride or daughter, is exactly measured by the property she has to bring into her alliance. This whole establishment has been recognized for many generations as a chief pillar of the State and not only in Austria. In towns the artisans including shop-keepers, came from and maintained this establishment.

There was always a proletariat, especially in mining and the metal industries, building, printing, textiles; but it was (and is) a trained work force and was until recently employed in small units near to its family bases. Both the new mobility of the railways and the concentration of manufacturing into larger units needing capital and credit above the capacity of single families, disturbed this old pattern. From an economic and strategic point of view the industrial expansion was not nearly large enough for such a big State; and its smallness was a considerable factor in the decisive loss of Austria's leading position in the German world in 1866. Dependence on German industry was indirectly responsible for the failure of Austrian diplomacy to influence German policy in the twenty years before 1914 and, fatally for Europe, during that war. The other cause of loss of control over Germany as a whole was the Hungarian question which tied the hands of the Emperor and his ministers in all departments of government. Which is not to say that Franz Joseph would have understood the need for a competent native industry; he might not have done but the continuous haggling and preoccupation with Hungary, the overriding need to hold the two parts of his Empire together, removed any possibility of it. The endemic uncertainty of relations between Austria and Hungary were, naturally, a serious cause of unease in themselves.

The new industries got their work forces from the general increase of population and from increasing movement towards large towns from all corners of the multi-lingual empire. This happened everywhere but in Austria with the added strains of language differences. These newcomers were of course by no means all, or even mainly, Jewish. But the Jews were the group that possessed a recognizable summit. Upper class Jews helped to operate the enlarged finance market and were, thanks to their love of learning and the uprush of intellectual vitality from emancipation, dominant in the press. They were not dominant but still noticeable and influential in the learned professions and the arts; and especially in the theatre this became unpopular, not only in Vienna. It may be mentioned in passing, since it is often ignored, that there is nothing disreputable in people who love the theatre and take it seriously, wishing it to remain in their own control, and to speak in their inherited idioms.

The main object of fear and dislike, however, was the finance market, the Stock Exchange. People did not want to need more money or to be in debt and the dislike was not confined to anti-Semites; some of Herzl's diatribes against 'money Jews' could have been incorporated into Hitler's speeches without changing much. Naturally all the financiers were not Jewish but 'Turkish' Hirsch and the Rothschilds, who all built railways, and their friends were very powerful and very visible. The almost complete lack of interest among aristocratic Austrians and Hungarians in industry, commerce and finance, added to this visibility and to narrow membership of the finance-operating market. They were much publicised in terms inciting hatred and mainly by Jews. Writers such as the owners of the *Presse*, Bacher and Benedikt, Herzl himself and above all the satirist Karl Kraus, did more than their part; they did their own people a savagely ill turn in their strictures and lampoons against the Stock Exchange. Ordinary people do not understand finance as distinct from money, and when finance fails, as in the great slumps and in inflations, its mysterious failures frighten people because money seems to acquire a malign life of its own.

The old town middle classes lived cheek by jowl with the new proletariat; quarters became overcrowded, everyone could see what awaited him in factory and slum if his small business failed in competition with the new commerce and industry. In spite of prosperity people feared the future because they felt their control over their own destinies loosen. The fear coming from rapid and prolonged change was acted upon by politicians and publicists for both moral and immoral reasons. Prosperity itself is often the cause of fear because people have more to lose and sudden increases in goods and money appear, and often are, of uncertain duration.

By the time Herzl returned to Vienna this complex of feeling was widespread and was already grafted on to the much older and taken-for-granted vague religious anti-Semitism. Certainly religious anti-Semitism is absurd and disgusting, but it plays little part in Herzl's story because he felt no attachment to his own or any other religion. He knew hardly anything of the Jewish faith or its customs and it is clear that if he had felt any respect for religion he could not have suggested, as he once did, a mass baptism of Viennese Jews in St Stephen's Cathedral. He was so much an unbeliever that it seems never to have occurred to him, not even when his publisher pointed it out, that this proposal was an insult to the Mosaic as well as to the Christian religion. Quite in the ethos of his time, his religion was nationalism. If anything, he disliked his own religion and always insisted on the worldly nature of his own Jewish patriotism. He was discovering at this time the ancient plight of his own people under

Russian rule, where a corrupt religiosity made them outcasts. His own consciousness, sharply increased by recent events in Paris, must have been touched by guilt that he had not known about this suffering and humiliation of his own people and this shows in many comments of his. He was becoming aware that the great dynamism of Zionist longing came principally from the Jews in Russia and with good reason.

Fired by his own vision of the Jewish State, Herzl was profoundly shocked by the now general anti-Semitism in Vienna which no longer made a clear distinction between Viennese citizens and 'easterners'. He saw the populist politician Lueger as first and foremost anti-Semitic; this was not so. The Christian Social movement was not more than incidentally, almost cynically, anti-Semitic; it used polemics against finance, big industry and the Jews to bind the loyalties of Lueger's followers to him. None the less shameful for that. They were unworthy of an able and devoted man who did much for his fellow citizens and would be a blot on Lueger's reputation even if they had not influenced the future. This influence was never as great as is often thought on Hitler. Hitler learned his jumble of disgusting notions from a sub-culture of half-educated fools such as are to be found in all large cities believing in the interpretation of the world by measuring the Great Pyramid and writing lascivious accounts of the kind of beautiful women they would like to dominate but cannot. What Lueger may have shown Hitler and others was the structure and control of mass-movements; it was certainly he who showed this skill to the Austrian Socialists. There is no reason, either, to suppose that Russian conspirators like Bronstein spent their exile time in Vienna without learning something from this master of mob-control.

There is a famous passage in Herzl's political diary which expresses his observation at this time; translated it runs:

'20 September 1895. Local elections were held in Vienna on the day before *Erew Rausch Haschonoh* (sic: the Jewish

229

New Year's Eve). Every seat fell to the anti-Semites. The Jews are in a mood of despair. The Christians are much inflamed.

'Actually, the movement is not noisy. For me, used as I am to the uproar of demonstrations in Paris, it is much too quiet. I find this calm more uncanny. Yet everywhere one sees looks of hatred, even if one does not search for them in the eyes of the people with the lurking fear of persecution mania.

'On election day I was in the Leopoldstadt [Second District, then and now the most Jewish quarter of Vienna] in front of the polling booth to see a little of the hate and rage for myself close to.

'Towards evening I walked up the Landstrasse [a main street of the Third District, Lueger's own district]. In front of the election centre a silent, excited crowd. Suddenly Dr Lueger came out into the square. Enthusiastic cheers; from the windows women waved white kerchiefs. The police held the people back. Next to me, someone said with tender warmth "that is our leader".

'More than any declamation or cursing this phrase showed me how deeply anti-Semitism is rooted in the hearts of this population.'

On the face of it, it is not easy to see why. If the phrase, which then meant nothing but what it said, had been intended as a jibe at Herzl, it would not have been spoken in a tone of tender warmth; clearly Herzl was not recognized as a Jew by the man next to him. And he records no hesitation in walking about the streets unaccompanied during the evening of the triumph of the anti-Semites. No violence was expected and there was none. It was the quiet itself that worried him. In other words it was the atmosphere.

No Mayor, no matter how large his majority, can change the laws of a country and Lueger was in any case not confirmed as Mayor – a matter that did cause the Viennese to show their anger, but to the monarch, who was treated with cold silence

in Vienna on several occasions in sharp contrast to the affection
and respect he normally received. So educated Jews cannot have
feared anti-Jewish measures. What Herzl and many others,
Jews and Gentiles, felt was the atmosphere of change, and
change for the worse. Jews felt it as anti-Semitism because of
the scurrilous electioneering of the Christian Social Party, but
it was felt all over Europe. The euphoria of scientific progress
was gone and this was beginning to issue in the arts as reaction
against the over-decorated vulgarity in the accepted styles of
painting, architecture and music. In England self-confidence
continued for another twenty years, but all over the mainland
of Europe fear of the future grew.

This was the beginning of the time of mass-movements and
Theodor Herzl himself was the originator of one of them which
only did not become a mass exodus because he died untimely.
With the rise of mass parties came the men who achieved power
by manipulating mobs.

Hag-ridden by this lowering atmosphere Herzl developed a
driving energy. At first he had believed that the great Jewish
fortunes would finance Zionism. But although the Rothschilds
and others founded colonies in Palestine and gave large sums
to their own charities, they neither wanted a Jewish State nor
did they feel any confidence in it. Nor did less the well-known
but still wealthy bourgeoisie. Rabbis preached against Herzl and
Zionism in the Viennese synagogues. He was not invited to the
drawing rooms of the charming and intelligent Viennese Jewish
ladies. Karl Kraus wrote an essay entitled 'A Crown for Zion'
making fun of him and not only the title slid close to blas-
phemy. The very people who pulled the *Presse* out of each
others' hands to read Herzl's essays and those of his many discoveries, did not want to know him or his ideas; that his view
of the future was prophesy was the last thing they wanted to
believe, and who can blame them? Indeed, they said that Herzl
encouraged the anti-Semitism of the vulgar populace and gave it
fuel. In many of his complaints against the Viennese Herzl

was in fact speaking of the Viennese Jews and particularly of his wife's family.

Most of what funds the Zionists had came from the membership subscriptions of the very poor. In his chase for money which he hated, and for the protection of Israel by a great power which he longed for, Herzl's life turned into a succession of journeys. He rushed from France to England, to Zionist Congress and Baden and Berlin and Turkey, then back again to France and England. Later he went to Russia to try to persuade the Tsar's ministers that by supporting Zionism they could rid themselves of many revolutionary conspirators; it was the time of constant terrorism in Russia when assassination was frequent. That the revolutionaries were often Jewish was a natural consequence of their being shut out of every form of public life; as soon as this tradition was slightly relaxed so that Jews could enter lay education to some extent, they devoted themselves to the concept of radical change in society simply because any change must for them be for the better. This consideration influenced the German government too, but in neither case was the wish to rid the State of radicals put into action.

The Zionist movement grew by leaps and bounds, especially after the first Zionist Congress at Basle in 1897. The Congress was at first to take place at Munich, the meeting place being changed at the instance of the Jewish community there who both believed in assimilation and feared anti-Semitism – the Jewish dilemma in a nutshell. But Herzl's dynamism and the tremendous pressure of eastern misery overcame all reluctance and the Congress was an immense success. Herzl was always on the move, raising funds, interviewing politicians, constantly on the brink of seducing some statesman by his fiery eloquence but never quite succeeding. Cranks and adventurers helped Herzl as much as his own people. An eccentric English parson, the chaplain at the British Embassy in Vienna, took him to the Grand Duke of Baden who in turn presented Herzl to the Emperor of Germany. Wilhelm II took up the cause briefly as a possible move in his game of rivalry with the British in the Near East. It was to meet Wilhelm that Herzl made his only visit to the promised land.

It was a multiple agent of espionage who introduced Herzl to the court of the Turkish Sultan and even to the Sultan himself. They tried to induce this slippery potentate to agree that if a group of millionaires would fund the immense Turkish State debts the Jews should be allowed to settle in Palestine, buying land from the indigenous Arabs. Perhaps fortunately, the Sultan could not quite be persuaded; because the millionaires were as cagey as he was. The money in fact never existed. Only the British were really sympathetic; for them the Jews were one more of the flourishing religious sects so beloved of the Islanders. All the journeys seemed to be fruitless but they were not. The idea of Zion was widely spread among the powers of this world and the churches, even if the Pope when he gave Herzl an audience, could not agree to support his cause. And the seed was sown that did in the end bear fruit. British dignitaries explained the modern Zionist idea to King Edward VII in pursuit of the project of British protection for Palestine. Somehow this idea remained alive and issued in 1917 as the Balfour Declaration promising to establish a National Home for the Jews. Just as important as engaging the imagination of the British (whose motives were no doubt political and strategic), was Herzl's organization of his own people. Scattered in small communities throughout eastern Europe, the vast majority of Jews were cut off both from their own coreligionists and from the outside world; once the international ties were established their impotence was over for they had a means of communication.

In a few years Herzl achieved the three things that founded Israel. He formulated an idea of genius so simple that every unlettered villager could grasp it; he harnessed the helpless longing of the Jews of the Russian Empire; and he engaged the sympathy of the most powerful State in the world for Zion.

Theodor Herzl, literary editor of the *Neue Freie Presse*, which many and perhaps a majority of its readers considered the most important part of the paper, was an absentee for much of the time. He was in Vienna often enough and long enough to keep his job and no more. His assistants ran the famous 'feuilleton' and he wrote his own contributions at odd moments, snatching time in trains and ships and hotel rooms. His Jewish employers and colleagues ignored his real activities and their purpose. But from sulky silence they were moved to ridicule and from laughter to a reluctant respect; in the end to something like awe. There is no doubt that the publishers Bacher and Benedikt continued to employ their wilful literary editor in tacit and perhaps guilty support of an idea they did not believe in but could not help admiring. Nothing was said, in spite of long discussions about Zionism, that could force the issue to the point at which Herzl would have to resign or his publishers would have to sack him. Except for his student days, this is the only truly Viennese aspect of Herzl's life; the compromise, silent in the midst of unceasing talk. They talked of everything except what they were really saying and they all knew that even more than his salary Herzl needed the prestige of his newspaper. When the great of the world received him, when he penetrated the studies of kings and their ministers, it was the *Presse* that opened the doors, often unmentioned, sometimes openly. He was frequently not grateful. He bought a small newspaper as vehicle for his views which were contrary to those of the paper to which he owed his living and his public loyalty; but his editorship on the *Presse* was continued. Sometimes he referred to Benedikt by a diminutive insulting to a man who was honoured by the Emperor, or changed his name in joke to Maledikt; the quips which were certainly known in a city where there are no secrets, were passed over in silence. That Herzl remained the literary editor of the *Neue Freie Presse* until his death was *urwienerisch* (fundamentally Viennese) as nothing else was in Herzl's life or character. He lacked altogether the Viennese temperament, with its indolence, its urbanity, its inborn tendency to arrange matters quietly, and its oblique, conciliatory sociableness. Herzl was fiercely intransigent, single-minded, direct in thought, speech and action. If temperament can be attached to place he was much more an Hungarian than a Viennese. He was a Jew who so profoundly disliked what he knew as Jewishness that he wanted to abolish it altogether; and in this, as everyone who knows Sabras must agree, he succeeded.

In doing so he killed himself. In the early summer of 1904 his overtaxed health broke down completely. His heart would no longer obey the tyranny of his will. He died in the Semmering hills outside Vienna in July. To the end his mother and his wife raged at each other. Some years before he had cut Julie out of his will as far as the law allowed, and given the legal guardianship of her children to his mother. But at the last Julie won, it seems, in the long battle with her hated mother-in-law, for it was she who nursed Theodor. Even her avowed enemies admitted that Julie waited on the husband with whom, or against whom, she had lived in bitter rancour with loving gentleness. It was perhaps the only time in their marriage that she had him all to herself; a sad tale of a disastrous love that could achieve neither unity nor indifference. Impossible not to feel a painful pity for both of them.

Herzl was only forty-four when he died in 1904. To the amazement of his Viennese colleagues and even his fellow-Zionists, his funeral cortège numbered thousands. From all over Europe and the Near East, especially from the Russian Empire, the poor and outcast came, weeping and tearing their garments. They flung themselves upon the coffin in uncontrollable grief. They knew that what Herzl feared was true for they lived it every day. They knew he had sacrificed himself for them and they had lost their only friend.

Thirteen years later a National Home for the Jews was announced, to be established in Palestine under British Mandate when the Turkish Empire at last fell to pieces. It is tempting and not too far-fetched to speculate that if Herzl had lived a few years longer the exodus might have begun before 1914. But timing is everything in public as in private life, and the time was out of joint for Herzl as for many millions. It was too late; the history of 'the real twentieth century' had begun.

Index

Index

Catholic Church, 71, 119, 220, 221
Cervantes, 124
Charlemagne, Emperor, 221
Christian Socialist Party, 83, 85, 86, 229, 231
Clemenceau, Georges, 23
Coburg, Prince Ferdinand, 106
Coburg, Prince Philipp, 30, 51, 53, 54–5, 104, 109
Coburg, Princess Louise, 104–5, 108, 109, 110–12
Cologne, 122
Committee for Social Questions, 82
Conservatory, Vienna, 168–71
Constantinople, 16
Croatia, 22, 98
Czechs, 2, 72–3, 98, 113–14, 143–4, 165–6, 215, 219

Danilevsky, 2
Danube Canal, 87
Darwin, Charles, 36
Davos, 143
Dreyfus, Alfred, 216, 222–3, 224
Duehring, Eugen, 221–2

Edward VIII, King of England, 16, 17, 30, 49, 233
Einstein, Alfred, 5
Elisabeth, Archduchess, 27
Elisabeth, Empress, 82, 101, 196; and the Mayerling affair, 12, 17–18, 23–4, 28–9, 53, 56–8, 63; unpopularity, 104; relationship with Franz Joseph, 119–20, 121, 127–8; friendship with Katharina Schratt, 127; assassination, 137–8
Enlightenment, 123
Epstein, Professor, 168, 169
Eydkuhnen, 145

Felder, Mayor, 74–5, 77, 89
Ferenczy, Ida von, 56–7, 58
Feydeau, 97
Fischer von Erlach, Johann Bernard, 195

Florence, 195
France, 2, 123, 149, 208, 222–3
Franco-Prussian War, 78–9
Franz Ferdinand, Archduke, 32, 98, 99–100, 103, 160
Franz Joseph, Emperor, 24, 28, 63, 97, 115–16, 214, 226–7, 230–1; introduces general suffrage, 2; friendship with Katharina Schratt, 8, 117–31, 135–41; popularity, 9; and the Mayerling affair, 12, 21, 34–5, 37–8, 39, 46, 56, 58; relationship with Crown Prince Rudolf, 23, 29–30, 33; disapproves of anti-Semitism, 80; attitude to Hungarians, 82; and Karl Lueger, 82–3, 86–7; frugal nature, 101, 103; and Archduke Johann Salvator, 107; overseas reputation, 108; and new Vienna Opera House, 180–1; visits Seccession, 201–2; death, 1, 141
Freemasons, 20, 71
French-Italian Treaty, 1902, 99
Freud, Sigmund, 34, 114, 189
Fuchs, Robert, 169

Galicia, 153, 157, 215
Geneva, 4, 137
Germany, 21, 226; reform in, 2; Habsburg foreign policy, 23; unification of, 71; battle of Königgrätz, nationalism, 72, 80, 220; Triple Alliance, 99; Jews in, 217; and Zionism, 232–3
Giesl von Gieslingen, Baron, 143, 151, 155, 160
Girardi, 197
Gödöllö, 17
Goethe, Johann Wolfgang von, 124
Great Britain, 2, 5, 8, 231, 233

Hamburg, 184, 186
Hanslick, Eduard, 185
Hasenauer, Baron, 196

238

Index

Index

Sarah Gainham

Sarah Gainham was born in London and is half Welsh and half English, the celtic side predominating. She has lived most all her adult life as a member of the moving village of journalists, diplomats and business people whose professions cause them to live away from home. When she began to write she adopted her great-grandmother's name and has used it ever since. There was never any decision to live outside her own country; she was simply married to a foreign correspondent and therefore lived "abroad." After the death of her husband in 1975 there appeared to be no pressing motive for change, so she stayed where she was and now lives in what was formerly the head gamekeeper's house, which she has rebuilt, of a large estate on the Danube east of Vienna.